THE ARAB INFLUENCE IN MEDIEVAL EUROPE

Folia Scholastica Mediterranea

EDITED BY

Dionisius A. Agius

AND

Richard Hitchcock

THE ARAB INFLUENCE IN MEDIEVAL EUROPE

Ithaca Press is an imprint of Garnet Publishing Limited

Published by
Garnet Publishing Limited
8 Southern Court
South Street
Reading
Berkshire RG1 4QS
UK

First paperback edition 1996
Reprinted 1997

ISBN 0 86372 213 X

British Library Cataloguing-in-Publication Data
A catalogue record for this book is available from the British Library

Jacket design by David Rose

Jacket illustration by Penny Williams Yaqub
reproduced with kind permission of Aramco

Typeset by Columns Ltd, Reading

Printed in Lebanon

Contents

Editors' Introduction

The contributions that make up this publication were, in their original form, delivered as addresses to a conference entitled *Arabic Influences upon Medieval Europe*, organised by the Department for External Studies, University of Oxford between 6th and 8th April 1990. The underlying themes are those of contact and interaction between the Arabs and Europe during the medieval period, not solely in the Iberian Peninsula although al-Andalus clearly had a major role to play in the transmission of material, but also, no less significantly, in the wider arena of the Mediterranean basin. There was vigorous literary and cultural impact in both Sicily and Italy, and in scientific disciplines Arabic knowledge was widely disseminated, and permeated European monasteries as early as the tenth century.

The papers are arranged in an order that is intended to reflect a movement from the Eastern Mediterranean via Sicily and Italy to al-Andalus. Thus the survey on frontier contacts by David Abulafia precedes the investigations of Donald Hill and James Allan who chart the gradual encroachment of Islamic technological knowledge into a Europe that had apparently lost contact with its classical heritage. What the Muslims absorbed and exploited from the classical world, the Europeans received, and eventually developed and embellished. Eduardo Manzano Moreno's focus on the concept of frontiers in al-Andalus paves the way for the insight into medieval Iberian life provided by Charles Burnett in his study of sheep's shoulder-blades. Philip Kennedy re-examines the vexed question of putative Islamic sources for Dante's *Divine Comedy*, and David Wulstan, drawing on musical theory, scrutinises the role of the Romance *kharjas* in Hispano–Arabic poetry, and sets his arguments in the context of the controversies surrounding the origins of European lyric poetry.

The papers were enthusiastically received at the conference at which they were delivered. Now, given a wider audience, they can, through their scholarship, stimulate and encourage others. The impact of the Arabs and Islam on medieval Europe is a vast subject; this volume, it is hoped, will demonstrate just some of the ways, both unusual and more obvious, in which this influence was experienced.

Dionisius A. Agius
Richard Hitchcock

Contributors

Dr David Abulafia is reader in Mediterranean History at the University of Cambridge, and has been a fellow of Gonville and Caius College, Cambridge, since 1974. He is the author of *The Two Italies* (1977) and of *Frederick II* (1988), both of which have also appeared in Italian translation. Several of his fifty articles on the economic and political history of the medieval Mediterranean have been collected in *Italy, Sicily and the Mediterranean* (1987), and more are due to appear in a further collection of studies scheduled for publication in 1993. His short study of *Spain and 1492: Unity and Uniformity under Ferdinand and Isabella* was published in 1992. His current research is focussed on the trade and politics of the Catalan Kingdom of Majorca, particularly during the period of its independence from Aragon–Catalonia (1276–1343).

Donald R. Hill, having served in the Royal Engineers during the Second World War, took a B.Sc. (Hons.) in engineering at the University of London. After qualifying he worked for the Iraq Petroleum Company in the Lebanon, Syria and Qatar. During this time he learned Arabic. Returning to England, he worked for Imperial Chemical Industries and in the subsidiaries of two major US petrochemical corporations. By spare-time study he earned a master's degree from the University of Durham and a Ph.D. from the University of London, both in Arabic history. He has published six books and numerous articles on the history of Islamic technology. He retired from industry in 1984 and now devotes his time to his historical work. He is a contributing author to the *Encyclopaedia of Islam.*

James W. Allan took his degree in Arabic at St Edmund Hall, Oxford, in 1966, and completed his Oxford University D.Phil. thesis on "The metalworking industry of Iran in the early Islamic period" in 1976. He has worked in the Ashmolean Museum, Oxford, since 1966, and was appointed Keeper of Eastern Art in 1991. He is also a fellow of St Cross College and a university lecturer in Islamic Art. He has written a number of books on Islamic art and architecture, including the following on metalwork: *Persian Metal Technology 700–1300 A.D.*, Oriental Institute Monographs no.2 (Oxford 1979), *Islamic Metalwork: the Nuhad Es-Said Collection* (London 1982), *Nishapur: Metalwork of the Early Islamic Period*, Metropolitan Museum of Art (New York 1982) and *Metalwork of the Islamic World: the Aron Collection* (London 1986). He is married with four children.

Philip F. Kennedy holds a B.A. in Oriental Studies (Arabic with Spanish) from the University of Oxford where he stayed on to complete a D.Phil. in Classical Arabic poetry. He was a junior lecturer in Arabic at the Oriental Institute, Oxford (1989–91) and is currently a junior research fellow at St John's College, Oxford. Though he has concentrated on pre-Islamic to ʿAbbasid poetry of the Arab East, his interests have also included the literature of Islamic Spain, in particular the polemical issues that have characterised the study of the *muwashshaḥ* and its *kharja.*

Eduardo Manzano Moreno is research fellow at the Department of Arabic Studies in the Consejo Superior de Investigaciones Cientificas (C.S.I.C.), Madrid. He has studied at Complutense University and at the School of Oriental and African Studies, University of London. His Ph.D. dissertation dealt with the problems of frontier organisation in al-Andalus during the Umayyad period. It has been published recently under the title *La frontera de al-Andalus en época de los Omeyas*, Madrid, 1991. He has also published works on other topics like the Berber settlements and historiography during the Umayyad period in al-Andalus. He is the author of *Historia de las sociedades musulmanas en la Edad Media*, Madrid, 1992. At present he is engaged in research on the military reforms of al-Manṣūr in al-Andalus and on the relations between North Africa and Muslim Spain during this period.

Charles Burnett has been Lecturer in the history of Islamic influence in Europe in the Middle Ages at the Warburg Institute, University of London, since October 1985, having held research fellowships at St John's College, Cambridge, and the University of Sheffield. He works on the transmission of Arabic philosophy, mathematics and medicine to Europe through translation into Latin made in Spain, Sicily and the Middle East in the Middle Ages. His works include the edition and translation of a Latin cosmological work using Arabic sources, Hermann of Carinthia's *De essentiis*, a collection of essays by several scholars on the twelfth-century English translator and scientist, Adelard of Bath, and a study of the introduction of Hindu–Arabic numerals and methods of calculation to Europe.

David Wulstan is research professor at the University of Wales, having recently retired as Gregynog Professor of Music at Aberystwyth. Initially pursuing a scientific career, he then took up music at Magdalen College, Oxford, where he stayed on as a fellow and lecturer. He was also visiting professor in the Department of Near Eastern Studies at Berkeley, California, and professor of music at Cork, Ireland, before moving to Aberystwyth.

He is well known as the director of the Clerkes of Oxenford, who have made many appearances at festivals, on radio and television and on record. His books include *Tudor Music*, *Musical Language* and editions of Orlando Gibbons, John Sheppard and several other composers of the period. His interests include the *Cantigas* of Alfonso el Sabio, the *kharjas*, Hebrew metre and the relationship of music and poetry in various languages, reflected in his forthcoming book *Echo to the Sense*.

The Role of Trade in Muslim–Christian Contact during the Middle Ages

DAVID ABULAFIA

I

The subject matter of this paper may seem to demand little justification. In 1962 Aziz Atiyah entitled a slim volume *Crusade, Commerce and Culture*, and had no serious doubts about the link between the three.[1] The evidence is surely clear enough: the arrival of Arabic numerals in Europe, used first by the very notaries who drew up contracts for trade in the Muslim world around 1200; the use in several European languages of commercial terms of Arabic or Persian derivation, such as bazaar, cheque, tariff, traffic, arsenal, *douane* or *dogana*,[2] and, once we enter the nautical world, the Islamic derivation of instruments, astronomical tables and cartographic methods is a common assumption, if not quite a certainty. This is to leave aside additional evidence provided by the vocabulary used to describe various expensive textiles, such as the damasks of Damascus and the *baldechini* of Baghdad, or cloths made from raw materials originally unfamiliar in the west, such as the fustians, partly of cotton, of Fusṭāṭ (Old Cairo).

A further area that Professor Atiyah might have investigated more deeply is the transfer of Arab agricultural technology to western Europe, generally in those areas, such as Valencia and Sicily, that had once been under Arab rule.[3] Seville oranges, bananas, rice, henna and sugar are a few of the products that continued to be produced by Christian conquerors, who also sought to acquire the technical skills required for the glass industry, for glazed pottery production, for the paper industry and possibly for the silk industry from the Muslim world. Such commodities acquired great importance in Mediterranean trade by 1400, and were carried much further afield, via the Atlantic all the way to England; even when produced in lands ruled by Christians, they were often cultivated or fabricated by Muslims or Jews, and their origin in the Islamic world is incontrovertible.

It is an impressive picture which has been qualified most notably by Joseph Needham's assertion that a good deal of what the west supposedly acquired from the Arab world was in reality ultimately of Chinese origin, not least paper and the compass.[4] Much the same could be said to apply to some of the fruits and specialised crops of Chinese or Indian ancestry that have just been mentioned.[5] Even if this were largely true, it would not contradict the assumption that it was from the Muslim world that all or most of this know-how arrived in western Europe; nor would it be easy to prove that in around 1300 or even 1400 western Europeans had much knowledge or understanding of Chinese and Indian culture, Marco Polo notwithstanding. But the idea of western borrowing from Islam by way of the international trade routes needs more careful definition from a western perspective as well as from a Chinese one. It is clear already that a distinction needs to be made between the borrowing of Arabic terms as a result of Christian conquest of Muslim lands, and borrowings actually effected through trade. The use of place-names in the Islamic world to describe particular types of cloth does seem to provide a faint echo of early trade relations, even though terms such as fustian rapidly came to be applied to western copies of what were originally cloths of a single place in Egypt.[6] There is, however, one western institution that provides eloquent testimony to the nature and effect of western trade with the Muslim world in the Middle Ages: it is the *fonduq* or *fondacho*, another word which (though ultimately of Greek origin, in the form *pandocheion*) arrived in Italian and Catalan from Arabic, and which was used to described the inns, warehouses and business headquarters that the western merchants operated in North Africa and other Muslim lands.[7]

The central question I want to pose is what it meant to a western merchant, a Latin Christian reared in an age of constant crusade propaganda, to penetrate the Christian–Muslim frontier not as a soldier but as a merchant. We must therefore start with an act of imagination. To live in the late thirteenth century as a Latin Christian in Majorca was to live among the vestiges of an Islamic civilisation that had been torn apart by the Aragonese–Catalan conquest of 1229. The Muslims were a minority, many of them unfree. To travel from there to Valencia was to stay under the rule of an Aragonese king, but to enter a second world in which Muslims were the majority and in which the royal government treated the inhabitants with well-calculated consideration.[8] But to move from there to Tunis or Alexandria was to enter a third world in which Christian merchants were able to practise their religion only on sufferance, and in which simple daily activities, like the quaffing of wine, were subject to government control. It was a world in which the nature of government interference in economic affairs was entirely different from what was found in Genoa, Pisa or even the strongly interventionist Venice. But above all, it was a predominantly Muslim world in which Christian merchants had daily contact with people of another religion.

In a recent, and in many ways inconclusive, book Philip D. Curtin has talked of the stimulating economic role of 'cross-cultural trade', expressed primarily through the presence of cohesive minorities settled in outstations in the midst of an alien civilisation; among the groups that he cites are the Armenian diaspora, and the Greeks who reached as far south as the Zambezi River as Africa was opened up. Often such groups are strikingly resistant to assimilation, retaining a distinctive religion and/or language.[9] Did similar contact between the Christian merchants and the Muslims in the Middle Ages leave any cultural legacy? In a material sense, certainly, it did: the arrival and imitation in the west of oriental luxury goods is proof of that, though there is obviously a difference between items treasured as curios, and items imitated and even excelled by western copyists. The example of Islamic glazed pottery shows how something at first regarded as exotic became the inspiration for a prosperous local industry in central Italy during the early Renaissance.[10]

The intellectual impact of mercantile contact with the Muslim world is far harder to judge. It will be necessary to take on board the statements of missionaries as well as merchants, notably Ramón Llull of Majorca, eccentrics who used the trade routes to try to convert the Muslims to Christianity. It is possible that Llull's generally good-tempered approach to Islam and Judaism reflects a mercantile culture in which it was difficult to demonise the non-Christian:

contact on the frontier was too persistent, and real friendships could be formed across the religious divide between Christian, Muslim and Jew.[11]

In the first part of what follows I shall outline the process by which western merchants began to penetrate the markets of the Islamic world, taking my discussion up to about 1400. This will mean looking as much at the exports from the west to the Muslim countries as at imports into Europe; the aim will be to show the increasing interdependence of the western and the Islamic economies. I shall then look at the way that communities of Latin merchants operated within the Muslim cities such as Tunis and Alexandria where they had been granted *fonduqs*. Finally, I shall assess the implications of this contact for Christian understanding of the Muslim world.

II

Around 1000 the trade links between western Europe and the Islamic world were few, and were dominated by a small group of cities. One or two of these cities, notably Naples and Marseilles, were very ancient trade centres which had continued to send ships or at least goods to the Maghrib and even the Levant throughout the early Middle Ages;[12] more noticeable, however, are the newer centres, above all Venice and Amalfi, which traced their origins to groups of Roman refugees fleeing the barbarian invasions. In each case, we are looking at trade in small quantities of prestige products. The papyrus of Egypt disappeared from use in western Europe in the eleventh century, but perfumes, spices, cloth and gold were among articles being imported by way of Gaeta in southern Italy around 1012.[13] The southern Italian towns supplied courtly demand in Benevento, Capua, Naples and not least the great ecclesiastical centres at Rome and Montecassino; at this period only small quantities of eastern cloth were filtering north of the Alps. We must not forget, either, that the Byzantine Empire was an alternative source of supply for luxury cloth, and that almost anything under the sun could be bought in Constantinople. It is thus possible that some Islamic products reached the west via Byzantium. Finally, it has to be stressed that the strong stylistic similarities between Byzantine and Islamic silks makes it hard to identify surviving examples found in western Europe as specific imports from Spain, Sicily, Egypt, Syria or Greece. However, some Islamic cloths, silks especially, were certainly arriving in northern France and even northern Germany well before 1100.

The opening up of the Levant trade coincides with the early crusades, and there has been vigorous debate over the importance to the rise of Italian sea-power of the conquest of the Holy Land by the crusaders. Commercial privileges, including promises of tax exemption and quarters in the coastal cities of Palestine, were granted to Genoa, Pisa and Venice, in return for naval help in the capture of Acre, Jaffa, Haifa and eventually Tyre; after the battle of Ascalon, in 1123, Egyptian fleets apparently ceased to pose a great threat to western shipping. In the traditional scenario, new naval powers, Pisa and Genoa, moved in swiftly to take advantage of the commercial privileges that had been granted them, and rose rapidly to a position where they could challenge, if not equal, Venice; better established centres of the Levant trade in southern Italy, such as Amalfi and Bari, failed to participate in the early crusades and thus did not reap the rewards that were offered Genoa and Pisa. The imposition of Norman rule in southern Italy is traditionally assumed to have deprived the region's cities of the political freedom necessary if they were to conduct a vigorous foreign policy aimed at supporting the crusader states.[14]

More recent research has tended to qualify this view in important ways. Pisa and Genoa were not total newcomers to the Levant in the 1090s. They clearly had an active trade in the Maghrib well before 1100. Their merchants occasionally appeared in Alexandria before the First Crusade. These cities saw themselves as front-line statelets with a special duty of clearing the western Mediterranean of Muslim pirates. They had expelled the Muslim warlord Mujāhid from Sardinia at the start of the eleventh century, and alone or together they worked hard against Muslim power in Sicily (attacking Palermo in 1063) and in Tunisia (attacking al-Mahdiyya in 1087). After the First Crusade their enthusiasm for the holy war against Islam in the west did not abate one whit: in 1113–15 the Pisans invaded Majorca and Ibiza with Catalan help; in 1147–8 the Genoese committed themselves to expensive campaigns against Muslim ports in Mediterranean Spain, Almería and Tortosa.

Recent research has also shown that the Holy Land was not the prime trading target of Italian merchants even when they reached the Levant.[15] The Venetians had big interests at Tyre, including landed estates in the environs (later known to have produced sugar cane, a plant that had quenched the thirst of the armies of the First Crusade).[16] But Tyre gives poor access to the interior, since it is cut off from the trade routes leading into Syria by the mountains of southern Lebanon. Acre was better placed, since from there overland routes crossed the rolling hills of Galilee and ascended the Golan Heights before pressing on to Damascus.[17] Acre in particular could function as an outport of Damascus, and Italian merchants gathered there from the mid-twelfth century in order to make contact with Syrian Christians and Muslims bringing goods from as far afield as Mosul. Yet we should not underestimate the bitter struggles that the Italian merchants had to undergo, not with the Muslim rulers of the Middle East but with the Latin kings of Jerusalem, who denied them confirmation of the rights that they claimed in virtue of the treaties drawn up at the time of the original conquest of the coast of the Holy Land.[18] In the 1160s the Genoese demanded, even at the papal court, the restoration of a Golden Inscription supposedly installed in the Church of the Holy Sepulchre in Jerusalem, detailing their special privileges.[19] So bitter was the conflict that in 1163 the Genoese appear to have withdrawn from trade in the Holy Land.[20]

It is now clear that the great age of Acre's trade was the thirteenth century, when changes in the international trade routes as a result of the Mongol conquests in Asia made the overland routes beyond Mesopotamia into Persia, and via Cilician Armenia through Turkey to Persia and beyond, into thriving business concerns.[21] Despite attempts to limit Italian participation on these routes by the rulers of Jerusalem (who saw the penetration of the interior as a threat to their revenues from trade) there were Italian visitors to such centres as Aleppo in the thirteenth century, in search both of luxury goods and of alum, a fixative used by western cloth manufacturers.[22]

But it was the lights of the Pharos of Alexandria that really beckoned. In the twelfth century, Egypt was a major exporter of alum to the west.[23] It was also an important souce of cotton, much of which was not in fact Egyptian but Indian.[24] And here lay the attractiveness of Egypt. It was an access point to a second set of trading networks, to which the Italians did not have access; like

Bruges in Flanders, Alexandria was the interchange point between otherwise largely self-contained trading systems, on the one hand the Hanseatic system in the North Sea and Baltic, on the other the elongated trade route via Cairo, the Red Sea and Yemen to India and the Spice Islands. Increasingly fearful of the danger of Christian assaults on Mecca and Medina, the Egyptians closed the Red Sea to non-Muslim shipping. By the end of the twelfth century a new generation of Muslim merchants, the *Karimis*, had gained ascendancy on the India route, taking over gradually from the well-documented Jewish merchants of Fusṭāṭ, the so-called Cairo Genizah merchants.[25]

Pepper and ginger certainly took first place in the Italian spice trade out of late medieval Egypt; it is noteworthy that these products, like much of the exported cotton, were not actually produced in Egypt, but were trans-shipped (and heavily taxed) through Egypt.[26] This is not to deny the gratitude felt by western rulers when they received gifts of Egyptian products from the sultans of Egypt; in 1306 James II of Aragon was sent embroidered and plain cloths in a variety of colours, produced in the state factories in Egypt, and made of silk, linen and cotton; some of the cloths were hand-painted, one possibly with pictures of peaches; the sultan also sent balsam and incense, and some crossbows.[27] The Aragonese–Mamlūk diplomatic exchanges illustrate the efforts made by western princes to keep open the trade routes and to guarantee the safety of Christians in Muslim lands; James II even sought to secure the reopening of Jacobite and Melkite churches in Cairo.[28] But it was normally a delicate enough task to look after the western Christian visitors to Egypt, let alone the native Christian communities.

Christian merchants found themselves in a difficult diplomatic position. On the one hand, there was the fact that they had helped create the Latin Kingdom of Jerusalem, and that they had a considerable stake in its survival. On the other hand, their presence in Acre, Jaffa and Tyre was made more valuable, in commercial terms, by the fact that the ports of the Holy Land were secure bases from which it was possible to make short trips to the Nile Delta. Acre was Alexandria's twin, in the sense that it provided facilities for merchants (and their ships) who intended to make the final hop into Muslim-controlled territory.

Winds and currents helped determine the relationship between

Acre and Alexandria.[29] The safest route from Italy to the Levant, from the point of view both of navigation and of immunity from Muslim pirates, was that running round southern Greece, past Crete, and along the island chain towards Rhodes, southern Turkey or Cyprus and the coast of Syria. Some ships did divert from southern Crete directly to the Nile Delta, but few followed the coast of Tripolitania and Cyrenaica, where there were dangerous sandbanks. The result was that a great part of the shipping bound for Alexandria passed the ports of the Latin Kingdom of Jerusalem, once again confirming the special standing of Acre as command centre of the Latin trade network in the Middle East. After the fall of Acre to the Mamlūks of Egypt in 1291, a similar role was assumed by Famagusta in Cyprus, from which trade routes radiated outwards to Laiazzo in Cilician Armenia, to the coast hard by Antioch, to Beirut, and above all to Alexandria and Damietta.[30]

The conquest of eastern markets was also made possible by the readiness with which those markets absorbed western goods. Yet in the older literature the western trading nations tend to be treated as poor relations with little of substance to offer.[31] It is true that until the late twelfth century there was little demand in the Muslim world for western industrial goods; but this changed dramatically as Flemish, north French and even English woollen cloths, made to very high specifications, became the preferred export of the Genoese, Pisans and Venetians to eastern markets.[32] However, the west still depended on Muslim sources for some of the raw materials required in the processing of these goods: alum arrived from Egypt or Syria, and in the late thirteenth century from western Turkey; high quality dyes, notably the bright red grana, came from a variety of sources — in the case of grana, often from Muslim Spain. The growing cotton industry of Lombardy depended, as has been implied already, on supplies of Middle or Far Eastern cotton imported from Egypt and Syria, though there were also supplies nearer at hand in ex-Muslim Sicily and (apparently of a rather better standard) in Malta, which formed part of the Kingdom of Sicily.[33] The conquest of eastern markets by western cloth involved not simply the exploitation of demand for the produce of the mother country among the Franks of the Latin Kingdom of Jerusalem; it also reveals a capacity to create demand at Muslim princely courts. In a sense, the late twelfth century marks the birth of the European fashion industry. In 1306 the Mamlūk sultan sent the king of Aragon Venetian linen as well as luxury goods of the Islamic world.[34] The task was facilitated by industrial decline in Egypt and the Islamic heartlands. The theme of industrial decline was the keynote of the work of the prolific Israeli historian of the Islamic economy, Eliyahu Ashtor; but it is hard to explain why this decline took place.[35] Western economic aggression is not a satisfactory explanation, at least on its own, and problems resulting from government intervention in the Egyptian and Maghribi economies must be taken into account too.

Another commodity that western merchants could offer the Muslim world was silver. Here again there have been many misunderstandings.[36] Silver was long seen as a sign of economic weakness: the western world almost entirely abandoned the minting of gold coins after the beginning of the ninth century, while in the Muslim world gold, silver and base metals all circulated. The only Christian kingdoms where a similar position held were those won recently from the Muslims: in some parts of Spain, in Sicily and in the Latin Kingdom of Jerusalem, whose gold coinage was closely modelled on Islamic types. The work of Andrew Watson has indicated, however, that the Muslim countries were short of silver in the early twelfth century.[37] Imports of western silver into the Muslim world, along with the opening of new mines in Khorasan, led to a return to the minting of silver in Syria and North Africa during the twelfth century.[38] The Cairo Genizah documents reveal that a wealthy Jewish merchant, Nahray ben Nissim (fl. 1045–96), carried western silver eastwards in the form of silver ingots.[39] A return to silver meant a return to the freer movement of middle-priced goods, the market for which was restricted by a lack of specie. Of course, another way of describing this process is to say that the balance of trade between east and west always favoured the east in the Middle Ages; such a statement does, however, impose modern economic concepts on the medieval world, and the silver exports must not be seen simply as a drainage of western money eastwards — in a sense, silver too was a commodity, some of which was mined and cast into ingots without being minted as coin.[40] There were also good opportunities for western merchants to buy gold (again, a commodity as well as coin) in the Levant rather more cheaply than they could in the ports of western Europe, and we begin to see an accumulation of Islamic gold coins in royal treasuries as far afield as that of Henry III of England.[41] Muslim gold was thus sometimes used to make very large payments within western Europe, and it was hardly a major revolution when, in 1252, the Genoese and the Florentines resumed the minting of European gold coins, made mainly of gold imported from Muslim lands, after a break of four and a half centuries.[42]

A third group of imports that was much esteemed among the Muslims was armaments. It is hardly surprising that arms appear among the exports to the Latin states in Syria; the scale of exports to Egypt was, however, sufficient to cause scandal throughout the Middle Ages. A type of shield known in Egypt as the *janāwiyya* has been plausibly identified as a shield from Genoa.[43] On occasion whole ships appear to have been sailed to Egypt and sold there, though more common was the trade in timber, vital for the Egyptian army, and in short supply in Egypt itself.[44] Since the great naval defeat at Ascalon at the hands of the Venetians, the Egyptians found it harder to gain access to the timber of southern Anatolia, though raiding parties continued to harass Cyprus, where, again, good timber was to be found. It is clear that the building of a fleet was a far more challenging proposition for the Egyptians than it was for the Italians or even for the relatively sea-shy Byzantines. And no Italian republic was prepared to go to the lengths of offering its fleet to the sultans of Egypt, in the way that the Italians regularly offered fleets in return for commercial privileges to Christian princes — to the Byzantines and to the rulers of Jerusalem.

The result was that the actual privileges the Italian merchants received in Muslim countries were less generous than those which they received in Christian regions. Rather than being granted quarters of towns, they were granted control of a *fonduq*, in which the merchants were confined under curfew at night. The question was one of gaining any access to Egyptian markets, rather than of being given preferential access. Some minor tax reductions were secured, but nothing on the scale of the massive reductions claimed in Constantinople and the Latin east. In 1154–5, the Pisans, perhaps disappointed at their failure to extend their trade rights in the crusader states as far as they had hoped, sent Rainerio Botaccio as ambassador to Fāṭimid Egypt, and were compensated for their pains by promises to grant Pisan merchants safe conduct in Egypt.[45] There are, however, few indications of attempts to penetrate beyond Alexandria and Damietta, though the south Italian merchant Solomon of Salerno, who was a Genoese resident, travelled to Cairo in 1156 to buy lac and brazilwood for a Genoese business partner.[46] In fact, there are several signs that the western merchants approved of crusader plans to establish Latin rule over the Nile Delta: in 1169 the Pisans were lured by King Amaury of Jerusalem into a plan for a joint Byzantine–Frankish attack on Egypt, the prize for Pisa being the promise of commercial privileges in conquered Egypt. But they were back trading in Alexandria in 1174, when an attacking Sicilian fleet surprised a Pisan ship that had arrived from Venice; at the same time, there were apparently Pisans, Genoese and Venetians in the invading fleet.[47] The Egyptians knew that the Italian merchants were involved, and regarded this as a betrayal of the good relations that had been built up over recent years. The original target of the Fourth Crusade, in which the Venetians were so heavily involved, was Alexandria, not Constantinople;[48] and the Fifth Crusade as well as the crusade of St Louis saw the capture of Damietta as the key to the recovery of Jerusalem.[49] Here again the Italians had a commercial stake, though the shameless activities of a group of nineteenth-century forgers, whose bogus charters still have the power to deceive Sotheby's, have perhaps magnified the Italian role out of real proportion.[50] It is certain, too, that the Italians did not always secure the protection they craved. In 1195 and 1200 there were Venetian and Genoese merchants held captive in Egyptian gaols. The Italians were all too easily held hostage for the good behaviour of the mother-city, especially at times of rising tension between the Ayyūbids of Egypt and Syria and the virtually encircled Latin kings of Jerusalem.

The intention here has been to make a very simple point: it was the western merchants who opened up the markets in the Levant. The north Italians were not forced to compete with Muslim merchants operating the same trade routes in reverse direction. Even in the tenth and eleventh centuries, the great age of the Cairo Genizah merchants, Amalfi and other western ports were not apparently visited by swarms of Muslim merchants, though Amalfi itself had a high reputation among Muslims as the western trading station par excellence. In fact, the ample records of twelfth-century Genoa make little reference to Muslim visitors. The major recorded incident in Genoa involving a visit by merchants of probable Muslim origin, themselves agents of a very powerful Muslim prince, actually concerns Sicilian Muslims living a full ninety years after the Norman seizure of Palermo from Islam.[51] It is true that the Jews sometimes acted as intermediaries between the Muslim and the Christian world; but the Jews of Fusṭāṭ, whose trade is so superbly recorded, gave their attention to the India route, to the land and sea trade routes along the coast of North Africa, to trade with Sicily and, in small measure, with southern Italy. What is striking is that the Jewish merchants did not penetrate Genoa or Venice, cities which actually discouraged Jewish settlement.

It was in the western Mediterranean that the role of the Jews as intermediaries took on reality; and it was in this arena that Jews, Christians and in some cases Muslims coexisted in the same cities: Jews and Christians in Marseilles or Barcelona; all three religions in Ciutat de Majorca or Valencia. It is possible, too, that Montpellier in southern France had a small Muslim trading settlement, since fragments of twelfth-century gravestones survive there that are otherwise very hard to explain.[52] It is now necessary to turn to the great arc of lands known to historians of the late Middle Ages as the Crown of Aragon, including Sicily, Sardinia, the Balearics and Montpellier as well as Catalonia, Aragon and parts of southern France. It was from here that a particularly intensive penetration of north-west Africa was launched.

III

Although North Africa was an important source of cloths, it would be wrong to assume that the areas to the west of Egypt had a similar economic profile to Egypt itself. The appeal of African trade lay at least as much in access to supplies of wool, leather and other raw or semi-processed materials as it did in the desire to obtain luxury goods. Morocco even functioned as a granary for western merchants by the fourteenth century, although Tunisia underwent a long economic crisis in which one of the early signs of collapse was the onset of very frequent famines, starting in the late eleventh century. Its towns also gradually succumbed to the industrial malaise which made them increasingly receptive to western finished textiles. The obvious means of payment was gold, as the ability to supply home-produced cloths, and demand for them in an increasingly self-sufficient west, both declined. Western penetration of North African markets perhaps reached its peak when the Catalans and the Italians carved out a monopoly in salt production and transport in the western Mediterranean, so that regular imports of Ibizan salt in exchange for African gold became a satisfying source of profit to the Catalan businessmen of Majorca.[53]

The emergence of the Catalan merchants is one of the great success stories of medieval business. In the twelfth century there was undoubtedly a limited Catalan trade out of Barcelona towards southern France, Muslim Spain and North Africa. The travel diary of the Spanish Jew Benjamin of Tudela, of about 1160, even suggests that Muslim merchants regularly visited Barcelona at this time.[54] However, Catalan fleets played no part in the great naval expeditions against al-Andalus, such as the brief occupation of Majorca from 1113 to 1115. It was a century later, in 1229–35, with the building of a fleet to capture the Balearics decisively in the name of Christendom, that the Catalans became a truly powerful economic and political force in the western Mediterranean. North Africa remained a very high priority for Catalan shipping. Commercial contracts from Barcelona, and a remarkable book of licences for ships leaving the port of Majorca in 1284, confirm the primacy of the Maghrib in Catalan trade at this period.[55] In 1282 the Aragonese conquest of Sicily, valuable both for itself and as a gateway to the Levant, enlarged the area in which Catalan shipping could eventually move freely, even though it by no means marked the inception of Catalan trade with the central and eastern Mediterranean.[56] This position of strength was not significantly weakened in the fourteenth century. The *Llibre de conoxenses de spécies e de drogues e de avissaments de pessoas, canes e massures de diverses terres*, a merchant manual of 1385, probably from Barcelona, refers to seventeen or more ports in the Maghrib and strongly suggests that this was the area of the Mediterranean that the Catalans knew best, other than their home waters.[57] If confirmation were needed, the great number of surviving treaties with the rulers of Tunis, Tlemcen, Bougie and Ceuta indicates the importance of Catalan trade in North Africa to the kings of Aragon and of Majorca, who drew substantial revenues from trade taxes remitted to them by the Muslim amirs.[58] The Catalans possessed more than one *fonduq* in several North

African towns: in Bougie the Catalan king of Majorca gained control of one of the Catalan *fonduqs* in 1302, despite the protests of his kinsman the king of Aragon–Catalonia.[59] There were even cases where the king of Aragon received a share of the trade taxes imposed on all Latin merchants, including Italians and southern French merchants as well as Catalans. This signifies very clearly the political and commercial ascendancy achieved by the Catalans in North Africa during the thirteenth century.

Another source of gold was payment by Muslim charitable organisations for the redemption of captives seized by Christian pirates (Valencia was a great centre of Christian pirates by 1300); however, this was a two-way traffic, and western merchants sometimes found themselves acting as agents for the two Redemptive Orders, the Trinitarians and Mercedarians, who collected funds in western Europe to pay ransoms for Christian prisoners in Muslim Spain and North Africa.[60] The image of the Christian captive in Muslim lands is brilliantly portrayed in such thirteenth-century French romances as *The Count of Ponthieu's daughter*, where the separation of two lovers results from capture and sale into slavery.[61] It was a trade in humans in which the Catalan merchants had a special stake. In addition, Catalan merchants were heavily involved in the trade in Muslim slaves, who were placed on sale in slave markets in Palermo, Ciutat de Majorca and other frontier ports. Many slaves, having been exported from the Muslim world, were then re-exported to North Africa and al-Andalus, so that the Catalans acted as intermediaries between Muslim and Muslim. The sale of the century occurred in 1287, when the Aragonese seized Muslim Menorca and enslaved nearly all those who could not afford to pay for their redemption; the island was almost completely depopulated, though most of its inhabitants did return, if only as slaves, to the Islamic world.[62]

The importance of medieval Catalan trade lies partly in maritime technology: the apparent ease with which Catalan sailors were able to navigate to the Balearics and to Africa in both winter and summer (by 1284) and the advanced cartography of the so-called school of Majorca provide two explanations for the use of Catalan ships even by Genoese and Tuscan merchants seeking to penetrate the markets of North Africa. It has been argued that the Catalans of Majorca were the first Mediterranean sailors to breach the Straits of Gibraltar around 1277 and to establish direct sailings to England and Flanders.[63] What is certain at least is that navigation along the Atlantic coast of Africa developed in the early fourteenth century. Ports such as Anfa (the modern Casablanca) were being visited with regularity around 1330.[64] The Bardi and Peruzzi, the two greatest banks of Florence in the early fourteenth century, turned to Catalan shippers when they sent grain and wine from Sicily to Tunis just before 1300.

The cartographic evidence is, however, very difficult to handle: what survive are the portolan charts of the fourteenth century, in some quantity, and the larger world maps or atlases that were a de luxe extension of the portolan charts, and in some cases formed part of royal libraries.[65] Whether any of these maps were ever used by captains on the high seas is a debated issue. The maps do show similarities to Muslim maps of the thirteenth century, and there is no reason to doubt that such mapmakers as Abraham and Judah (Jafuda) Cresques in fourteenth-century Majorca had access to Arabic geographical sources.[66] They were Jews who could exploit the close cultural and economic links between the Jewish communities of the Balearic Islands and those of North Africa, whence part of the Majorcan community in fact originated. As Felipe Fernández-Armesto has recently stressed in an elegant study of exploration and colonisation before Columbus, the extension of geographical knowledge to include detailed information on the west coast of Africa, as far as the Canaries, and to include also rough data on the gold routes linking black Africa to the Mediterranean, was partly achieved through the physical penetration of these regions by western merchants, Catalan and Italian.[67] Arab geography alone did not solve all the problems of the mapmakers.

Catalan missionaries, seeking to convert the Muslims of the Maghrib to Christianity, did not neglect the opportunities created by the trade relations between the Crown of Aragon and the North African rulers. Dominicans and Franciscans set up schools of Arabic and Hebrew, in which Jewish and Muslim sacred texts were studied in the original, in order to equip the friars for preaching campaigns in Muslim Spain, the Maghrib and, of course, in areas such as Valencia that were now under Christian rule but that retained a large non-Christian population. The most prolific exponent of the mission against Islam was Ramón Llull, born in 1232, who by his death in

1316 had set up a school of Arabic in his home island of Majorca, had written a great number of tracts on the relative merits of Judaism, Christianity and Islam, and had gained access to the courts of Majorca, Paris and Rome in attempts to mobilise new Christian missions in North Africa.[68] His own knowledge of Muslim culture was exceptional, though probably not unique; the general mark of his approach was a degree of politeness and respect towards his Muslim interlocutors that perhaps was unique. Once in Tunis, he was able to gain access to the emir's court, and to hold religious discussions with Muslim scholars; but his presence was only tolerated when political relations between Tunis and the Latin west were close and when the ruler of Tunis teased western sensibilities by appearing to hint at his future conversion to Christianity.

IV

It is in Tunis that we can observe the day-to-day interaction of Christian merchants and Muslim rulers. This is in part because of the survival of a remarkable book of minutes by a Genoese scribe, Pietro Battifoglio, dating from 1289.[69] More than three hundred westerners are mentioned in these acts from Tunis, over a period of seven months. Yet the Christian community of Tunis was already very large at the start of the thirteenth century, when the Pisan merchant Leonardo Fibonacci lived there and studied Arabic numerals, on which he wrote a famous treatise in 1202.[70] Tunis is perhaps not typical: the Christian community, consisting of merchants, sailors, mercenaries, loose women, priests and so on, occupied by the mid-fourteenth century a vast area of the city, about equal to the Muslim fortified city.[71] But, precisely because it is an exceptional case, it is worth examining for possible evidence that the merchants of Genoa, Pisa, Barcelona and elsewhere who lived there enjoyed not simply a business relationship with their Muslim hosts.

The evidence of Pietro Battifoglio shows that the problems faced by Christian merchants in gaining recognition of their rights in Tunis were quite severe. On 21 April and on 1 May 1289 the Genoese consul in Tunis, Balianno Embrono, declared to the head of the customs service that the agreements between the city of Genoa and the ruler of Tunis must be respected by that ruler, and that he must grant an audience to the consul, as accredited head of the Genoese colony, no less than twice each month.[72] In other words, the consul was having some difficulty in gaining access to the ruler's ear, and yet the latest treaty between Genoa and Tunis dated from as recently as 1287.[73] The guarantees provided by the royal court included a promise of protection for the goods of the Genoese, and of indemnity when they were seized illicitly. A vast sum (20,393 besants) was granted to the Genoese as a refund for damage inflicted by Pisan aggressors on Genoese goods and shipping in the port of Tunis, at La Golette; the ruler of Tunis was liable here since he had failed to give proper protection to his allies.[74] One of the pillaged ships was said to have contained over 2,000 jars of oil. However, wine was an even more sensitive issue, not least since the Genoese were able to operate their own tavern in the *fonduq*. When the amir tried to increase taxes on wine, the consul protested with vigour; afraid of trouble, the consul locked the warehouse where wine was stored, and gave the key to the resident Genoese priest, Tealdo.[75] Such disputes over taxes on oil and wine could erupt in violence: it was apparently easy to mobilise a crowd to hurl not just abuse but sticks and stones at the wine-swilling, pork-eating, uncircumcised polytheists in their midst. The sense of insecurity felt by the Christians in Tunis comes across easily; it was simply not the same existence as they experienced when living in the Italian quarter in Acre or Majorca. Nor did the Italians and Catalans conduct intensive business in the interior of Tunisia. To some extent Tunis functioned as the command post for a local network of trade routes, but the main commercial links were with the Christian world, to Sicily, the Balearics and beyond.[76]

The community of Genoese in Tunis naturally consisted mainly of birds of passage. There were, however, long-term residents: the priest has been mentioned, and it is known that the churches of the different merchant communities were subject to restrictions. Bells were not to be rung and campanili were not to be built, although the Venetians tried hard to build one.[77] They were small chapels, one or more for each merchant community, and another one for the large regiment of Aragonese mercenaries who also lived in Tunis; despite Ramón Llull's wishes, the churches never really functioned as missionary centres, though for about twenty years from 1250 there was a Dominican school of Arabic in Tunis, one of the earliest of those missionary colleges which aimed to teach a knowledge of Arabic and of Islam to future preachers in North Africa and Muslim Spain.[78] It was presumably tolerated because its members sought only to learn from Muslims, and not actually to preach to Muslims. All told, the amirs valued Italian and Catalan trade too much to deny the merchants reasonable facilities; yet the merchants did live in a large, but nevertheless confined, area, and they had to renegotiate their rights regularly. This was an especial problem at the end of the thirteenth century, when the Mediterranean was convulsed by the War of the Sicilian Vespers, and shifting political alliances created great uncertainty about trade prospects.

V

The *fonduq* and merchant quarter thus constituted an island in the Muslim world. It is hard to see how, except in the rare cases of active missionaries seeking to penetrate Islam, these islands were linked by bridges to the surrounding culture. This is not to deny that certain skills in numeracy and cartography did derive from Muslim sources. Trade between Christians and Muslims, conducted by Christian visitors to Muslim lands (and not normally Muslim visitors to continental Europe), had enormous implications for the development of the western economy, as can be seen from the rise of the European textile industries and from the associated changes in the European monetary system after 1252. We can only guess at the extent to which Christian merchants observed and took an interest in the Muslim civilisation they came to know through trade. They travelled to the Muslim lands in search of the products of the east, in search of markets for their own goods and above all in search of profits. Moreover, one of the main attractions of the bazaars of Alexandria was the availability of spices, which had in large measure arrived from beyond the frontiers of Islam, and had been carried all the way across the Muslim world; so too the gold which they sought on the coasts of North Africa had been panned beyond the southern edge of Islam, in black Africa.[79]

While it would be wrong to deny the intrinsic attractions to western buyers of many items produced within the lands of Islam, it is important to remember too that Islam presented a frustratingly large block of lands impeding free access to supplies of non-Muslim regions far to the south and east. As early as 1291, with the Vivaldi expedition to India via West Africa (which never reached its destination) hopes were being expressed of bypassing the Arab countries entirely.[80] The Mongol trade routes also for a few decades facilitated overland links to China that avoided the heartlands of Islam. Thus two hundred years before Christopher Columbus (d. 1506) and Vasco da Gama (d. 1524) merchants saw the Islamic world as much as a physical impediment, as a source of exotic goods and of wealthy clients able to pay in gold.

It was, rather, in those areas of Europe such as Andalusia, Valencia and Sicily where Arab culture survived, at least briefly, the shock of Christian conquest that the economic influence of the Islamic world was most profound. Sicily actually experienced a brief florescence of Arab learning after the Norman conquest; Valencia retained and improved its irrigation systems, still commemorated in the water courts of Valencia City.[81] But even here there is an optical illusion. When in the fifteenth century western merchants visited Valencia and Sicily in search of rice, sugar and up-market fruits, they were buying goods whose production had not necessarily been maintained continuously since Muslim times. Sicilian sugar, henna and indigo were disappearing around 1200, and Frederick II made a determined effort to restore their cultivation, using Jewish labour, in the mid-thirteenth century.[82] The Turkish advances in the eastern Mediterranean were stimulating the planting of so-called Islamic crops in the west, as far west, in fact, as Madeira and the Canary Islands.[83] Valencian irrigation had serviced the needs of grain producers in the thirteenth and fourteenth centuries, and specialised crops apparently grew in importance only in the late fourteenth and fifteenth centuries, even if the know-how had always been there. Even Muslim Granada, a major source of quality fruits, became a virtual economic colony of the Genoese financiers in the fifteenth century, who made Málaga into a major base for Italian and Catalan trade.[84] The lesson of all this is that it was increasingly possible to conduct trade in the produce of the Muslim world without having to set foot in that world. It is true, as has been said, that in formal terms the western merchants never managed to adjust in their favour the balance of trade with the Islamic world. However, following on from the defeat of Muslim navies and from the triumph of western textiles in the Mediterranean, the capture of Arab agricultural technology confirmed the massive ascendancy of western merchants in their trade with Islam by the end of the Middle Ages.

Notes

1 A.S. Atiyah, *Crusade, Commerce and Culture* (Bloomington, Indiana/Oxford, 1962).

2 Atiyah, pp. 240–1.

3 A. Watson, *Agricultural Innovation in the Early Islamic World* (Cambridge, 1983).

4 J. Needham and collaborators, *Science and Civilisation in China* (Cambridge, 1954 onwards), a massive multi-volume work still in progress.

5 Watson, pp. 31–44.

6 Other terms, derived from the absorption and remodelling of Muslim administration under Christian conquerors, do not offer real proof of trade contacts: there are the amirs of Sicily, who developed by the thirteenth century into the office of Admiral; there are also the *rais* or headmen of Latin Syria, and the separate *rais* of the tunny fishing fleets of western Sicily, who are said still to survive. On the former, see L.R. Ménager, *Ammiratis-'Αμηρᾶς. L'émirat et les origines de l'amirauté* (Paris, 1960).

7 Robert Lopez, "The trade of medieval Europe: the South", *Cambridge Economic History of Europe*, revised edn, vol. 2 (Cambridge, 1987), p. 347.

8 See for Valencia the works of R.I. Burns, e.g. *Medieval Colonialism. Postcrusade Exploitation of Islamic Valencia* (Princeton, N.J., 1975).

9 P.D. Curtin, *Cross-cultural Trade in World History* (Cambridge, 1984).

10 David Abulafia, "The Pisan bacini and the medieval Mediterranean economy: a historian's viewpoint", *Papers in Italian Archaeology*, IV: *the Cambridge Conference*, pt. iv, *Classical and Medieval Archaeology*, (British Archaeological Reports, International Series, 246), ed. C. Malone and S. Stoddart (Oxford, 1985), pp. 287–302.

11 On the general phenomenon of conversion of Muslims in the thirteenth century, see B.Z. Kedar, *Crusade and Mission. European Approaches toward the Muslim* (Princeton, N.J., 1984).

12 R. Pernoud, "Le moyen-âge jusqu'à 1291", *Histoire du commerce de Marseille*, ed. G. Rambert, vol. 1 (1949); P. Arthur, "Naples: notes on the economy of a Dark Age city", *Papers in Italian Archaeology*, IV: *the Cambridge Conference*, pt. iv, *Classical and Medieval Archaeology*, (British Archaeological Reports, International Series, vol. 246), ed. C. Malone and S. Stoddart (Oxford, 1985), pp. 247–59.

13 M. Merores, *Gaeta im frühen Mittelalter* (Gotha, 1911), pp. 96–8. The debate about the supply of oriental commodities was, of course, given new life by H. Pirenne, *Mohammed and Charlemagne* (London, 1939).

14 See, e.g. A. Schaube, *Handelsgeschichte der Romanischen Völker des Mittelmeergebiets bis zum Ende der Kreuzzüge* (Munich/Berlin, 1906).

15 C. Cahen, *Orient et Occident au temps des Croisades* (Paris, 1983), pp. 123–8.

16 J. Prawer, *Crusader Institutions* (Oxford, 1980), p. 160.

17 The routes thus crossed the present no-man's land between Israel and Syria, passing Banyas in modern Golan, where there was a major castle: *The Travels of Ibn Jubayr*, ed. and transl. R.J.C. Broadhurst (London, 1952), p. 315. Some travellers bound for Tyre stopped in Acre en route (Ibn Jubayr, p. 319).

18 See now Marie-Luise Favreau-Lilie, *Die Italianer im heiligen Land vom ersten Kreuzzug bis zum Tode Heinrichs von Champagne (1098–1197)* (Amsterdam/Las Palmas de Gran

Canaria, 1989) for a masterly survey of the relations between the Italians and the kings of Jerusalem in the twelfth century.

19 M.-L. Favreau and H.E. Mayer, "Das Diplom Balduins I. für Genua und Genuas Goldene Inschrift in der Grabeskirche", *Quellen und Forschungen aus italienischen Archiven und Bibliotheken*, 55/6 (1976), 22–95, repr. in H.E. Mayer, *Kreuzzüge und lateinischer Osten* (London, 1983), essay V; B.Z. Kedar, "Genoa's golden inscriptions in the Church of the Holy Sepulchre: a case for the defence", in *I comuni italiani nel regno crociato di Gerusalemme*, ed. G. Airaldi and B.Z. Kedar (Genoa, 1986), pp. 317–35.

20 David Abulafia, *The Two Italies. Economic Relations between the Norman Kingdom of Sicily and the Northern Communes* (Cambridge, 1977), p. 131.

21 On the general problem, see David Abulafia, "Asia, Africa and the trade of medieval Europe", in *Cambridge Economic History of Europe*, revised edn. vol. 2 (Cambridge, 1987), pp. 443–4, and, for Turkey, pp. 455–8.

22 J. Riley-Smith, "Government in Latin Syria and the commercial privileges of the foreign merchants", in *Relations between East and West in the Middle Ages*, ed. D. Baker (Edinburgh, 1973); and, for merchants bound to Aleppo, David Abulafia, "Crocuses and Crusaders: San Gimignano, Pisa and the Kingdom of Jerusalem", in *Outremer: Studies in the History of the Crusading Kingdom of Jerusalem presented to Joshua Prawer*, ed. B.Z. Kedar, H.E. Mayer and R.C. Smail (Jerusalem, 1982), pp. 227–43.

23 Abulafia, "Asia, Africa", pp. 434, 436.

24 For Egyptian cotton, Abulafia, "Asia, Africa", 432; for Indian cotton, see M. Mazzaoui, *The Italian Cotton Industry in the Later Middle Ages, 1100–1600* (Cambridge, 1981), pp. 15, 35 and *passim*.

25 Abulafia, "Asia, Africa", pp. 437–43, and the bibliography, pp. 906–8.

26 See the studies collected together in: E. Ashtor, *Studies on the Levantine Trade in the Middle Ages* (London, 1987); E. Ashtor, *East-West Trade in the Medieval Mediterranean*, ed. B.Z. Kedar (London, 1986).

27 A.S. Atiyah, *Egypt and Aragon. Embassies and diplomatic correspondence between AD 1300 and 1330* (Abhandlungen für die Kunde des Morgenlandes, 23:7) (Leipzig, 1938), pp. 26–34. Further evidence, this time of a physical nature, of interest in fine Egyptian cloths comes from a series of vestments found at the Marienkirche in Danzig (Gdansk): W. Mannowsky, *Der Danziger Paramentenschatz. Kirchliche Gewänder und Strickereien aus der Marienkirche*, vols. 1–4 (Berlin, 1931–8), I, 1:13, II, 1:15; cf. Atiyah, *Egypt and Aragon*, pp. 28–9.

28 Atiyah, *Egypt and Aragon*, pp. 20–5.

29 This is the convincing thesis of J.H. Pryor, *Geography, Technology and War: Studies in the Maritime History of the Mediterranean, 649–1571* (Cambridge, 1988).

30 D. Jacoby, "The rise of a new emporium in the eastern Mediterranean: Famagusta in the late thirteenth century", *Meletai kai hypomnemata, Hidryma Archiepiskopou Makariou III* (Nicosia, 1984), pp. 145–79, repr. in D. Jacoby, *Studies on the Crusader states and on Venetian Expansion* (Northampton, 1989), essay VIII.

31 R.S. Lopez, "Il problema della bilancia dei pagamenti nel commercio di Levante", *Venezia e il Levante fino al secolo XV*, vols. 1–2 (Florence, 1973), I.431–52.

32 David Abulafia, "Maometto e Carlomagno. Le due aree monetarie italiane dell'oro e dell'argento", *Economia naturale, economia monetaria* (Storia d'Italia, Annali, 6) ed. R. Romano and U. Tucci (Torino, 1983), pp. 223–70.

33 For Maltese cotton, see Abulafia, *Two Italies*, 218, 230; A.T. Luttrell, "Approaches to medieval Malta", *Medieval Malta. Studies on Malta before the Knights* (London, 1975), p. 31.

34 Atiyah, *Egypt and Aragon*, p. 32.

35 See most conveniently E. Ashtor, *A Social and Economic History of the Near East in the Middle Ages* (London, 1976); E. Ashtor, *Technology, Industry and Trade: the Levant versus Europe, 1250–1500*, ed. B.Z. Kedor (Aldershot, 1992).

36 For a new view, see Abulafia, "Maometto e Carlomagno".

37 A. Watson, "Back to Gold — and Silver", *Economic History Review*, 2, 20 (1967), 1–34.

38 On western sources, see P. Spufford, *Money and its Use in Medieval Europe* (Cambridge, 1988), pp. 109–31.

39 S.D. Goitein, *A Mediterranean Society:* vol. 1 *Economic Foundations*, (Berkeley/Los Angeles, 1967), pp. 153–4; Abulafia, "Maometto e Carlomagno", 253.

40 Abulafia, "Maometto e Carlomagno", 231–6, for the implications; Spufford, 209–24, for the physical realities.

41 P. Grierson, "Oboli de musc", *English Historical Review*, 66 (1951), 75–81; P. Grierson, "Muslim coins in thirteenth-century England", *Near Eastern Numismatics, Iconography, Epigraphy and History. Studies in Honor of George C. Miles* (Beirut, 1974), pp. 387–91; M. Bloch, "Le problème de l'or au moyen âge", *Annales d'Histoire Économique et Sociale*, vol. 5 (1933), pp. 1–34; but cf. Abulafia, "Maometto e Carlomagno", pp. 249–50.

42 R.S. Lopez, "Back to Gold", *Economic History Review*, 2, 9 (1956/7), pp. 219–40; R.S. Lopez, "Settecento anni fa: il ritorno all'oro nell'occidente ducentesco", *Rivista storica italiana*, 45 (1953), pp. 19–55, and 161–98 (and published as a separate volume, Naples, 1955); Spufford, pp. 176–7.

43 Cahen, pp. 133, 176.

44 For an example of a ship being repaired in Genoa and then sailed to Egypt to be sold there, see Abulafia, *Two Italies*, p. 244.

45 K.H. Allmendinger, *Die Beziehungen zwischen der Kommune Pisa und Ägypten im hohen Mittelalter. Eine rechts und wirtschaftshistorische Untersuchung* (Wiesbaden, 1967), pp. 45–54; Cahen, pp. 125–7.

46 Abulafia, *Two Italies*, p. 240.

47 Abulafia, *Two Italies*, pp. 140–1.

48 D. Queller, *The Fourth Crusade* (Leicester, 1978), p. 13.

49 J.M. Powell, *Anatomy of a Crusade, 1213–21* (Philadelphia, 1986), pp. 137–8; the Fifth Crusade did, however, include preparatory expeditions aimed at targets around Mount Tabor in the Holy Land. Joinville's *Life of St Louis* is the major source for the planning of Louis IX's Crusade: *Mémoires de Jean sire de Joinville ou histoire et chronique du très Chrétien roi Saint Louis*, ed. F. Michel (Paris, 1867).

50 David Abulafia, "Invented Italians in the Courtois Charters", *Crusade and Settlement: Papers Read at the First Conference of the Society for the Study of the Crusades and the Latin East and Presented to R.C. Smail*, ed. P.W. Edbury (Cardiff: University College Cardiff Press, 1985), pp. 135–43; some Courtois material was put on sale at Sotheby's in the summer of 1989 on the assumption that it was genuine.

51 Abulafia, *Two Italies*, pp. 247–50.

52 Casts of these stones are on display in the crypt of Nôtre-Dame des Tables, Montpellier.

53 C.E. Dufourcq, *L'Espagne catalane et le Maghrib au XIIIe et XIVe siècles* (Paris, 1966).

54 David Abulafia, "Catalan merchants in the western Mediterranean: studies in the notarial acts of Barcelona and Sicily, 1236–1300", *Viator*, vol. 16 (1985), p. 209, repr. in David Abulafia, *Italy, Sicily and the Mediterranean, 1100–1400* (London, 1987), essay VIII.

55 Arxiu del regne de Majorca, Palma de Majorca, Real Patrimonio, Llicències per a Barques. See A. Riera Melis, "La Llicència per a barques de 1284. Una font important per a l'estudi del comerç mallorquí del darrer quart del segle XIII", *Faventia*, vol. 2 (1980): 91–125, (also printed in *Fontes Rerum Balearium*, vol. 3 (Palma de Majorca, 1978–83);

David Abulafia, "Les Llicències per a barques et le commerce de Majorque en 1284", *Les Catalans et la Mer*, ed. H. Bresc (Paris, forthcoming).

56 Fines imposed on Catalan merchants trading with Egypt became a major source of revenue to the Aragonese kings in the early fourteenth century; a supposedly illicit trade was thus transformed into a trade merely subject to additional taxes, and in 1302 these taxes supplied about half the king's known revenue from Catalonia: J. Hillgarth, "The problem of a Catalan Mediterranean Empire, 1229–1327", *English Historical Review*, supplement no. 8 (London, 1975), pp. 7, 41–2.

57 F. Fernández-Armesto, *Before Columbus: Exploration and Colonisation from the Mediterranean to the Atlantic, 1229–1492* (London, 1987), p. 141.

58 For Tlemcen see Dufourcq, pp. 145–56, 311–36.

59 A. Riera Melis, *La Corona de Aragón y el reino de Majorca en el primo cuarto del siglo XIV*, 1: *Las repercussiones arancelarias de la autonomía balear (1298–1311)* (Madrid/Barcelona, 1986), p. 299.

60 The main account of the Mercedarians in the Crown of Aragon is J. Brodman, *Ransoming Captives in Crusader Spain: The Order of Merced on the Christian–Islamic Frontier* (Philadelphia, 1986).

61 *La fille du comte de Pontieu*, ed. C. Brunel (Paris, 1923, 1926).

62 Elena Lourie, "La colonización cristiana de Menorca durante el reinado de Alfonso III el Liberal rey de Aragón", *Analecta sacra Tarraconensia*, 53/4 (1983), pp. 135–86; Ramón Roselló Vaquer, *Aportació a la història medieval de Menorca. El sigle XIII* (Ciutadella, 1980); Micaela Mata, *Conquests and Reconquests of Menorca* (Barcelona, 1984), pp. 9–62. In a paper at the 13th Congress of the History of the Crown of Aragon, Palma de Majorca, September 1987, H. Bresc argued that the events of 1287 were a novelty, marking a new attitude to the Muslims among Christian Mediterranean rulers: H. Bresc, "L'esclavage dans le monde méditerranéen des XIVe et XVe siècles: problèmes politiques, réligieux et morales", *XIII Congrés d'Història de la Corona d'Aragò*, 4 vols. (Palma de Mallorca, 1989–90), 1.89–102; see also David Abulafia, "Monarchs and minorities in the western Mediterranean in the later thirteenth century: Lucera and its analogues", *Christendom and its Discontents*, ed. S. Waugh (Center for Medieval and Renaissance Studies, University of California, Los Angeles, forthcoming).

63 David Abulafia, "Les relacions comercials i politiques entre el Regne de Majorca i Anglaterra segons fonts documentals angleses", *XIII Congrés d'Història de la Corona d'Aragò*, 4.69–79, argues for a continuous series of Mallorcan visits to England and Flanders throughout the early fourteenth century.

64 Dufourcq, Table 3, pp. 596–7.

65 See Fernández-Armesto, p. 151. Indispensable is T. Campbell, "Portolan Charts from the late thirteenth century to 1500", *The History of Cartography: Cartography in Prehistoric, Ancient and Medieval Europe and the Mediterranean*, ed. J.B. Harley and D. Woodward, vol. 1 (Chicago, 1987), pp. 371–463.

66 See the Arab chart illustrated as plate 4 of C. de la Roncière, *La Découverte de l'Afrique au moyen âge: L'intérieur du continent*, vol. 1, published as tome 5 of *Mémoires de la Société royale de Géographie d'Égypte* (Cairo, 1924).

67 Fernández-Armesto, pp. 151–68.

68 The best introductions to Llull are those of J. Hillgarth, *Ramon Lull and Lullism in Fourteenth-century France* (London, 1971), and A. Bonner, "Introduction", *Selected Works of Ramon Llull (1232–1316)*, ed. A. Bonner, vols. 1–2 (Princeton, 1985).

69 Geo Pistarino, ed., *Notai genovesi in Oltremare. Atti rogati a Tunisi da Pietro Battifoglio (1288–1289)*, (Collana storica di Fonti e Studi, 47) (Genoa, 1986). There is also a summary of the acts in G. Jehel, "Catalogue analytique et chronologique des actes du

notaire Petrus Batifolius rédigé à Tunis du 20 décembre 1288 au 24 juin 1289", *Cahiers de Tunisie*, 25 (1977), pp. 69–137.

70 C.H. Haskins, *Studies in the History of Mediaeval Science* (Cambridge, Mass., 1924), pp. 249, 259; cf. David Abulafia, *Frederick II. A Medieval Emperor* (London, 1988), p. 254.

71 See the map of late medieval Tunis in R. Brunschvig, *La Berbérie orientale sous les Hafsides*, vols. 1–2 (Paris, 1940–7), I, 339. The first recorded trade representatives of a Christian ruler date from 1117, when Count Roger of Sicily had commercial agents in Tunis, who may, at this period, have been Muslims themselves, though by the late thirteenth century the Christian merchants of Messina controlled a *fonduq* and Sicilian church in Tunis. Bickering between the Sicilian kings and their brothers, the kings of Aragon, over who should control this consulate was one of many irritants creating tension between the various kings of Aragonese origin in the Mediterranean around 1300. By 1231 there was a Venetian consul at Tunis, representing his city's political and economic interests; evidence for representatives of other Italian cities appears soon after this.

72 Pistarino, nos. 68, 87, pp. 99–100, 126; Jehel, nos. 68, 78–9, pp. 99–100, 103–4. There are some very minor discrepancies between the ordering of the documents which result from Jehel's reasonable decision to produce a calendar of acts in chronological order rather than in the order of the documents.

73 L. de Mas Latrie, *Traités de paix et de commerce et documents divers concernant les relations des Chrétiens avec les Arabes de l'Afrique septentrionale au moyen âge*, parts 1–2, vol. 2 (Paris, 1866), pp. 125–7.

74 Pistarino, no. 78, pp. 113–14.

75 Pistarino, no. 1, pp. 3–4.

76 Pistarino, nos. 75, 78, 86, 106, pp. 109–10, 113–14, 125, 153–4, etc.

77 Brunschvig, vol. 1, pp. 452–4.

78 André Berthier, "Les écoles de langues orientales fondées au XIIIe siècle par les Dominicains en Espagne et en Afrique", *Revue Africaine*, 73 (1932), pp. 84–102. Jeremy Cohen, *The Friars and the Jews. The Evolution of Medieval Anti-Judaism* (Ithaca, N.Y., 1982), p. 107, cites the evidence and additional literature; the reality of the existence of the Tunis school perhaps needs further thought.

79 Abulafia, "Asia, Africa", p. 473.

80 Fernández-Armesto, p. 152.

81 T.F. Glick, *Irrigation and Society in Late Medieval Valencia* (Cambridge, Mass., 1970).

82 Abulafia, *Frederick II*, pp. 335–6.

83 Fernández-Armesto, pp. 198–9; C. Verlinden, *The Beginnings of Modern Colonization* (Ithaca, N.Y., 1970) contains several studies of the transfer of agricultural technology from the Mediterranean to the Atlantic; cf. Watson, p. 154, for the Islamic perspective.

84 J. Heers, "Le royaume de Grenade et la politique marchande de Gênes en Occident (XVe siècle)", *Le Moyen Âge*, 63 (1957), pp. 87–121, repr. in J. Heers, *Société et Économie à Gênes (XIVe–XVe siècles)* (London, 1979), essay VII.

Arabic Fine Technology and its Influence on European Mechanical Engineering

DONALD R. HILL*

By fine technology we mean those types of machines or instruments that were designed to give pleasure to courtly circles, or for timekeeping or for the use of scientists (mainly astronomers). Fine technology is thus distinguished from utilitarian technology which is concerned with machines such as mills, water-raising devices and textile machinery. These were essential to the economic prosperity of society but were very much simpler technically than the constructions of fine technology. Also, the sources for the two categories are different. Information on utilitarian technology comes largely from archaeology (including the examination of existing machines), and references in the works of geographers, travellers and other non-technical writers. For fine technology we find most of our information in a few precious technical treatises. There is some overlap between the two categories, since the writers of the treatises borrowed some of their vocabulary from the craftsmen, such as millwrights and metalworkers. Sometimes they incorporated in their devices miniaturised versions of components from large machines. Occasionally they also described improvements they had made to the traditional machines. In general, however, the division into two separate categories is justifiable.

The traditions of fine technology began in the Hellenistic world in the third century BC. The most important works that have survived were those of Philo of Byzantium (*c.* 200 BC) and Hero of Alexandria (fl. mid-AD 100). Philo's *Pneumatics* exists only in an Arabic version;

* The author acknowledges with gratitude the generosity of the Royal Society in providing him with a grant to assist him in his researches into Islamic technology.

it consists mainly of trick vessels operated by siphonic action, together with descriptions of various types of water-wheels. A number of Hero's works are extant, mainly in Greek, although the *Mechanics* has survived only in an Arabic version made by Qūstā b. Lūqā (d.*c.* 300/912–13) in Armenia towards the close of the third/ninth century. His *Pneumatics* is clearly derived from Philo's work of the same name, but includes more ingenious mechanisms, including a miniature steam turbine. His *Automata* describes two types of automatic theatre, one of which consists of a console that moves by means of a weight-driven motor.[1]

The works of Philo and Hero, as well as some shorter treatises of Greek origin by various authors, were certainly known to the Arabic writers. There is no space here, however, to make a detailed comparison among the various treatises — Greek and Arabic. Suffice it to say that the Arabs, although they took the Greek works as their starting-point, were considerably more advanced. In the following pages any ideas that were in existence in Hellenistic times will be mentioned where relevant, but the distinctive contributions of Arabic engineers will of course occupy most of our attention.

It is highly likely, from references we find in the works of Greek, Roman and Arab historians and travellers, that a tradition for the construction of ingenious devices had existed in the eastern Mediterranean from Hellenistic times and through the periods of the Roman and Byzantine empires into the world of Islam. Written works that actually describe machines in any detail are, however, very rare. The only two important Greek writers have already been mentioned. In Arabic also, although there are a number of short treatises, there are only two writers of major importance. The first of these was Aḥmad, one of three brothers known as the Banū (sons of) Mūsā from their father Mūsā b. Shākir who had been a close companion of Maʾmūn when the latter was residing in Khurāsān before he became caliph (he reigned from 198/813 to 218/833). The brothers were among the most prominent figures in the first flowering of Arabic culture that took place in Baghdad in the third/ninth century. They were patrons of scientists and translators, undertook public works and took part in the turbulent palace politics that characterised the ʿAbbāsid caliphate as the empire began to break up into regional units. Above all, they were erudite scientists and engineers in their own right. About twenty works are attributed to the brothers — Muḥammad, Aḥmad and al-Ḥasan — by the Arab biographers, but only three of these have survived. One is a mathematical treatise that exists only in a Latin translation, the second is the *Book of Ingenious Devices* by Aḥmad, and the third is the description of a musical automaton that we shall have occasion to refer to later. It is probable that this work is also largely attributable to Aḥmad. The most important of these works, however, is undoubtedly the *Book of Ingenious Devices.* About eighty of the devices described in it are trick vessels of various kinds, and the remainder include fountains, lamps, a "gas mask" for use in polluted wells and a clamshell grab. Despite the apparent triviality of many of the devices, Aḥmad's mastery of aerostatic and hydrostatic pressures and his use of automatic controls and switching systems places him well in advance of his Hellenistic predecessors. Indeed, his work in this field, though limited in scope, was not surpassed until modern times.[2]

The great machine book of Ibn al-Razzāz al-Jazarī (fl. seventh/thirteenth century) was completed in Diyār Bakr in 602/1206. This is certainly the most important of the Arabic treatises and probably the most important engineering document from any cultural area before the Renaissance. The work is divided into six categories: (1) water-clocks and candle-clocks, (2) wine dispensers, (3) phlebotomy measuring devices and water dispensers, (4) alternating fountains and musical automata, (5) water-raising devices and (6) miscellaneous. Several of the machines, mechanisms and techniques that appear for the first time in al-Jazarī's work were later to enter the vocabulary of European mechanical engineering. The work is also important because al-Jazarī described his methods of manufacture and construction with the avowed purpose of enabling later craftsmen to reconstruct his machines. Indeed, several have been successfully reconstructed by modern craftsmen using his instructions and illustrations. Detailed instructions and specifications are very rarely found in early mechanical treatises; in fact from this aspect al-Jazarī's work is almost unique before modern times. Other writers were usually unable to give clear instructions either because they had little practical experience or because they did not wish to reveal all the secrets of their profession.[3]

Reference to only two major treatises should not mislead readers into thinking that there were no other Arabic works of significance to the history of machine technology. Indeed, as will be made clear later, some significant ideas occur in some of the shorter treatises. It seems unlikely however, that any major works comparable to those of Aḥmad b. Mūsā and al-Jazarī await discovery. It may seem rash to make such an assertion, given the number of manuscripts in the libraries of universities, mosques and other institutions that have not been examined. The evidence suggests strongly that treatises such as the two mentioned above are of rare occurrence. All the major Arabic biographical dictionaries dealing with scientists have entries on the Banū Mūsā and on no other writers of comparable works on machines. Al-Jazarī lived too late to be included in the *Fihrist* of Ibn al-Nadīm (d. 385/955), and later biographers do not mention him, either because they usually copied from the *Fihrist* or because al-Jazarī's reputation did not spread beyond the limits of the Jazīra until some time after his death. He is, however, mentioned by the Egyptian scholar al-Qalqashandī (d. 821/1418) as pre-eminent in the science of machines.[4] The many manuscripts of al-Jazarī's work, dating from the seventh/thirteenth to the twelfth/eighteenth century, also testify to the esteem in which he was held in the world of Islam.

Al-Jazarī himself always acknowledges his predecessors. Thus he mentions the Banū Mūsā as the most illustrious workers in this field in earlier times.[5] He also mentions by name two Greek and two Arabic writers on machines. All these men are known to us. It seems likely that he knew of all the works of his predecessors that had a direct bearing on his work. From the available evidence, therefore, it appears that we possess the two major works of medieval Arabic machine technology, together with a number of minor works. Major works on machines were equally rare in Hellenistic times, for which we have only the works of Philo and Hero, whose writings were the only Greek works on this subject to reappear in medieval Europe. Clearly, the ability to describe machines accurately and fully has been a rare talent in earlier centuries.

For the remainder of this article we shall be considering some of the more important features of Arabic machine technology. Some of the ideas to be discussed are of Greek origin and such cases will be identified. Otherwise it may be assumed that ideas that occur for the first time in the writings of a given Arab engineer are inventions that were due to that engineer. (References to the Banū Mūsā and al-Jazarī, given in parentheses, are to the page numbers in Hill's translations. References to other writers are given in notes in the usual manner.)

It would be tedious to list all the components and ideas that were known in Islam before their appearance in Europe. Only some of the more significant will therefore be listed. Many of these come from al-Jazarī's works, partly because he was an innovative engineer and partly because his detailed descriptions permit us to understand the construction and purpose of most of the devices that he described. One of the most important components, however, the conical valve, was used to the greatest effect by the Banū Mūsā. It may have been of Greek origin, but nowhere is it used in more applications than by the Banū Mūsā throughout their work. (The normal practice among Arab writers of referring to the *Book of Ingenious Devices* as the work of all three brothers is followed from here onwards, even though its main author was Aḥmad.) The manufacture of these valves was not described until the latter part of the fourth/tenth century in *Mafātīḥ al-ʿUlūm* (The Keys of the Sciences), a dictionary of the sciences written by a certain Abū ʿAbd Allāh al-Khuwārizmī (d. 370/980–1).[6] Further details are given by al-Jazarī, who tells us that plug and seat, usually made of bronze, were cast together in the same mould, then ground together with emery powder until a watertight fit was obtained (20). Emery powder was also used in the calibration of orifices. Al-Jazarī tells us how he accurately calibrated an orifice for a monumental water-clock. He must have known the approximate bore needed and intentionally made the orifice, bored through a piece of onyx, too small. The orifice was then gradually enlarged, with continuous checks on its throughput, until the required rate of flow under a given head of water was achieved (24–5). Conical valves first appear in Europe in the notebooks of Leonardo da Vinci (d. 1519).

The crank is one of the most important components of many modern machines. Manual cranks were known in Europe by the ninth century but the incorporation of cranks in machines did not appear until the fourteenth. Rudimentary cranks appear in the Banū Mūsā; these did not make a complete rotation and were used for the automatic opening and closing of valves (204–9). In one of al-Jazarī's water-raising machines, however, a crank is an integral part of the machinery. It turns continuously to transmit power through a slot-rod to the water-raising apparatus (184–5). This section of al-Jazarī's work is the only one in which he describes large utilitarian machines, probably in order to record improvements that he had made to the traditional types. The fifth and last of these machines is very significant in the history of technology. It is a twin-cylinder water-driven pump with true suction pipes. The pumps of classical and Hellenistic times had vertical cylinders that stood directly in the water. Al-Jazarī tells us that this pump was similar to the "Byzantine siphon" used for discharging Greek fire, except that it was larger. This is the first evidence we have of the construction of this flame-thrower (186–9).

Among other techniques described by al-Jazarī were the static balancing of wheels on a mandrel using small lead weights (27); the use of paper models to assist in the design of intricate mechanisms (68); and the lamination of timber to prevent warping (80). In describing the casting of a large door made of brass and copper for the palace of Āmid (now Diyār Bakr) he mentions two methods of casting: one is the *cire-perdu* or lost-wax process, which had been known since antiquity; the other was using closed mould-boxes with green sand, a method that was not introduced into Europe until the end of the fifteenth century (192).

A very important feature of the thinking behind many of the devices described in the treatises is the preoccupation of the Arab engineers with controls, particularly with controls that would allow a given machine to continue working for long periods — hours, days or even longer — without human intervention. Many types of control, most of which are thought of as quite modern, were employed to achieve these results: feed-back control and closed loop systems, various types of automatic switching to close and open valves or change direction of flow, and precursors of fail-safe devices. In the space available it is possible to describe briefly only four such systems, two by the Banū Mūsā and two by al-Jazarī.

Figure 1 shows a constant-level vessel by the Banū Mūsā (196–7). The main container *DJHT* is divided into two chambers, the upper one, *DJCK*, being the reservoir for the water which is poured in at hole *X*. In the lower chamber is a tank *S* in which is a float *Z*, soldered to the top of which is a valve rod. The plugs of two conical valves are soldered to the upper part of this rod, their seats being fitted to a hole in plate *CK*; valve *L* opens upwards, valve *M* downwards. A pipe *BE* connects tank *S* to a tank *G* outside the main

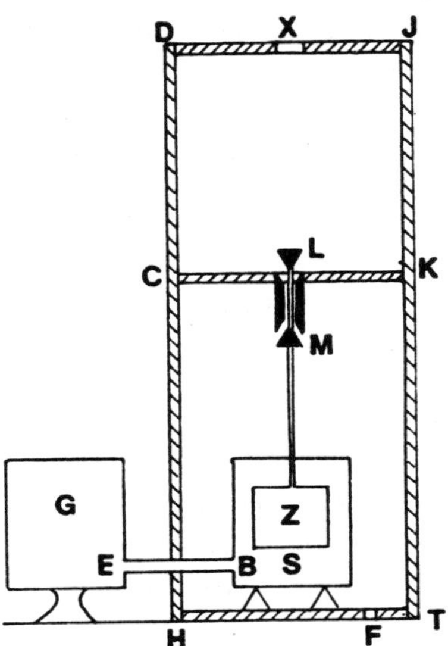

Figure 1 Banū Mūsā: Constant-level device

container. The water-levels in tanks *S* and *G* are the same. When a moderate amount of water is withdrawn from tank *G*, valve *M* opens to replenish the two tanks, then closes when the water reaches its original level. If however, a large amount is withdrawn, valve *L* closes, and no replenishment can take place. Although this device was intended only to mystify onlookers it embodies a principle that was to be important in fail-safe mechanisms. Also, for the first time, we have a double-acting valve.

A fluting machine attributed, probably correctly, to the Banū Mūsā, does not appear in the *Book of Ingenious Devices* but in a separate unique manuscript.[7] The flow of air to the flute is achieved by hydraulic means. Water is directed to one of two chambers alternately, the switching being done by means of a water-wheel, a worm-and-pinion gear, a semicircular cam and a system of valves. When one chamber is filled the air expelled from it goes through a non-return valve into the flute. The flute was provided with eight pallets that were operated by cams on the surface of a cylinder. The cylinder was rotated by a water-wheel on whose axle was a small toothed pinion meshing with a large gear-wheel co-axial with the cylinder. Unfortunately, the manuscript does not include any illustrations, but Figure 2, from a German work of the year 1650, shows essentially the same system. The air supply system shown at the right is cruder than that of the Banū Mūsā, and the instrument is an organ, not a flute, but the method of causing a tune to be played is very similar. The Banū Mūsā's machine, only a very sketchy outline of which is given here, was very sophisticated both hydraulically and mechanically.

The water-machinery shown in Figure 3 was used by al-Jazarī to provide motive power for the first of his monumental water-clocks (17–41). The bottom *A* of the large reservoir is shown. In the reservoir was a float *B*, to which cord *C* was attached; this cord operated the various time-recording mechanisms, and it was of course essential that float *B* descended at constant speed and hence that the discharge rate from the reservoir was also constant. This was achieved as follows: a tube of cast bronze was led out from the bottom of the reservoir, its end turned down at right angles and

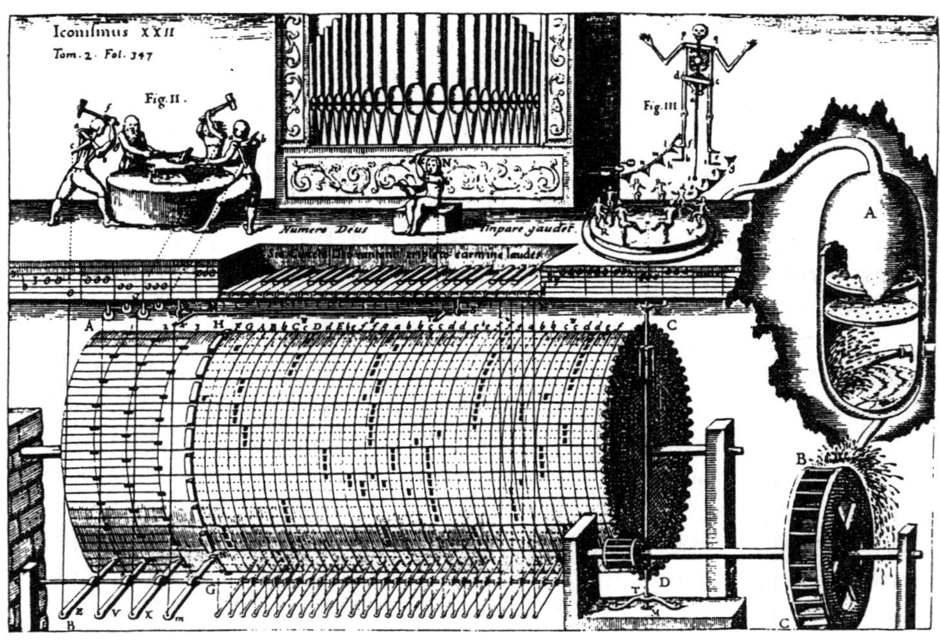

Figure 2 Hydraulic organ from a German treatise of AD 1650

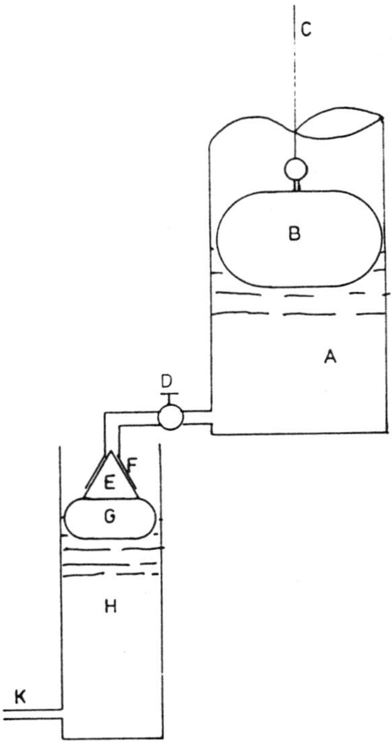

Figure 3 Al-Jazarī: Water-machinery of first clock

formed into the seat *E* of a conical valve. The pipe was provided with a tap *D*. Below the valve seat a small cylindrical float-chamber *H* was erected, having an orifice *K* at its lower end. In it was the small float *G* carrying the plug for the conical valve. To begin the operation the outlet *K* was temporarily closed and tap *D* was opened. The float-chamber *H* filled, float *G* rose and closed valve *E*. Now outlet *K* was opened, and water was discharged, allowing float *G* to fall. Water flowed through valve *F* which closed momentarily, then opened momentarily, and so on. The water-level in the float-chamber and hence the rate of discharge were therefore almost constant. This is a brilliant application of the principle of feed-back control. Al-Jazarī attributed its invention to Archimedes (d. 212 BC) and indeed there exists an Arabic manuscript attributed to

Archimedes that includes a description of this system. Even so, it is a little strange that no other Greek work mentions conical valves.[8]

A system in another of al-Jazarī's clocks is probably his own invention. Figure 4 shows the essential machinery on his third clock (51–7). Inside the model of a boat a water tank *n* is concealed. On the surface of the water is a submersible bowl, *tarjahār*, that has an orifice in its underside that allows it to submerge in one hour precisely. The bowl is attached to the side of the tank by the links *b*. Diametrically across the top of the bowl *a*, a rod *k* is soldered. This has a hole in its centre to which a wire *h* is attached. This wire goes vertically upwards and is connected inside the "castle" to a ball-release mechanism (not shown). A staple is soldered to the underside of the bowl, opposite the orifice, to which a light chain *d* is connected. Above the boat four tubular metal columns are erected and these support the "castle", a metal box, inside which, as already mentioned, is the ball-release mechanism. From this mechanism a channel leads to the head of a falcon *f*, soldered to the outside of the

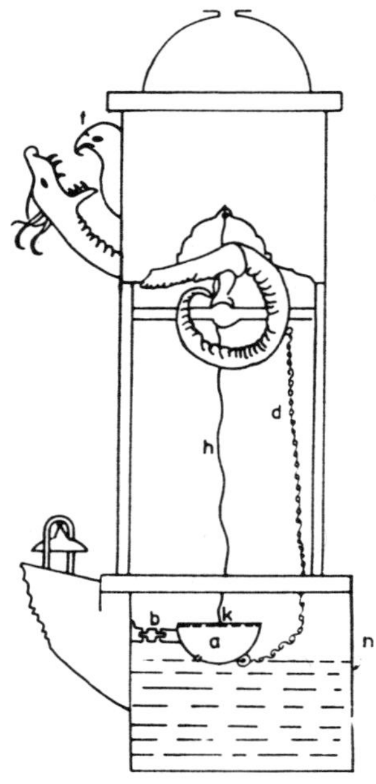

Figure 4 Al-Jazarī: Water-machinery of third clock

castle. Between the columns, below the castle, are two crosspieces between which is an axle to which the feet of a serpent are soldered. The tail of the serpent is bent into a circle which is in fact a pulley; its neck extends outside the castle, bringing its open jaws close to the beak of the falcon, this being the position at the beginning of the operation, when the empty bowl is on the surface of the water. Chain *d* is connected to a staple on the tail of the serpent, and the balls are loaded into the magazine of the release mechanism through a detachable dome at the top of the castle. The action is as follows: the bowl sinks slowly until at the end of an hour it submerges suddenly. Wire *h* then tautens and jerks the ball-release mechanism. A ball rolls into the head of the falcon and emerges from its beak into the jaws of the serpent whose head descends. At the bottom of its travel it drops the ball onto a cymbal, which rings, and the falcon, made lighter by the release of the ball, resumes its former position. When the serpent descended chain *d* tautened and the combined action of this and links *b* raised the bowl and tilted it. It therefore discharged its contents, settled back on the surface of the water and the whole sequence recommenced. A closed loop was therefore in operation: the clock would continue to work as long as balls were loaded into the magazine. This gives only the essential parts of the clock. There were several more automata on this clock and ever more on the following one, the clock of the elephant.

The foregoing examples of techniques, mechanisms and control systems described in the treatises will, it is hoped, give some idea of the level of sophistication achieved by Arab engineers. It has been indicated in several cases that Arabic ideas preceded their introduction into the west, but it is felt that the influence of Arab engineering on the development of European machine technology can best be demonstrated in a structured manner by examining the antecedents of a single machine. The mechanical clock was perhaps the most significant machine to have been introduced in the Middle Ages. The mechanical escapement, a mechanism for slowing down the descent of a heavy weight, was without doubt the invention of an anonymous western European clockmaker towards the close of the seventh/thirteenth century. It can be shown, however, that all the other elements of the mechanical clock, as it emerged in Europe in the fourteenth century, were present in Arabic horology many years before that time. The elements of the early European mechanical clocks were as follows: (1) weight drive, (2) escapement, (3) "going-train" of gears, (4) "striking-train" of gears, (5) assembly of clockwork into a limited space, (6) audible signals, e.g. striking bells, and (7) visual signals, e.g. dials, but more importantly moving jackwork figures of humans and animals; celestial automats. Let us see which of these elements were present in Arabic horology.

A. Weight drive and escapement, (1) and (2)

It can be argued that the large floats that were used in Greek and Arabic water-clocks were weight drives controlled by hydraulic escapements. Also, Hero of Alexandria, writing about the year AD 60, described automata activated by a heavy weight resting on a bed of millet seed in a container. As the seeds slowly escaped from a hole in the bottom of the container, so the weight descended. The idea of using a freely suspended weight, however, seems to have exercised the minds of medieval Arab engineers. There is a treatise, dating to the fifth/eleventh or sixth/twelfth century, that exists in a number of manuscript copies. The manuscripts all contain other material, but the section in question is entitled "Wheels that move by themselves".[9] These devices are usually dismissed as dead-end essays in perpetual motion, but there is more to them than that, although they are admittedly obscure. They were probably serious investigations into the possibility of using gravity as motive power in machines.

One of the devices shows two chain-of-pots pumps mounted on a horizontal axle, in the centre of which was a wheel fitted with curved tubes each partially filled with mercury. The wheel was supposed to turn by the movement of the mercury within the tubes and so operate the pumps. This is of course impossible. The second device shows two weight-driven gear-wheels which meshed with a third gear-wheel that could be connected to a machine. No method for controlling the speed of descent of the weights is given. It is often assumed that this treatise was written for the amusement of courtly circles and not for practical application. It is possible, however, that the writer knew quite well what it was about and that he omitted certain essential components in order to safeguard "trade secrets". Weight is lent to this supposition by the existence of a practical machine that combines the main principles of both machines — mercury escapement and weight drive.

The *Libros del Saber* were prepared in Spain in 1277 under the direction of Alfonso X of Castile (1226–84), with the express purpose of making Arabic knowledge available in Castilian. It is a compilation of translations and paraphrases of Arabic works, some with known authors, some anonymous. In the latter category come the five timepieces described in the last section of the work; only one of these is relevant to our present theme. This clock consisted of a large drum made of walnut or jujube wood and sealed with resin. The interior of the drum was divided into twelve compartments, each with small holes through which mercury flowed. Enough mercury was enclosed to fill just half the compartments. The drum was mounted on the same axle as a large wheel which had a rope wrapped around its perimeter, to the end of which the driving weight was attached. Also on the axle was a pinion with six teeth that meshed with thirty-six oaken teeth on the rim of an astrolabe dial. The drum and the pinion made a complete revolution every four hours and the astrolabe dial made a complete revolution in twenty-four hours.[10] The inclusion of astrolabe dials or similar celestial representations was not uncommon in Islamic monumental water-clocks. The remains of two such clocks can still be seen in Fez, Morocco, and one of them includes an astrolabe dial. Incidentally, the remains of these clocks, built in the eighth/fourteenth century are an important attestation of the tradition of building large water-clocks in Islam.[11]

The compartmental cylinder clock had been in Islam since the fifth/eleventh century — two hundred years before the first appearance of the mechanical clock in Europe. This type of clock, probably derived from the example in the *Libros del Saber*, became very popular in Europe. In the European variety the liquid was water and the drum itself descended. The clock consists essentially of an upright frame which is open and has hours marked down one or both sides. The drum is supported at the centre on two cords wound around the centre of the drum. The arbor is extended to cut the hour scale(s). Under its own weight the drum is free to revolve slowly down the cords, and if the quantity of water within and the sizes of the cords and the orifices are properly adjusted it will indicate the time on the hour scale at the side. Starting in the seventeenth century and throughout the eighteenth and nineteenth centuries, especially in agricultural regions, the falling drum clepsydra in its various forms was extremely popular as a cheap and reliable timekeeper.[12]

B. Gear trains, (3) and (4)

In a mechanical clock, there are two distinct systems of gearing. One of these, the "going-train" consists of the gears that are used to transmit power from the weight drive through the escapement and keep the movement of the clock in correct line. The "striking-train" is also connected indirectly to the drive; its purpose is to cause the bells or other audible signals to sound at regular intervals. One of the gear-wheels in the striking-train is of the segmental type, that is to say it has teeth on only part of its perimeter, thus permitting intermittent action.

The standard types of gearing had all been known since Hellenistic times: parallel meshing; meshing at right-angles; worm-and-pinion; rack-and-pinion. A very complex astronomical calculator, discovered in a shipwreck near the island of Antikythera, probably dates to about 80 BC. It contains many intermeshing gear-wheels and also a differential turntable. Although it could be used for a number of astronomical computations, it was manually operated and so did not have to transmit high torque.[13] Gears that did transmit high torque were the mill with a vertical water-wheel and the water-raising machine known as the *sāqiya*, both introduced in Hellenistic times. In these machines, however, the gears were simply a pair of right-angle meshing wheels.

The Arabs were of course familiar with all the normal types of gearing. Gears that begin to resemble the gears of clockwork occur in some geared calendars and astrolables. Geared calendars were known in Byzantium by the late fifth century AD, and were also constructed by the Arabs, as shown in a treatise written by the famous scientist al-Bīrūnī (d. 440/1048–9) about the year 1040. The gear-wheels were fitted to the inside of a flat circular brass box, bearings being soldered to the base of the box to receive the arbors of the wheels. Three pairs of wheels were mounted concentrically. On the surface of the box, for three of the wheels, there were pointers mounted on extensions of the arbors. One of these moved over a scale divided into the days of the week, the other two, one for the sun and the other for the moon, moved over scales divided into the zodiac and its divisions. The gear ratios were carefully calculated so that the calendar remained synchronous. The pointer for the week was moved each day, causing the pointers for the sun and the moon to move to their correct degree of the zodiac for that day. There was another wheel which displayed the shape of the moon in its correct phase for each day.[14]

In Greek and Arabic instruments we therefore have fairly complex manually-operated gearing, and in the utilitarian machines we have simple gearing that transmitted high torque. Until recently, however, we had no evidence for the combination of the two, i.e. complex gears that transmitted high torque. In the mid-70s a treatise on automata and water-clocks was discovered. This was written in the fifth/eleventh century by a Spanish Muslim called Ibn Khalaf al-Murādī (fl. fifth/eleventh century). The unique manuscript is very badly damaged, the descriptions are too short and the illustrations are badly drawn. It is therefore impossible to discover exactly how any of the thirty devices worked. It can be determined unequivocally, however, first that the devices were large and robust, and secondly that complex gear-trains were used to transmit power from the prime movers to the mechanisms and automata. Sufficient text remains for us to be sure that these included segmental gears, which can also be clearly seen on the illustrations. We have already seen that such gearing was used in the striking-trains of medieval mechanical clocks (al-Murādī may also have used epicyclic gears, but this cannot be established with certainty).[15] Al-Jazarī also used segmental gears in two of his water-raising machines for the transmission of intermittent power (179–81). Taking the evidence as a whole, there is no doubt that the Arabs' knowledge of gearing was at least as sophisticated as that of the European makers of early mechanical clocks.

C. Assembly of clockwork into a limited space, (5)

There are a number of cases where automata and mechanisms were assembled in a limited space, foreshadowing the compact arrangement of the parts of mechanical clocks. Perhaps the most noteworthy example is the assembly of the mechanisms in the "machine-box" of al-Jazarī's fourth clock (63–8). The box was a cube, its sides approximately 30 cm. Into this volume the following mechanisms had to be assembled: ball-release mechanism and magazine for the balls; "balance" for directing the balls alternately to the left and right sides of the clock; a wheel for rotating the figure of a bird on top of the clock; a toothed wheel and a one-way hinge for slowly causing a set of roundels to turn from black to silver (63–9). Some of the Banū Mūsā's devices are masterpieces of intricate assembly, but the description of one such device would occupy too much space.

D. Audible and visual signals, (6) and (7)

Again we may profitably use one of al-Jazarī's machines as an example. This is his first clock. The description of the manufacture, assembly and operation of this clock is long and detailed, but, as is usual with al-Jazarī, he gives a summary of its outside appearance and operation at the start of the chapter. This summary is on pages 18–19 of Hill's translation. The clock consisted of a working face about one and a half metres across and three and a half metres high. At the top of the clock was a disc marked with the signs of the zodiac that turned with constant speed throughout the day. Below this, across the face of the clock were two rows of twelve doors each. In front of the lower row a small crescent moved with constant speed. Every hour, as it reached the sides of the doors, the upper door leaves opened to reveal a standing figure, and the lower door rotated to reveal a different colour. At either side of the clock was a falcon in a niche; every hour each falcon spread its wings, leant forward and dropped a ball onto a cymbal, which rang. Between the two falcons was a semicircle of twelve glass roundels. During the night one roundel became fully illuminated every hour, until at the end of the night all twelve were fully illuminated. Finally, on a platform across the bottom of the clock were the figures of two trumpeters, two drummers and a cymbalist. These performed at the sixth, ninth and twelfth hours. The motive power for all this array of automata was the water-machinery described in an earlier part of this article. Very similar displays were described in the clock built in the sixth/twelfth century at the Jayrūn Gate in Damascus, and another public clock built in Tlemcen, North Africa, in the eighth/

fourteenth.[16] Arrays of automata were to be seen on the early mechanical clocks of medieval Europe, in which dials were one of the less important features. To quote Lynn White:

> Something of the civic pride which earlier had expended itself in cathedral-building now was diverted to the construction of astronomical clocks of astounding intricacy and elaboration. No European community felt able to hold up its head unless in its midst the planets wheeled in cycles and epicycles, while angels trumpeted, cocks crew, and apostles, kings, and prophets marched and countermarched at the booming of the hours.[17]

It is never easy to trace the diffusion of technological ideas, since these ideas are usually transmitted by non-literary means: for example by contacts among craftsmen, by travellers' reports and by the inspection of earlier constructions. It is therefore not always possible to find absolutely firm evidence for the passage of a given idea from one cultural area to another. This is true of horological ideas. Even so, it is simply not credible that the mechanical clock suddenly appeared in Europe without any antecedents. Although our contention that many of the ideas upon which the mechanical clock was founded were Arabic ideas is partly conjectural, nevertheless it is felt that these conjectures are more credible than the genesis of the mechanical clock *ex vacuo*.

Writing in the year 1271, Robertus Anglicus indicated clearly that the invention of the mechanical escapement was imminent and that the invention was being sought among the ranks of the makers of water-clocks.[18] The earliest description we have of a European water-clock appears in MS Ripoll 225 from the Benedictine monastery of Santa María de Ripoll at the foot of the Pyrenees. The MS is tentatively dated to some time in the fifth/eleventh century. The description of the main water-machinery is missing but the section describing the striking-train is complete.[19] There are other, later references to water-clocks in Europe; indeed the existence of a considerable market for water-clocks in Europe in the twelfth century is implied by the establishment of a guild of clockmakers in Cologne in 1183.[20] There is also evidence to indicate considerable improvements in hydraulic timekeeping in the sixth/twelfth century.

Several routes for the transmission of Arabic ideas on fine technology can be suggested, but the most likely route was from

Muslim to Christian Spain and from there into northern Europe. We know for certain that the knowledge of the astrolabe entered Europe by that route. It has now been established that the first European treatises on the astrolabe were of Arabic inspiration and were produced in the monastery of Santa María de Ripoll in the fifth/tenth and sixth/eleventh centuries.[21] This new knowledge was probably disseminated into Europe by Gerbert d'Aurillac, later Pope Sylvester II (999–1003), after he visited Ripoll about the year 967. But we have already seen that the first known European description of a water-clock was written in the monastery of Ripoll. Since the church was keenly interested in methods of timekeeping, it seems likely that information about Arabic advances in horology was carried to the rest of Europe by churchmen.

All the ideas and components embodied in the mechanical clock, except the escapement, had long been present in Arabic fine technology. Apart from the Iberian peninsula, these ideas could also have entered at other points where the two cultures were in contact, e.g. Byzantium, Sicily, and Syria during the Crusades. The mechanical escapement, an invention of genius, undoubtedly originated in western Europe, but it was an invention that was grafted onto an array of ideas that were Arabic in origin.

Notes

1 A.G. Drachmann, "Ktesibios, Philon and Heron: a study in Ancient Pneumatics", *Acta Historica Scientiarum Naturalium et Medicalium* (Biblioteca Universitatis Hauiensis Copenhagen, 4, 1948), pp. 1–197.

2 Banū Mūsā, *The Book of Ingenious Devices*, trans. and annotated Donald R. Hill (Dordrecht: Reidel, 1979); Arabic text, ed. Aḥmad Y. al-Ḥasan (Aleppo: Institute for the History of Arabic Science, 1981).

3 Ibn al-Razzāz al-Jazarī, *The Book of Knowledge of Ingenious Mechanical Devices*, trans. and annotated Donald R. Hill (Dordrecht: Reidel, 1974); Arabic text, ed. Aḥmad al-Ḥasan (Aleppo: Institute for the History of Arabic Science, 1979).

4 Al-Qalqashandī, *Ṣubḥ al-Aʿshā*, ed. Muḥammad ʿAbd al-Rasūl Ibrāhīm, vol. 1–XIV (Cairo, 1913–30), p. 1,477.

5 Al-Jazarī, p. 157.

6 E. Wiedmann, *Aufsätze zur Arabischen Wissenschaftsgeschichte*, vol. 1 (Hildesheim: Georg Olms, 1970), pp. 209–10.

7 Banū Mūsā, "Al-Āla allatī tuzammar bi-nafsihā", Arabic text ed. L. Cheikho, *Al-Machriq*, 9 (1906), pp. 444–56; English trans. by H.G. Farmer, *The Organ of the Ancients*, (London: Reeves, 1931), pp. 88–118.

8 Pseudo-Archimedes, *On the Construction of Water-clocks*, trans. Donald R. Hill (London: Turner & Devereux, 1976).

9 H. Schmeller, "Beiträge zur Geschichte der Technik in der Antike and bei den Arabern", *Abhandlungen zur Geschichte der Naturwissenschaften und der Medizin*, 6 (Erlangen, 1922).

10 *Libros del Saber* . . ., ed. M. Rico y Sinobás (Madrid, 1863–7); see also Silvio A. Bedini, "The compartmented cylinder clepsydra", *Technology and Culture*, 3 (Spring 1962), pp. 115–41.

11 Derek de Solla Price, "Mechanical water clocks of the 14th century in Fez, Morocco", *ITHACA* (Paris, 1962), 26 VIII–2 IX.

12 Anthony Turner, *The Time Museum*, vol. 1, Part 3 (Rockford, 1984), pp. 40–3.

13 Derek de Solla Price, *Gears from the Greeks* (New York: Science History Publications, 1975).

14 Donald R. Hill, "Al-Biruni's mechanical calendar", *Annals of Science*, 42, (1985), pp. 139–63.

15 Donald R. Hill, *Arabic Water-clocks* (Aleppo: Institute for the History of Arabic Science, 1981), pp. 36–46.

16 For the Damascus clock, see Hill, *Arabic Water-clocks*, pp. 69–88. For the Tlemcen clock, see Abū Zakariyyā Yaḥyā ibn Khaldūn, *Bughyat al-Ruuwād*, ed. A. Bel, vol. 2 (Algiers, 1904–13), pp. 40–1.

17 Lynn White Jr., *Medieval Society and Social Change* (Oxford, 1964), p. 124.

18 Lynn Thorndike, "Invention of the mechanical clock about 1271 AD", *Speculum*, 16 (1941), pp. 242–3.

19 Francis Maddison, Bryan Scott and Alan Kent, "An early medieval water-clock", *Antiquarian Horology*, 3 (1962), pp. 348–53.

20 White, p. 120.

21 Emmanuel Poulle, "Les instruments astronomiques de l'Occident latin au XIe et XIIe siècles", *Cahier de civilisation médievale*, 15 (1972), pp. 27–40.

The Influence of the Metalwork of the Arab Mediterranean on that of Medieval Europe

JAMES W. ALLAN

Among the problems facing any research into origins and influences are the limitations imposed by the quirks of survival. For example, in a recent article on the fourteenth century Wartburg carpet, Strohmaier[1] rightly observed that one particular figural grouping, the depiction of Jupiter in Pisces at the top of the carpet, was derived from an Islamic source. The large numbers of planetary and zodiacal schemes on surviving examples of Islamic metalwork gave him a ready source for these images, and so he attributed them to metal objects introduced into medieval Europe. In the long run, however, we may find that such comparisons are inappropriate, for in this context the existence in the Ashmolean Museum of a fourteenth-century Egyptian embroidery with a repeat design of this very motif[2] suggests that the carpet design may have been based on a source much more appropriate to its own medium, namely textiles.

It is in this light, perhaps, that we should see a very bizarre example of possible influence from Islamic metalwork in medieval Europe: the hares adorning the fifteenth-century entrance to Paderborn Cathedral. Strohmaier[3] found an obvious comparison in the three hares decorating the base of a *c.* tenth-century Persian silver flask, and similar designs recur on Islamic metalwork, for example in the three sphinxes which adorn the centre of Badr al-Dīn Luʾlu's tray in Munich, dating from the early thirteenth century.[4] But such a source should be viewed very tentatively: a more likely one in a more appropriate medium may well one day appear.

Two thirteenth-century statues on the other hand, do seem to have something important to say about metalwork. A statue of the Margrave Eckhardt in St Peter's Cathedral, Naumberg, dating from *circa* 1250 wears what is almost certainly an Islamic belt.[5] It is a rendering in stone of what was evidently a wide leather belt with upright metal spacers attached at regular intervals around it. Each of these spacers has a circular centre, perhaps a setting for a precious or semi-precious stone, a flaring lower element, and a straight vertical upper element which appears to terminate in a small hemisphere. This is a design very closely allied to that found in Ayyūbid Syria and Egypt, from which two sets of belt fittings have survived, one in the name of a nephew of Ṣalāḥ al-Dīn, al-Malik al-Ṣāliḥ Ismāʿīl, who died in 1266.[6] Here the centres are diamond-shaped and the upper and lower elements triangular. The upper element of Eckhardt's belt, however, is more reminiscent of the form of spacer used in two other sets of belt fittings, one in the British Museum, and another which appeared on the art market recently.[7] The former may well be Anatolian, while the latter probably comes from elsewhere in the Jazīra or Iran during the period which followed the collapse of Great Saljūq rule.

The second thirteenth-century European statue of interest is in Magdeburg Cathedral. Here, a sculpture of two figures, variously interpreted as the Emperor Otto I and his wife, Editha, or as Christ and Mary, shows the crowned male figure holding a circular object containing nineteen spheres. Whatever painted designs originally decorated this object have now disappeared. Traditionally thought to be representations of the nineteen tonnes of gold presented to the cathedral on its foundation by Otto I,[8] Strohmaier suggested a more likely link with Islamic planetary imagery.[9] For, to the Islamic art historian, the layout of the spheres in the dish suggest the sun, with the six planets around, and then, in an outer ring, the twelve signs of the zodiac. This type of layout is so common in Islamic metalwork, appearing regularly on bowls, basins, pen-boxes and trays,[10] that it is conceivable that some object with the planets and zodiacal signs depicted as spheres in concentric rings around a central spherical sun could indeed have existed in medieval Islam. In the context of Magdeburg Cathedral, the statue, whether of the Emperor or Christ, would then have been holding the cosmos as a symbol of power, and moreover displaying a rare and exotic object from the east.

Certainly there is evidence that Islamic metalwork reached Europe in the medieval period. For example, Rupin relates how Raymond III, Count of Rouergue, who had gone to the help of the Count of

Barcelona, gave the booty he had captured to the Abbey of Conques. This consisted of twenty-one engraved and gilded silver vases and a silver saddle, and from them the monks made a splendid cross "tout en conservant les riches ciselures des Sarrasins".[11] He also quotes Adémar de Chabannes, who, in discussing gifts made to the Abbey Saint-Martial in Limoges, refers to "duo candelabra saracenice fabricata".[12]

Surviving examples in their original European collections or treasuries are, however, virtually non-existent, and it is only the occasional echo which survives. One of the most famous pieces of church furnishing from northern Europe in the early Middle Ages is the pulpit of Henry II in Aachen.[13] Illustrations of this pulpit show that, in addition to the famous ivory plaques which are thought to be Umayyad, the rock crystal objects which seem to come from early Islamic Iran, the Islamic ivory and rock crystal chessmen and the semi-precious stones which adorn the pulpit, there are also twelve shallow hemispherical depressions in the gilt copper covering of the pulpit, each decorated with the same design in the "vernis brun" technique (fig. 1).

"Vernis brun", or "Braunfirnis", is the name given to a technique used to decorate copper in the Rhineland and Meuse from the eleventh to the mid-thirteenth century. "Vernis brun" was produced in four phases. In the first the copper was carefully polished. In the second linseed oil was applied in one or more layers, and heated as long as necessary to obtain a uniform crystalline covering, a sort of varnish varying from clear brown to black in colour. In the third stage the varnish was scraped away from the surfaces to be gilded, either the motifs themselves or the ground. The fourth phase consisted of gilding the cleaned metallic surfaces using an amalgam of gold and mercury. The result was a contrast between the areas of gilt surface and those coloured brown through the sort of varnish produced by the oil.[14]

Although the depressions in the gilt copper covering of the pulpit are not separate objects, like the others mentioned, their positions on the pulpit and lectern suggest that they should have similar significance, and not simply be decorated with the first motif the craftsman could think of. Since all of the objects are foreign and suggest the imperial aspirations and worldwide kingly contacts of Henry II, could not this design also in some way invoke the same idea?

Figure 1 Design of the "vernis brun" hemispherical depressions on the Ambo of Henry II, Aachen Cathedral.

Now radial patterns are very common in Islamic ceramics. This is especially true of the twelfth and thirteenth centuries, from which comparatively large numbers of Iranian and Syrian objects survive. But the nearest to the design on the pulpit are those which occur on ʿAbbāsid lustreware of Iraq in the ninth–tenth century. At that period radial patterns were extremely common in tilework, as is clear from the lustre tiles preserved on the *miḥrāb* of the Great Mosque in Qairawan.[15] The single tiles with diagonal designs must originally have been designed as sets of four, which, when put together, would have given strong radial patterns. Reconstruction of such radial patterns shows that the designs included wing-like leaves growing from half-way up a stem, and other elements, such as the palmette in an ogival cartouche, recalling those on the pulpit. More important, two particular surviving lustre bowls, one of them in Copenhagen (pl. 1), bear radial designs which are surely simplified versions of those on the pulpit.[16] Lustreware was heavily dependent on luxury metalwork for its original inspiration, as the metallic colour schemes and the dotted grounds of these objects, the latter derived from ring-punching on silver, testify. Consequently, designs are likely to have followed metalwork as well.

The designs used on the Aachen pulpit are therefore most likely derived from ʿAbbāsid Iraqi silver bowls with niello inlay. These must have not only provided models for the designs used by the Iraqi lustre potters of the day, but also been exported, through trade or gifts, to Europe. There, although perhaps too practical and useful for inclusion in the Aachen pulpit, their designs, with "vernis brun" taking the place of the Islamic niello, could be used to symbolise the exotic east.

This, of course, raises an interesting possibility about the origins of "vernis brun". Lemeunier has proposed that such a specific art form alongside enamelling could have been suggested to the early eleventh-century jewellers by some of the great products of the Carolingian illuminators, and that this might account for the epigraphy in "vernis brun" on the ambo of Henry II, and the common use of the technique for rinceau designs. While this is obviously true, one could perhaps postulate in addition that pieces of Islamic silver decorated with niello could also have played their part in the establishment of this tradition.

In form the decorated depressions suggest small shallow hemispherical saucers, which would presumably have been used in their original context for wine-drinking. Such a shape has not been recorded up till now in ʿAbbāsid metalwork. It does, however, occur in a later piece of royal Islamic silver, a small silver gilt bowl in the Hermitage which, following Marshak's interpretation, depicts the eleventh-century ruler of Afghanistan and northwest India, Maḥmūd of Ghazna.[17] All the more does our proposed ʿAbbāsid silverwork origin for the Aachen pulpit design ring true.

The influence of the original silver wine bowl or bowls, and of the design derived from them, was destined to be negligible. Alongside the other examples of exotica in Aachen Cathedral, they remained a world apart, too remote physically and intellectually to inspire any local craftsmen, or a taste for Islamic designs among local patrons.

Other Near Eastern objects reaching Europe, on the other hand, were destined to have a much more profound, albeit localised, influence. Here our discussion must turn to the niello spiral. The history of the niello spiral has been most fully investigated by Boris

Marshak.[18] He has shown that the taste for this type of ornament was Iranian in origin, and a silver bowl in the name of Sharaf al-Maʿālī Anushirvan, ruler of Gurgan (1029–49) (pl. 2), provides an example of its popularity in the eleventh–twelfth century. But Marshak has also pointed out that Byzantine Antioch in the late tenth and early eleventh century shared with Iran a taste for spirals against a niello ground. A key example is the Aachen atrophorium, most probably made in Antioch *c.*970. Antioch, through its geographical location, was probably a very important centre for the distribution of Iranian artistic ideas. This is suggested by a nielloed silver reliquary box in the Vatican (pl. 3), which is to be attributed to Antioch through its imagery (it has St Peter, patron saint of Antioch, in place of the Virgin Mary), but has typical Iranian niello ornament.[19] It would thus be through centres such as Antioch that Europe, via the Crusaders, would have been exposed to this fashion for niello spirals and arabesques.

An extremely important example of this fashion has recently come to light in the German excavations at Rusafa in Syria.[20] The Rusafa treasure consists of five pieces of twelfth-century church silver, and interestingly includes a Crusader object bearing contemporary European coats-of-arms, showing that Crusader objects permeated the Christian areas of Syria, where they could be used in appropriate church settings. Of much greater interest here, however, is a chalice in the Rusafa treasure bearing a Syriac inscription and spirals against a niello ground (pl. 4). Whatever the origin of the actual chalice — and it could well be a European object — the decoration must be the product of a twelfth-century Syrian, perhaps Antiochan workshop, and it was undoubtedly the arrival of pieces of silver in this style in Europe that was to lead to the establishment of an extraordinary fashion in silverwork of the late twelfth century, localised in Lower Saxony.

Henry the Lion, Duke of Saxony from 1139 to 1195, was married to Matilda, eldest daughter of Henry Plantagenet of England, and was the father of the future Holy Roman Emperor Otto IV. In 1172 Henry set out on pilgrimage to the Holy Land, returning to Brunswick the following year. He was accompanied by a retinue of over five hundred, including an archbishop, and several counts and abbots. The diary of Abbot Heinrich, one of those who accompanied Henry, tells of Henry's great veneration for relics. During his return from Palestine, Henry was presented with fourteen mules loaded with gold and silver and silken vestments by the Byzantine Emperor, Manuel Comnenus. While expressing "immense thanks", the Duke let it be known that however precious these objects were he would by far prefer relics of certain saints. The relics he coveted were readily given him, the emperor adding "much glory of precious stones" to the gift.[21] Two surviving objects in the Guelph treasure may have come from Constantinople at this time, though they could also have reached Otto IV through the hands of Crusaders returning from the sack of Constantinople in 1204: an icon of St Demetri and a portable altar.[22] But sadly we can only speculate on the full range of precious metal items which Henry may have brought back from Byzantium and the Crusader and Islamic Near East.

Among these objects, however, must have been silver vessels and reliquaries with niello inlay and the spiral scroll which we have been discussing. For, in the last quarter of the twelfth century, the use of the spiral scroll against a niello ground becomes extensive in silver objects produced in Lower Saxony. For example, it appears on the Arm Reliquary of St Lawrence, now in the Kunstgewerbe Museum in Berlin (*c.*1175–80),[23] on the Head Reliquary of St Oswald in Hildesheim Cathedral treasury (*c.*1180),[24] the chalice of Count Berthold III of Andechs (1148–84) in Wilten Abbey (Innsbruck) (pl. 5),[25] the chalice in Tremessen Abbey, (Poland *c.*1170), which may well have been a gift from Henry the Lion,[26] the Paten of St Bernward in Cleveland (*c.*1185),[27] and many more. It was presumably through a similarly decorated object brought back from the Crusades that a craftsman in England had the inspiration for the late twelfth-century clasp of the Bible of Hugh du Puiset in Durham.[28]

Other late twelfth-century objects from Lower Saxony give us additional, significant evidence for the import of Islamic metalwork into Germany at this period, presumably through the same channels as the objects decorated with niello scrolls. For example, in the Wilten chalice we find two styles of interlacing roundels, both widespread in Islamic art. The cup of the chalice follows a simpler style of interlace common on Islamic metalwork, exemplified by a medallion of the planets and signs of the zodiac on the lid of a thirteenth-century Jazīran pen-box in Bologna;[29] the more complex interlacing roundels on its foot may be compared to those on the base of a late thirteenth-century or early fourteenth-century Mamlūk bowl in the Bargello.[30] On the chalice's foot the roundels are arranged six on the inner row and twelve on the outer row, following the zodiacal layout of the Islamic tradition, even though they no longer hold planetary or zodiacal images. The export of such images from Islam to Christian rulers is clear from the fact that the same planetary and zodiacal images in interlaced roundels decorate the basin made by mid-fourteenth-century Syrian craftsmen for Hugh IV of Lusignan, who was in theory King of Jerusalem but in practice resident in Cyprus.[31]

On occasional pieces, too, we find copies of Arabic inscriptions, as for example on the chalice and paten from the Petrikirche in Salzburg, now in the Kunsthistorisches Museum in Vienna (pls. 6–7).[32] Both have pseudo-kūfic inscriptions, similar in style to those of a Limoges enamelled gemellion in the Victoria and Albert Museum in London (to which we shall return) and deriving almost certainly from Fāṭimid art. The trefoil surmounting an arch copies a ninth–tenth century western Islamic form of *ʿayn* or *mīm*, the uprights with three cusps copy hastae of the same period, and so too the stems and leaves curling right over to form the beginnings of a spiral.[33]

Lower Saxony was not the only locality to be influenced by Arab metalwork. In France, at approximately the same time, a comparable situation was to be found, but this time in enamel and centred on Limoges. It was Buchthal[34] who in 1946 first suggested a relationship between Limoges gemellions and Islamic art. He pointed out that the earliest surviving gemellion is Islamic: an enamelled example, now in Innsbruck, made for the Urtuqid ruler of Diyarbekir and Hisn Kaifa, Dāʾūd b. Suqmān (d. 1144) (pl. 8). He also noted that both the layout (a central circle with six circles around) and individual elements in the decoration of this object (the dancing girls, the trees, the animals and the spiralling vine ornament) can be paralleled on enamelled gemellions from Limoges, and he drew attention to other parallels betwen Islamic metalwork and thirteenth-century Limoges enamel designs: the use of the falconer, and the use of a central heraldic device. He concluded:

> [The Innsbruck dish] is only one representative example of the products of a school of craftsmen which must have worked in Islamic countries, probably in northern Mesopotamia, and of whose work

> several pieces must have been brought to France by the crusaders. They gave the idea of enamelled gemellions to the craftsmen of Limoges, who adhered rather closely to their models in the general organization and subject matter of their works.

Recent research makes it possible to support Buchthal's argument with additional evidence. For example, we may now compare Limoges gemellions with western Islamic ceramics. Sgraffiato wares are generally acknowledged to owe much to metalwork, since they were so often incised with dividers, producing the circle-based designs for which metalwork is also famed. There are striking parallels with Limoges gemellion layouts in Mesopotamian and Persian sgraffiato wares.[35] The shapes of these vessels, however, are unrelated. Significantly, there are better parallels for the shape from Egypt. Here, sgraffiato designs are uncommon, but one finds in lustreware both a field divided in a related way and the gemellion shape: for example, a piece in the Islamic Museum in Cairo,[36] and another example in the Benaki Museum in Athens,[37] both of which also have the dog-tooth edging of the Limoges gemellions. *Bacini*, the bowls cemented into the fabric of medieval churches in Pisa and other Italian towns, include many bowls from North Africa and the Levant, apparently following the gemellion shape,[38] suggesting that this was a popular form in Fāṭimid times. Moreover, two such *bacini* are obviously related to the Limoges style, for they are decorated with a central bird or flower in a roundel, and eight groups of outward-turned semi-circles around the upper body and rim.[39] Finally, there are a number of surviving Limoges objects bearing pseudo-Arabic inscriptions. Two examples may be conveniently cited, a gemellion in the Victoria and Albert Museum (pl. 9),[40] where the inscription may be seen around the central roundel, and an enamel plaque in the Musée de Cluny in Paris.[41]

Intriguing evidence of the presence of metal vessels of Muslim origin in Limoges at a slightly earlier date has recently come to light in a manuscript in the University Library in Leiden (Cod.Voss.Lat.0.15),[42] which was copied in the early eleventh century in the Benedictine monastery of Saint-Martial in Limoges by the monk Adémar of Chabannes. One particular page includes drawings of parts of three kūfic inscriptions which must have decorated objects kept in the monastery. In one of them, Adémar has included the background to the script, and his little circles clearly copy the ring punching so common on Islamic silver, showing that this inscription at least must have decorated a piece of Islamic silver. Incidentally, a fragment of decorated Islamic silver, found in Gotland in Sweden, must illustrate the type of object seen by the Limoges scribe.[43]

Recent research into the chemical composition of Limoges enamel has suggested another possible relationship between Limoges and Islam. West European glass of the period is either a high potassium glass used for windows, or a low magnesia, soda-lime silicate glass, used for vessels and some enamels. Limoges enamel, on the other hand, though low magnesia glass does occur, is usually a high magnesia, soda-lime silicate glass. Such a glass composition is characteristic of the Islamic world, and has been found in bodies of Fusṭāṭ glass objects and in one of the enamels used on Mamlūk glass. Though one must be cautious, given the small amount of work done in this field, there is at the very least an unexpected similarity of materials between Limoges and Egypt in this medium.[44]

In both the cases discussed above, however, the influences are very localised; the niello spiral is only rarely found outside Lower Saxony, while the enamels showing clear Islamic influence are as uniformly products of Limoges. A much wider geographical range of influence is suggested by various other European metal objects. First let us take the base-metal, three-legged ewer, so widespread in Northern Europe in the thirteenth and fourteenth centuries [pls. 10–11].[45] There seems to be no precedent for the form of these objects in Europe, but there does seem to be a possible origin for them in the earlier Islamic ewers of the eastern Mediterranean. Examples of the latter are quite numerous but very varied in form. An example in the Museum of Islamic Art, Cairo (fig. 2), has a strongly concave-sided body with slight facetting on it, and can be dated to *c.* AD 900 on the basis of its inscription;[46] an example in the Keir collection (fig. 3) has a very slightly inward-curving cylindrical body;[47] a piece in the Dauphin collection (fig. 4) has six sides and a strongly facetted shoulder;[48] a ewer in Ani (fig. 5) has a body of inverted pear shape;[49] a piece in Berlin-Dahlem (fig. 6), found with the famous Marwān ewer at Abu Sir al-Malaq in the Fayyum (Egypt), has six concave sides;[50] a further piece in Berlin-Dahlem (fig. 7) has a squat cylindrical body.[51] Outstanding among the features which occur on different examples of these objects are the three feet, the

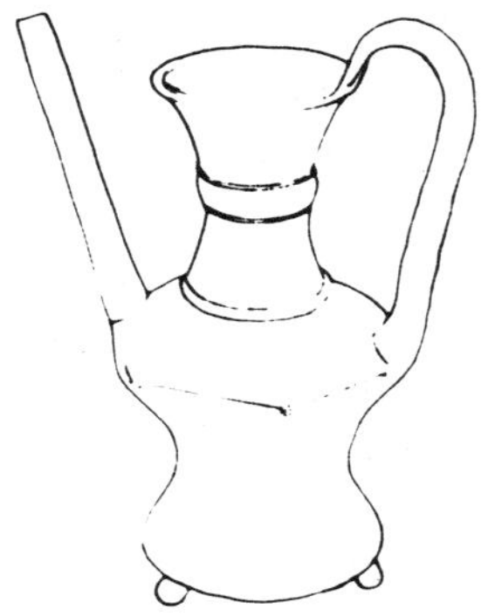

Figure 2 Islamic Museum, Cairo, no.24261

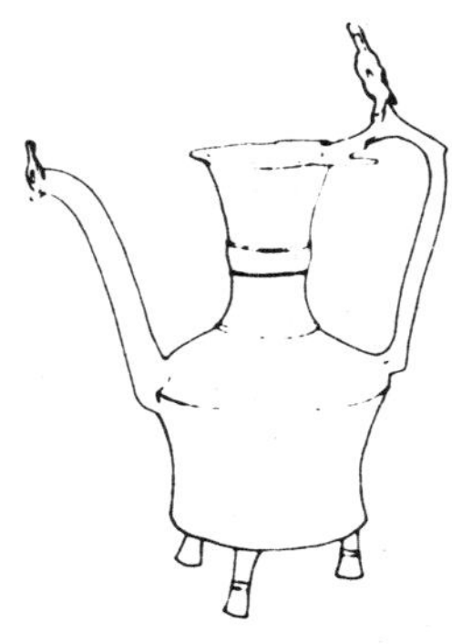

Figure 3 Keir collection, no.3

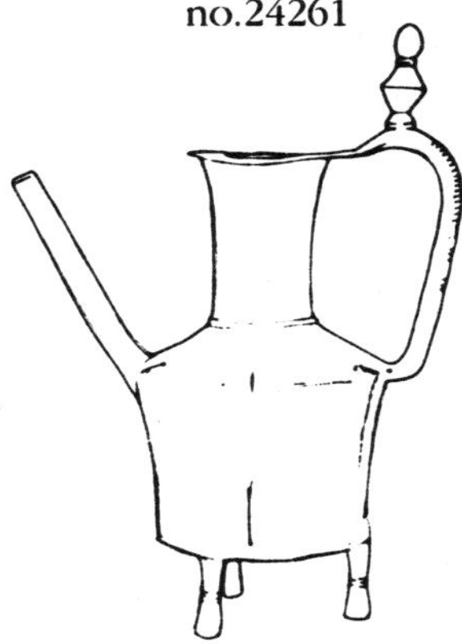

Figure 4 Dauphin collection, Geneva

Figure 5 Ani

Figure 6 Berlin-Dahlem, no.I 3553

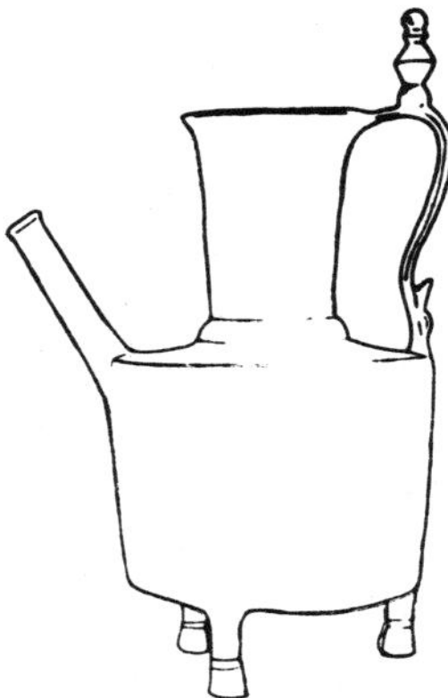

Figure 7 Berlin-Dahlem, no.I 6758

spout rising from the shoulder, the curving handle which joins the shoulder to the rim, and in its more decorative form, a neck with a knop around the centre and a ridge at its base. There seems to be a real possibility that a more spherical-bodied variation of this type of Fāṭimid ewer could have been the origin of the European form, both the style with the more decorative neck (pl. 11), and the commoner style with a much more elegant, smoothly curving form (pl. 10). Such inexpensive, practical, base-metal objects could well have been carried for drinking and washing purposes by returning Crusaders, and could easily have introduced a general taste for this shape into Europe.

Certainly, Mediterranean Islamic influence must lie behind a twelfth- or thirteenth-century mortar from England, now on loan to the British Museum, and on display in the medieval gallery there. This object, with its heavy squat form, flaring lip, tall triangular flanges around the sides (pointing alternately upwards and downwards), and its ring handle, is quite different in form from the normal European mortar shape, e.g. a piece in the British Museum dated 1514 AD.[52] Instead it follows the standard form of Mediterranean Islamic mortar of the Fāṭimid period and later.[53]

It is perhaps appropriate at this point briefly to consider one other object form common in Europe in the thirteenth century — the ciborium. Here a very straightforward question may be asked: what is the relationship between the Vaso-Vescovali, produced in Afghanistan *c.*1200, now in the British Museum (pl. 12),[54] and the Balfour ciborium, produced in England at almost the same date, now in the Victoria and Albert Museum (pl. 13)?[55] And where does an object like the Surgut cup,[56] ascribed by Marshak to a frontier area, like the Dukedom of Edessa, or perhaps Armenia, fit in? One might ask the same question of two other cups: that from thirteenth-century Anatolia or northern Syria, in the Keir collection,[57] and that from Vil'gort, in the Hermitage. Marshak suggests that the latter is probably a twelfth-century Armenian product.[58] Similarly, a cup from the Crimea under the Golden Horde, also in the Hermitage;[59] a cup found in Gotland, which is attributed by Marshak to a possible English origin, and by Anderrson to Cologne, in the late twelfth century;[60] and other such cups, attributed by Darkevich to Limoges in the twelfth–thirteenth century,[61] though an English origin is also possible.[62] Marshak's conclusion is that these cups are all related, and that, on the basis of the Crusades and the movement of the niello scroll, priority must be given to the Near East, and influence of the Islamic world on Europe assumed, rather than the other way round.

A still more detailed study of these objects and their interrelationships cannot be undertaken in the present article. However, another iconographic feature which supports Marshak's argument for an eastern origin is worth noting. Around the upper part of the body of the Balfour ciborium is a meander which may be compared to a more complex band of interlacing strapwork found on early thirteenth-century inlaid Syrian metalwork,[63] which is in its turn most probably derived from Fāṭimid art.[64] If Marshak's theory is correct, then Islamic metalworking is providing a source not only for very ordinary, European, secular objects like the base metal ewers, but also for European objects of great splendour with a specific, sacred function.

Without question, however, the greatest influence from Islam to Europe in the field of metalwork is that of the aquamanile. Since earlier scholars have covered this subject far more thoroughly than any of the other topics treated in this article, a summary of the evidence will be sufficient here. The most substantial work on aquamaniles is that of Erica Dodd, in her article on the origins of medieval *dinanderie*.[65] Dinanderie is the name given to the decorative figures of brass, copper or bronze, made in Dinand (Belgium) and other European centres in the twelfth, thirteenth and fourteenth centuries. Very large numbers of these objects have survived, and were brought together by von Falke and Meyer in their classic volume *Die Bronzegeräte des Mittelalters*, published in 1935.[66] There are major problems in interpreting the evidence, as Dodd was well aware. She wrote as follows:

> One reason that the origin of the *dinanderie* is difficult to determine is that the number of Latin figures far exceeds the number of surviving Islamic ones and direct comparisons do not come readily to hand. To discover its origin, each species must first be studied separately in comparison with an Islamic model. Secondly, where direct comparison is not possible, Islamic examples in other media have to be found. This must be done for every shape, however, since it is possible that certain forms were taken over from Islam whereas others originated in an indigenous Latin environment, or stemmed

> from other medieval sources. Finally, one figure that attracts particular attention is the popular one of a rider astride a horse or a lion. This figure occupies a unique postion among the *dinanderie* because human representation is involved. Although the Near East may be regarded as the source for many of the bizarre beasts of the Romanesque repertoire, few scholars believe it could also be responsible for human figures, especially in the round. Since no bronze Islamic aquamanile in the shape of a rider has survived from earlier than the 15th century, it is easy to assume that this type of vessel represents a Latin addition to the inventory of medieval shapes.[67]

The starting point for assuming an Islamic origin for the *dinanderie* figures is chronology. The simple fact is that among the very large number of surviving medieval Islamic aquamaniles, water spouts and free-standing sculptures in the form of animals and birds, are many which predate the appearance of *dinanderie* in Europe by up to three centuries. As examples, one might cite a bird aquamanile in the Hermitage of Egyptian or Syrian origin, and dated AH 180/ AD 796,[68] and a stag in Munich which is probably tenth–eleventh century Fāṭimid Egyptian.[69]

Dodd approaches her study by taking three forms of European aquamanile, the lion, the griffin, and the mounted horseman, and bringing together the more specific evidence for each of them originating in the Islamic world. The most important Islamic example of a lion aquamanile is the lion now in Kassel in Germany [pl. 14], which is probably an eleventh century Egyptian object.[70] It has lost its tail, which would have formed the handle, but its Islamic origin is clear from the fact that it is signed in Arabic by ʿAbdallāh *maṭhthāl* (sculptor). Meyer's comparison of this piece with Romanesque lion aquamaniles (pl. 15) provides clear links between the two.[71] Not only is there a striking likeness in facial features, but, as Dodd shows, a number of early Islamic aquamaniles, produced in Egypt or Syria in the eighth–eleventh centuries (e.g. the bird aquamaniles in Berlin-Dahlem and St Catherine's Monastery, Mount Sinai),[72] have animal handles from which the Romanesque handle must surely derive.

Dodd's second creature, the griffin, is a more problematic animal, since exact parallels for extant European griffins are hard to find in Islamic art. There are, on the other hand, a large variety of real and mythical animals in the round in the Islamic world from which they might have derived. One might cite for example the eleventh-century Egyptian or North African Pisa griffin,[73] a twelfth–thirteenth-century ceramic fountain head from Syria in the shape of a cockerel,[74] another in the shape of a sphinx,[75] a small, related bronze sphinx probably from twelfth–thirteenth-century Anatolia,[76] and others.

Turning to the mounted horseman, a number of facts point to an Islamic source for both the idea and the form. First of all there is a European bronze falconer in the Lehman collection in New York.[77] Falconers are rare in medieval Europe but common in Islamic art, and Dodd shows that details of his bridle, his robe, and his hair and hat, suggest an Islamic source. Less obviously Islamic in origin perhaps is a mounted horseman now in the Victoria and Albert Museum (pl. 16),[78] but here too there is important evidence of an Islamic connection. The form of horse — small head, arched neck, bulging chest, and small hind legs, is very similar to that of the Bobrinski horse in the Hermitage,[79] which is a tenth-century East Persian object. Moroever the handle of the Victoria and Albert aquamanile follows the Islamic tradition already mentioned. Finally, we know that statues of horsemen, both functional and ornamental, were used to adorn Islamic buildings. A glazed pottery fountain-head in the form of a horseman, now in Damascus Museum (pl. 17), is said to have been found in 1924 in commercial excavations at Raqqa in Syria.[80] It is reputed to have been one of a set from what must have been a fine house. To this set also belong the cockerel and sphinx mentioned above, both in the David Collection, Copenhagen. For horsemen in a palatial context we have clear literary evidence: thus, for example, al-Khaṭīb al-Baghdādī describes the figures of horsemen in the palace of al-Muqtadir (AD 908–23):[81]

> On either side of this palace, to the right and left of the tank, stood figures in two rows, each row consisting of fifteen horsemen, mounted upon their mares, both men and the steeds being clothed and caparisoned in brocade. In their hands the horsemen carried long-poled javelins, and those on the right appeared to be attacking their adversaries in the row of horsemen on the left-hand side.

The vast quantity and variety of base metal aquamaniles produced in such centres as Dinand and Hildesheim in the twelfth and thirteenth centuries, as well as English examples, and local ceramic copies, makes it clear that the impact of this Islamic sculptural tradition on Europe was enormous, and would have had a very direct artistic impact on those who used these magnificent objects. It is somewhat ironic, therefore, that the greatest legacy of Islam to Christian Europe in metalworking terms was that very form of art most distrusted by Muslim piety, human and animal sculpture in the round.

Notes

1 G. Strohmaier, "Der Dekor islamischer Metallgefässe in der europäischen Kunst des Mittelalters", *Metallkunst von der Spätantike bis zum ausgehenden Mittelalter*, ed. A. Effenberger (Berlin, 1982), pp. 272–3.

2 G. Eastwood-Vogelsang and J.W. Allan, "Mamluk embroideries in the Ashmolean", *Islamic Art in the Ashmolean Museum, Oxford Studies in Islamic Art*, ed. J.W. Allan, vol. 10 (Oxford, forthcoming).

3 Strohmaier, pp. 268–9.

4 F. Sarre and F.R. Martin, *Die Ausstellung von Meisterwerken Muhammedanischer Kunst in München 1910* (Munich, 1911), taf. 145.

5 D. Schubert, *Von Halberstadt nach Meissen* (Cologne, 1974), pl. 171.

6 L.A. Mayer, *Mamluk Costume* (Geneva, 1952), pl. IX, now in the L.A. Mayer Memorial Museum, Jerusalem; *The Arts of Islam*, Arts Council (London, 1976), no.653, in the Benaki Museum.

7 *The Anatolian Civilisations* III, Topkapi Palace Museum 22 May–30 October 1983 (Istanbul, 1983), D.127; Sotheby's, *Islamic Works of Art*, Wednesday 25 April 1990, lot 118.

8 Schubert, pl. 107 and pp. 285–7.

9 Strohmaier, pp. 269–70.

10 Strohmaier, p. 271 Abb.4 illustrates the base of a fourteenth-century bowl in Florence as an example of this layout. Compare also a thirteenth-century Syro-Mesopotamian basin in Palermo, a thirteenth-century Jaziran pen-box in Bologna in F. Gabrieli and U. Scerrato, *Gli Arabi in Italia* (Milan, 1979), figs. 108 and pp. 579–80, etc.

11 E. Rupin, *L'oeuvre de Limoges* (Paris, 1890), p. 47.

12 Rupin, p. 48.

13 E. Doberer, "Studien zu dem Ambo Kaiser Heinrichs II. im Dom zu Aachen", in *Karolingische und Ottonische Kunst* (Wiesbaden, 1957), p. 311 fig. 136; H.Fililitz, "Das Evangelisten-Relief von Ambo Kaiser Heinrich II", *Karolingische und Ottonische Kunst* (Wiesbaden, 1957), p. 361 fig. 146.

14 I owe this information to Prof. Albert Lemeunier of the University of Liège, who kindly sent me a copy of a paper he had prepared on the subject entitled, "Le vernis brun. Splendeurs du décor dans l'orfèvrerie mosane".

15 G. Marçais, *Les faiences à reflets métalliques de la Grande Mosquée de Kairouan* (Paris, 1928), *passim.*

16 R.J. Charleston, *Masterpieces of Western Ceramic Art* vol. IV *Islamic Pottery* (Tokyo 1979), pl. 12, from the David Collection, Copenhagen no.14–1962; M.Pézard, *La céramique archaique de l'Islam et ses origines* (Paris, 1920), pl. CXXXII.

17 B.I. Marshak, *Sogdiiskoe Serebro* (Moscow, 1971), pl. 29.
18 B.I. Marshak, "Zur Toreutik der Kreuzfahrer", *Metallkunst von der Spätantike bis zum ausgehenden Mittelalter*, ed. A. Effenberger (Berlin, 1982), pp. 166–84.
19 Marshak (1982), Abb.5; H. Grisar, *Die römische Kapelle Sancta Sanctorum und ihr Schatz* (Freiburg, 1908), pp. 110–11, no.5, Abb.54.
20 T. Ulbert, *Resafa III. Der kreuzfahrerzeitliche Silberschatz aus Resafa-Sergiupolis* (Mainz am Rhein, 1990).
21 P.M. de Winter, "The Sacral Treasures of the Guelphs", *Bulletin of the Cleveland Museum of Art*, 72, i, (March 1985), pp. 55–6.
22 De Winter, figs. 61, 63.
23 De Winter, figs. 104–5.
24 De Winter, fig. 107.
25 De Winter, fig. 108.
26 H. Swarzenski, *Monuments of Romanesque Art* (London, 1954), figs. 434–5. Additional examples will be found in Skubiszewski (1982) (see n. 32).
27 De Winter, front cover, and colour pl. XIII.
28 De Winter, fig. 110.
29 E. Baer, *Metalwork in Medieval Islamic Art* (New York, 1983), fig. 210.
30 Baer, fig. 211.
31 G. Sievernich and H. Budde (eds.), *Europa und der Orient 800–1900* (Berlin 1989), p. 207 figs. 234–5, no.4/85.
32 P. Skubiszewski, "Die Bildprogramme der romanischen Kelche und Patenen", *Metallkunst von der Spätantike bis zum ausgehenden Mittelalter*, ed. A. Effenberger (Berlin, 1982), Abb.29–30.
33 A. Grohmann, *Arabische Paläographie* (Wien, 1971), vol. II, Abb.94–5, p. 248.
34 H. Buchthal, "A note on Islamic enamelled metalwork and its influence in the Latin West", *Ars Islamica*, 11–12 (1946), pp. 195–8.
35 A.U. Pope (ed.), *A Survey of Persian Art* (Oxford, 1938–9), pls. 569A, 583A, 584B, 587.
36 *La céramique égyptienne de l'époque musulmane*, Musée de l'art arabe (Cairo, 1922), pl. 34 top.
37 H. Philon, *Early Islamic Ceramics*, Benaki Museum (Athens, 1980), pl. XVI.
38 G. Berti and L. Tongiorgi, *I bacini ceramici medievali delle chiese di Pisa* (Rome, 1981), *passim*.
39 G. Ballardini, "Pomposa e i suoi bacini", *Faenza*, 24 (1936): pl. xxix a,b.
40 Acc.no.1860–6959, illustrated in J.W. Allan, *Metalwork of the Islamic World: the Aron Collection* (London, 1986), fig. 11. For this inscription compare the form of *hā'* and the trefoil topped hastae of other letters in the AD 988 building inscription of the Great Mosque in Sfax in Tunisia, A. Grohmann, *Arabische Paläographie* (Wien, 1971), Vol. II, Abb.95h and 97a.
41 *Europa und der Orient 800–1900* (Berlin, 1983), pp. 570–1, no. 4/45.
42 *idem* p. 169 Abb.182, and p. 570 no. 4/44.
43 *Islam. Konst och Kultur*, Statens Historiska Museum (Stockholm, 1985), pp. 189–90, no. 33.
44 Analytical work on Limoges enamels is being undertaken by Dr Julian Henderson of the Research Laboratory for Archaeology and the History of Art at Oxford University and Marion Campbell of the Victoria and Albert Museum. For the analyses of enamels from Fusṭāṭ, see Julian Henderson and James Allan, Enamels on Ayyūbid and Mamlūk glass fragments, *Archaeomaterials*, 4 (1990), pp. 167–83.
45 For European three-legged ewers see W. Dexel, *Das Hausgerät Mitteleuropas: 2. Auflage Deutschland, Holland, Osterreich, Schweiz* (Berlin, 1973), Abb.125–7; A.-E. Theuerkauff-Liederwald, *Mittelalterliche Bronze- und Messinggefässe* (Berlin, 1988), Abb.188–254.

46 J.W. Allan, "Concave or convex? The sources of Jaziran and Syrian metalwork of the 13th century", *The Art of Syria and the Jazira 1100-1250, Oxford Studies in Islamic Art*, ed. J. Raby (1985), vol. 1, p. 135, fig. 6.
47 G. Fehérvári, *Islamic metalwork of the eighth to the fifteenth century in the Keir collection* (London, 1976), no. 3, pl. 2a.
48 T. Falk (ed.), *Treasures of Islam* (London, 1985), no. 253.
49 B.N. Arakelyan, "Razvitie remesel i tovarnogo proizvodstva v Armenii v IX–XIII vekakh", *Sovietskaya Arkheologiya* 26 (1956), pp. 120–1, fig. 1.
50 O. Rubensohn, F. Sarre, "Ein Fund frühislamischer Bronzegefässe in Ägypten", *Jahrbuch der Preuszischen Kunstsammlungen* 50 (1929), fig. 3; *Museum für Islamischer Kunst. Katalog* (Berlin, 1971), no. 139, pl. 29.
51 *Museum für Islamischer Kunst. Katalog* (Berlin, 1971) no. 214; *Islamische Kunst. Loseblattkatalog unpublizierter Werke aus Deutschen Museen* Band 2; A. Hauptmann von Gladiss, J. Kröger, *Museum für Islamische Kunst. Metall, Stein, Stuck, Holz, Elfenbein, Stoffe* (Mainz/Rhein, 1985), no. 232.
52 Acc.no.1836.9–1.144.
53 A.S. Melikian-Chirvani, *Islamic Metalwork from the Iranian World, 8th–18th centuries*, Victoria and Albert Museum Catalogue (London 1982), no. 67, which I have elsewhere pointed out is Fāṭimid not Persian; see J.W. Allan, *Metalwork from the Islamic World. The Aron Collection* (London 1986), p. 19.
54 W. Hartner, "The Vaso Vescovali in the British Museum", *Kunst des Orients*, 9 (1973–4), pp. 99–130.
55 N. Stratford, "Three English romanesque enamelled ciboria", *The Burlington Magazine*, 126 (1984), pp. 204–16.
56 Hermitage Museum, Leningrad; Marshak (1982), Abb.7; B.I. Marshak, *Silberschätze des Orients* (Leipzig, 1986), fig. 150.
57 G. Fehérvári, *Islamic Metalwork of the Eighth to the Fifteenth Century in the Keir Collection* (London, 1976), no. 127, colour pl.G; "Working in metal: mutual influences between the Islamic world and the medieval West", *Journal of the Royal Asiatic Society*, 1 (1977), pp. 4–16; A.S. Melikian-Chirvani, "Argenterie et féodalité dans l'Iran médiévale", *Art et société dans le monde iranien* (Paris, 1982), pp. 144–51.
58 Hermitage Museum, Leningrad; Marshak (1982), Abb.9 and 19; Marshak (1986), fig. 152.
59 Marshak (1982), Abb.13.
60 Marshak (1982), Abb.11; A. Anderrson, *Medieval Drinking Bowls of Silver Found in Sweden* (Stockholm 1983), p. 86 no. 16.
61 V.P. Darkevich, "Proizvedeniya zapadnogo khudozhestvennogo remesla v Vostochnoi Evrope (X–XIV vv.)", *Arkheologiya SSSR* E.1–57 (Moscow, 1966), pl. 19.
62 Marshak (1982), Abb.10.
63 Sotheby's, *Islamic Works of Art, Carpets and Textiles* (London), Wednesday 12 April 1989, lot 62.
64 An unpublished Fāṭimid silver bowl in a private collection has a simpler version of the Syrian strapwork design.
65 E.C. Dodd, "On the origins of medieval *Dinanderie*: the equestrian statue in Islam", *Art Bulletin*, 51 (1969), pp. 220–32. She gives a full bibliography.
66 O. von Falke and E. Meyer, *Die Bronzegeräte des Mittelalters* (Berlin, 1935).
67 Dodd, p. 222.
68 J. Sourdel-Thomine and B. Spuler, *Die Kunst des Islam, Propyläen Kunst Geschichte* (Berlin, 1973), colour pl.XVI.
69 Sarre and Martin, taf.155.
70 Dodd, fig.1.

71 E. Meyer, "Romanische Bronzen und ihre islamischen Vorbilder", *Aus der Welt der Islamischen Kunst, Festschrift für Ernst Kühnel* (Berlin 1959), pp. 317–22.
72 Dodd, figs. 3–4.
73 Gabrieli and Scerrato, fig. 525.
74 "Art from the World of Islam", *Louisiana Revy* 27, iii (March 1987), no. 83.
75 *idem.*, no. 82.
76 *idem.*, no. 92.
77 Dodd, fig. 17.
78 Acc.no. M.70–1949.
79 Dodd, fig. 9.
80 M.A. al-ʿUsh, *Catalogue du Musée National de Damas* (Damascus 1969), pl.XIII.
81 Dodd, p. 228.

Plate 1 Lustre dish, Iraq tenth century AD, David Collection, Copenhagen no. 14/1962.

Plate 2 Nielloed silver dish, Iran 1029–1049 AD, Los Angeles County Museum of Art, The Nasli M. Heeramaneck Collection, gift of Joan Palevsky, no. M.73.5.149.

Plate 3 Nielloed and gilded silver reliquary, Antioch *circa* 1000 AD, Vatican (after Grissar 1908).

Plate 4 (*left*) Nielloed and gilded silver chalice, Rusafa treasure, twelfth century, National Museum, Damascus. **Plate 5** (*right*) The Wilten chalice, nielloed and gilded silver, third quarter of the twelfth century, Kunsthistorisches Museum, Vienna, no. 8924.

Plate 6 The Petrikirche chalice, silver gilt, detail of pseudo-kūfic inscription, late twelfth century, Kunsthistorisches Museum, Vienna, no. 9983.

Plate 7 The Petrikirche paten, silver gilt, detail of pseudo-kūfic inscription, late twelfth century, Kunsthistorisches Museum, Vienna, no. 9983.

Plate 8 Enamelled gemellion in the name of Dā'ūd ibn Suqmān (d. 1144 AD), Urtuqid, Tiroler Landesmuseum Ferdinandeum, Innsbruck.

Plate 9 Enamelled gemellion, Limoges twelfth century, Victoria and Albert Museum, no. 1860-6959.

Plate 10 Brass ewer, English fourteenth century, Victoria and Albert Museum no. M.25-1939 (photo: J. W. Allan).

Plate 11 Bronze ewer, English fourteenth century, Burrell Collection, Glasgow, no. 5+6/1976.

Plate 12 (*top*) The Vaso-Vescovali, bell-metal inlaid with silver, Afghanistan *c.* 1200 AD, British Museum no. 1950.7-25.1 (courtesy of the Trustees of the British Museum).

Plate 13 (*foot*) The Balfour ciborium, enamelled and gilded copper alloy, England *c.* 1160–1170 AD, Victoria and Albert Museum no. M.1-1981.

Plate 14 (*top*) Bronze lion aquamanile, Egypt eleventh century, Staatliche Kunstsammlungen, Kassel, no. B VIII 115.

Plate 15 (*foot*) Bronze lion aquamanile, Lower Saxony twelfth century, Staatliche Museen Preussischer Kulturbesitz, Kunstgewerbemuseum, Berlin no. 34,5.

Plate 16 Bronze horseman aquamanile, Scandinavian thirteenth century, Victoria and Albert Museum, no. M.70-1949.

Plate 17 Glazed ceramic horseman, Syria thirteenth century, National Museum, Damascus no. A 5819 (After al-ʿUsh 1969).

The Muslim Sources of Dante?

PHILIP F. KENNEDY

Whilst we can accept that Dante's *Divine Comedy*, written at the turn of the fourteenth century, is a marvel of European literature and the finest of Christian allegories, our understanding of the text in the twentieth century is a process which demands inquiry into the various layers of its social, historical and religious background; this includes its symbols and personages, its political backdrop and the ultimate, essentially mystical, goal which the text seeks to express. One aspect of its background which has been the cause of great controversy is the question of what it owed to Muslim sources; Dante scholars, themselves Christian and many indeed Italian,[1] seem to have viewed the subject, which now has its own history,[2] as an assault on the sublime author's very Christianity, as well as his identity as a European and not least an Italian. The anxiety of scholarship resulted from what was perceived; viz. the singling out of the most exalted of medieval Euro-Christian texts to be stripped of their originality. Ultimately, however, the question of Araby in the *Divine Comedy*[3] resolves itself by viewing the poem, in part, as a gauge to an age in which the cultures of Christian Europe and Islam were far from being hermetically sealed; thus just as the *Comedy* reflects the culture, politics and religion of Dante's native Florence and Italy both on a personal and general level, so in a wider sphere it reflects (less conspicuously) a Europe which in moulding its intellectual identity was in the shadow of elements of Islamic culture.[4]

The *Divine Comedy* is an allegorical depiction of Dante's journey through Hell, Purgatory and Paradise "Midway this way of life". It possesses a rigid structure: the eight concentric circles of Hell, divided between the five circles of upper Hell and the three circles of Lower Hell lying within the city of Dis; at the centre lies the Well in which the giant Lucifer stands up to his waist in the icy waters of Cocytus. The progression of circles forming a cone shape towards the centre of the Earth is an ethical progression, each circle harbouring the protagonists of sins of an increasingly higher order. Mount Purgatory, arrived at via the stream of Lethe at the other side of Hell, is of a similar structure; it is a mountain at the antipodes of Jerusalem, consisting of the two terraces of Ante-Purgatory and the seven cornices of Lower, Middle and Upper Purgatory, leading at the summit to the Earthly Paradise; again the physical site of Purgatory's conical mount is an ethical structure, each Terrace or Cornice hosting the expurgation of a particular sin (in Purgatory proper these are the seven sins). Dante's Paradise is constructed from the Ptolemaic system of astronomy; it has nine concentric spheres which carry the heavenly bodies: the Moon, Mercury, Venus, the Sun, Mars, Jupiter, Saturn and the Fixed Stars; the ninth sphere is the *Primum Mobile* which imparts motion to the spheres within itself; the tenth is the Empyrean where the souls of the blest dwell with God — the site of Dante's virtual apotheosis. These three parts of the *Divine Comedy* are contained within the narrative of one hundred cantos. The rigid structure thus outlined has no precedent in pre-existing Christian literature, whence the debate about the work's sources.

From even a cursory reading it is clear that the *Comedy* is replete with personages, real and mythical, from the classical age of Greece and Rome; they stand alongside characters pertaining to Dante's life and times, whereby the text becomes a veritable melange of the classical and middle ages. This feature of the work is best represented by the all-important roles of Virgil (d. 19 BC),[5] Dante's guide through Hell and Purgatory, and Beatrice, his beloved and guide through Paradise; the former is a symbol of the highest virtues of the classical world, the latter the most sublime encounter of Dante's personal life. Dante's *Comedy* transformed the classical world, with all its mythology, into important reference points of a Christian allegory, which sought to reiterate the identity of thirteenth-century Europe as an inheritance of the Ancient World. This expression of a cultural and even religious continuum may in itself constitute a statement of the work's intent — the revindication of a European identity in the shadow of the incursions of another culture.

Virgil's role is also important for providing a literary precedent of a trip to the underworld; clearly Dante was in part inspired by Virgil's depiction of Aeneas' descent into Hades in Book Six of the *Aeneid.* This episode of the *Aeneid* does indeed seem to have inspired details of the Inferno; for example the Sybil's appeasement of Cerberus is parallelled in Dante's work by Virgil's appeasement of the guardian of the underworld.

What then of Muslim influence? With no prior knowledge of the debate, which I will summarise below, we would discern only a few details through which Dante acceded recognition to the Muslim world. These exiguous elements are confined to cantos IV and XXVIII of the Inferno; in the former, depicting Limbo, Dante beholds amongst a host of classical characters the great Saladdin (Salāḥ al-Dīn; d. 589/1193), as well as Avicenna (Ibn Sīnā; d. 428/1036–7) and Averroes (Ibn Rushd; d. 595/1198–9).[6] To the circle of the schismatics Dante condemns both Muḥammad and his cousin ʿAlī; the towers of the city of Dis itself are perceived as mosques. Together, however, these elements constitute but a drop in the ocean.

In 1919 the Spanish Arabist, Miguel Asín Palacios, published *La Escatologia Musulmana en la Divina Comedia.*[7] In this extensive, erudite work Asín discusses a variety of subject matter, or source material, both religious and literary which can be divided simplistically into three categories: first, Muslim traditions of the Prophet Muḥammad's ascent into heaven, secondly a related mystical ascent written by the greatest of all Arab mystics, the Murcian Ibn al-ʿArabī (d. 638/1240–1) and thirdly a literary *Divine Comedy* written in the tenth century by the Syrian philosopher-poet al-Maʿarri (d. 449/1057–8). All three are related to the first — the *miʿrāj.*

From brief references in the Qurʾān, the *miʿrāj,* the Prophet's ascent into heaven, was expanded and diffused through the ages via the *ḥadīth* literature (the traditions of the Prophet on which the *sunna* was based) into an elaborate, growing legend. The word *miʿrāj,* originally meaning 'ladder' and later 'ascent', attached essentially to verse 1 of Sūra XVII of the Qurʾān: "Praise him, who travelled in one night with his servant from the *masjid al-ḥarām* [in Mecca], whose surroundings we blessed, in order to show him our signs." The *miʿrāj* appears to have taken place early in Muḥammad's prophetic mission becoming "a kind of dedication of him as a Prophet . . .".[8]

Asín shows clearly that from its Qur'ānic roots the legend was elaborated, in a largely popular manner, into three cycles. His summary and conclusion relating to the *mi'rāj* is, therefore, based on no single text but an amalgamation of a vast tradition through which he leads his reader. It is a veritable sea of collected material which defies résumé in a manner that properly allows one to share in the sense of conviction and acquiescence which accompanies a studied first reading.

Of the *mi'rāj* material (a journey to Heaven, Hell and Purgatory — in that order)[9] I will simply quote examples of intriguing reminiscences to the *Divine Comedy*, themselves mostly culled from Asín's own summary. This summary requires a prefatory caution that applies to all material analysed:[10] "Let [the reader] divest the *Divine Comedy* of its discourses and dialogues, the theological doctrine it breathes, its philosophical and astronomical lore and the allusions to Italian history with which it is replete (i.e. elements essential to the quality of the *Comedy*) and he will be able to proceed with a methodological comparison." For another important caution I paraphrase the author: "The monotonous style, the excessive hyperbole and the constant repetition, coupled with an absence of spiritual effect make it difficult to associate the *mi'rāj* legend with the artistic poem of Dante." A sample of Asín's observations:[11]

Muḥammad like Dante is made to tell the story. Virgil appears before Dante exactly like Gabriel before Muḥammad — each guide does his best to satisfy the pilgrim's curiosity.[12]

> "The general architecture of the Inferno is but a faithful copy of the Muslim hell. Both are in the shape of a vast funnel or inverted cone and consist of a series of stories, each the abode of one class of sinner . . . the ethical system in the two hells is much alike; both are beneath the city of Jerusalem."[13]

Asín perceives a resemblance of tortures: thus the first circle of Muslim hell equals Dis — a sea of flames on whose shores stand countless tombs aglow with fire.

> "The warning of the approach to hell in both legends is identical, viz. a confused noise and violent bursts of flame . . . The fierce demon who pursues Muḥammad with a burning brand at the outset of his nocturnal journey has his duplicate in the devil who pursues Dante in the fifth pit of the eighth circle."[14]

It should be noted that the similarities Asín observes are seldom exact duplicates of each other in every detail: thus the maddening thirst of the forgers in the *Divine Comedy* is suffered by the Muslim drunkards; Griffolino of Arezzo and Capocchio of Sienna (both condemned for Alchemy) scratch the scabs off their leprous sores, as do the slanderers in the hell of Islam.

> "The woman who, despite her loathsome ugliness, endeavours in the fourth circle of Purgatory to lure Dante from his path is almost a counterpart of the hag[15] who tempts Mahomat at the beginning of his journey . . . both Gabriel and Virgil agree that the vision is a symbol of the false attractions of the world."[16]
>
> "The architecture of both the Christian and Muslim heavens is identical, inasmuch as it is based upon the Ptolemaic system. The denomination of the nine spheres is in some cases the same, namely, that of their respective planets. Occasionally too the ethical systems are alike."[17]
>
> "The phenomena of light and sound are alone used by both travellers to convey their impression of the ethereal spheres."[18]
>
> "Just as Beatrice leaves Dante at the last stage of his ascension, so Gabriel leaves Muḥammad when the Prophet is wafted to the Divine Presence by the aid of a luminous wreath."[19]
>
> "It is not merely in general outline that the two ascensions coincide; even the episodes in the visions of Paradise are at times alike, if not identical: Dante for example in the heaven of Jupiter sees a mighty eagle formed of myriads of resplendent spirits all wings and faces, which, chanting exhortations to man to cleave to righteousness, flaps its wings and then comes to rest. Muḥammad sees in heaven a gigantic angel in the form of a cockerel, which moves its wings whilst chanting hymns calling mankind to prayer and then rests. He sees other angels, each an agglomeration of countless faces and wings, who resplendent with light, sing songs of praise with tongues innumerable. These two visions merged in one, at once suggest Dante's heavenly eagle."[20]

The apotheoses in both legends are exactly alike.

Amongst other details too numerous to list Asín makes a good case for similarities between Lucifer and Iblis, especially in the icy torture they suffer; he also clarifies that there is in the *miʿrāj* tradition a possible precedent for both Limbo and Purgatory (*al-Aʿraf* and *al-Sirāṭ* respectively).

Asín was aware of precedents to the Muslim legends and Christian precedents to elements of the *Comedy*; he was also aware of the wealth of scholarship which had studied these elements before him; however, he claimed a stronger case for his own observations. Thus in contrast to the Muslim purgatory of the *miʿrāj* he writes: "Nothing in Christian eschatology seems to warrant so detailed and precise a description of the site of Purgatory [as the one found in the *Divine Comedy*]. Not until a century later, after the appearance of the *Divine Comedy* did the existence of Purgatory as a special condition of the soul, engaged in temporary expiation of sin, become a dogma of the Christian faith."[21] As for the site of Hell he tells us in a footnote: "St Thomas finds no precise topography of Hell in Christian tradition and can only record the probable opinion of the theologians that *ignis inferni est sub terra* . . ."[22]

Asín added great weight to his hypothesis of Muslim influence by finding a spiritual paradigm for the *Divine Comedy* in the work of the thirteenth-century Muslim mystic Muḥiyy al-Dīn b. al-ʿArabī, who died twenty-five years before Dante's birth. Ibn al-ʿArabī followed precedents of Muslim mystics who, in adapting the *miʿrāj* towards mystical expression, "arrogated to themselves the role of protagonist that had hitherto been reserved for Muḥammad".[23] Already in the ninth century Yazīd al-Bistāmī was credited with an ascent to the Divine Throne. Ibn al-ʿArabī's own treatment of the ascension appears in a voluminous work entitled *al-Futuḥāt al-Makkiyya.* It is the main theme of an entire chapter, the heading of which — "The Alchemy of Felicity" — in itself implies an esoteric allegory. There are two protagonists — a theologian and a philosopher.

"The ascent is modelled on the *miʿrāj*: the first seven heavens correspond to the astronomical heavens: Moon, Mercury, Venus, Sun, Mars, Jupiter and Saturn."[24] In each sphere Ibn al-ʿArabī "ingenuously introduces many points from his theological system, such that the work becomes a veritable encyclopaedia of philosophy, theology and the occult sciences."[25] At the end of this stage of the ascent the theologian leaves the philosopher behind. In the second stage the theologian, passing through the last two spheres, beholds the ineffable mysteries of the divine essence. After apotheosis the theologian rejoins the philosopher, who then converts to the Muslim faith.

This marriage of philosophy with a higher faith is reminiscent of the anxieties of which the teachings of St Thomas Aquinas (d. 1274) were a product; Dante was in tune with Aquinas, thus the respect given to the philosophers is subsumed by the mystical allegory. That Dante was abreast of his age in all its tensions and complexity is exemplified in canto XII of the *Paradiso* in which the Averroist rationalist Siger of Brabant (d. 1281) is placed alongside Thomas Aquinas, his intellectual antagonist. Asín himself picked up on this tension between philosophy and theology:

> "Dante may be said to be acting in a dual capacity; firstly as a philosopher, by the experience gained from Virgil's teaching; and secondly as a theologian now taught by Beatrice or the blessed, who, on the other hand, enlighten him on supernatural or mystical problems. And this is precisely what happens in Ibn al-ʿArabī's story. The philosopher learns in each sphere of the natural phenomena produced in the sublunar world by its physical virtues; the theologian, on the other hand receives from the prophets the same instruction as the philosopher on matters pertaining to nature, supplemented by illumination of mystical and theological subjects."[26]

On another tack Asín provides a particularly arresting analysis of Ibn al-ʿArabī's use of light, treatment of which is strongly reminiscent of the *Lumen Gloriae* of Thomas Aquinas who undoubtedly had a profound influence on Dante. Asín claims that St Thomas Aquinas himself admits seeking inspiration, not among the Holy Fathers and scholastic theologians, but among the Muslim philosophers:

> "It is the authority of Alfarabius, Avicenna, Avempace and Averrhoes that he quotes, when he attempts to explain the Beatific Vision in terms of philosophy, and it is the theory of Averroes, of the vision of the substances separated by the soul, that he accepts as one most suitable for the elect's vision of God."[27]

Asín observes that Muslim precedents of belief in a spiritual rather than a sensual paradise were known to Christian scholastics — especially to the thirteenth–fourteenth-century Catalans Raymond Llull (d. 1316) and Raymond Martin (d. *c.* 1284) — the latter quotes passages from Algazet (al-Ghazālī; d. 505/1111–2) full of the loftiest metaphysical thought. It is Raymond Martin, if anyone, that may have rendered Muslim Ṣūfī texts into Latin; yet there is no evidence that these scholastics were interested in Ṣūfism *per se* (as opposed to what was perceived as more orthodox matters of Islam); this fact strongly weakens Asín's case that Dante was influenced by the very images of Ibn al-ʿArabī.

One detail which draws attention is Asín's observation that just as Dante and Virgil always move to the right in the *Inferno*, Ibn al-ʿArabī "taught that in hell there is no right hand, just as in heaven there is no left hand; from a Qurʾānic passage Ibn al-ʿArabī inferred that the damned move towards the left."[28]

Asín's conclusion is that Ibn al-ʿArabī's work "is of all Moslem types the most akin to the *Paradiso* in particular and the whole *Divine Comedy* in general, insofar at least as the latter may be regarded as a moral and didactic allegory."[29]

For a literary model the Spanish scholar turned to the *Epistle of Forgiveness* by the tenth-century Syrian–Arab poet, Abū l-ʿAlāʾ al-Maʿarrī:

> "The *Treatise of Pardon* is written in the form of an epistle but is really a skilful imitation of those simpler versions of the Nocturnal Journey in which Muhammad does not rise to heaven. The author appears to have had a dual purpose in view. With a touch of irony so delicate as to be almost imperceptible, he censures the severity of moralists as contrasted with God's infinite mercy, and protests against the damnation of men of letters. The epistle is a reply to a literary friend, Ibn al-Qāriḥ of Aleppo, who had inveighed against those poets and men of letters who lived in impiety or debauchery."[30]

Unlike the *miʿrāj* the *Epistle of Forgiveness* contains virtually no descriptive hyperbole of the topography of Heaven and Hell – the popular element of this material – rather there is a narrative of consecutive conversations with poets in both regions. Into this framework al-Maʿarrī inserted ironical criticisms of his own society. An amusing example depicts Ibn al-Qariḥ, on the eve of his visit to Hell, anxious at having lost his certificate of repentance. Whilst he was wary of religious hypocrisy al-Maʿarrī did not, however, display the serious grievances and anger of Dante; the *Inferno* is far more serious-minded, as evinced by canto XIX. Here Dante meets the shade of Pope Nicholas III — one of the Simoniacs — plunged downwards in a hole in the rock of malbowges iii; alluding to his Simony Dante remarks bitterly:

> Nay, tell me now how great a treasure of gold
> Our Lord required of Peter; ere that He
> Committed the great Keys into his hand;
> Certes He nothing asked save Follow Me.

Nor Peter nor the others made demand
Of silver or gold when, in the lost soul's room,
They chose Matthias to complete their band.
Then bide thou there; thou hast deserved thy doom.[31]

Asín tries to forge links of significant similarities between the two works, "the human and realistic touch imparted by Dante to the first two parts of the *Divine Comedy* is to be found in this earlier Moslem work". However much his comments are interesting in showing up the literary parallels between the two texts, his case of direct contact between Dante and al-Maʿarrī is far less convincing than the case presented for the *miʿrāj* and related mystical tracts. There is no evidence of this kind of high literature (*adab*) entering into the medieval canon of translated works.

One author,[32] convinced of Dante's debt to al-Maʿarrī, sees the latter himself as having absorbed his sense of irony with respect to a trip to the underworld from Aristophanes' (d. *c.* 388 BC) *The Frogs.* The author by implication suggests a link, therefore, between Dante and Aristophanes. Yet it is in the end surely unreasonable to expect Dante to have absorbed directly or indirectly every work that bears a resemblance to his. Such a burden of material would have killed the artistic merit and spontaneity of his genius.[33]

In an important additional part of his book Asín investigates Muslim features in the Christian legends precursory of the *Divine Comedy.* Thus, for example, though the vision of St Paul — his ascent into the Third Heaven — was derived from the second epistle to the Corinthians, the legend acquired elements which to Asín were of an Islamic provenance.[34]

Here the Spanish scholar adopts his most extreme position.

In the latter part of his book Asín deals with the transmission of Islamic models — a subject which requires a thorough knowledge of the nature of medieval Europe. He pointed to the communication between Islam and Christian Europe during the twelfth and thirteenth centuries, singling out first of all the Sicilian court of the Norman king Frederick II (d. 1250) who surrounded himself with Arab learning. In general, however, Spain eclipsed the importance of Sicily. The Mozarabs, Christians living under Muslim rule, formed the first link between the two peoples. As early as the ninth century the Christians of Córdoba had adopted the Muslim styles of living. Their delight in Arabic poetry and fiction, and their enthusiasm for the study of the philosophical and theological doctrines of Islam, are lamented by Alvaro of Córdoba in his *Indiculus Luminosus.*

In the twelfth century with the beginning of the Reconquista Toledo became important as a centre of learning and belles lettres in Christian Europe. It was then in the thirteenth century that the patron king Alfonso the Wise of Castile (1252–84) established a school in Toledo with collaborators and translators from the three monotheistic religions. Following in the footsteps of his father, Ferdinand the Saint, who had encouraged the compilation of wisdom literature, Alfonso nevertheless played a wider field commissioning works of history and science deeply reliant upon Arabic sources. As the Reconquista advanced to Murcia and Seville it opened up new points of contact.[35]

Asín tells us that Spain was the country most addicted to the study of the *miʿrāj* legend; in the ninth century it was regarded as the home of these traditions. Knowledge of these legends would filter through the slender barrier separating the two peoples in their conception of the hereafter. There is indeed evidence that Christians knew the legend (though at this stage Asín could not have known exactly which version of the legend this was); he sets out this evidence:

(a) In the ninth century Mozarabs of Córdoba (Alvaro and St Eulogius) mention *ḥadīths* (the actual source of the legend) containing such material.

(b) St Eulogius (d. 859) had found a biography of Muḥammad at the monastery of Leirre in Navarre in the ninth century.

(c) The *Historia Arabum* of Archbishop Rodrigo Jimenez of Toledo (twelfth–thirteenth century) furnishes further proof. In Chapter 5 he inserts a literal version of the *miʿrāj* legend, culled from what he terms the second book of Muḥammad (presumably the *ḥadīth* literature). From the *Historia Arabum* it passed to the *Crónica General* or the *Estoria d'Espanna* which king Alphonso the Wise had completed between 1260 and 1268 (see Chapters 488 and 489: "De como Mahomat dixo que subira fasta los syete cielos").

(d) At the end of the thirteenth century St Peter Paschal, Bishop of Jaen (1249–50), wrote the *Impunación de la Seta de Mahoma* whilst in captivity in Granada. He quotes in this work from a book variously titled *Elmiregi, Miragi, Miraj* or *Elmerigi* and he dismisses these episodes as "mere fancy, vanities, lies, humbug and idle talk". Furthermore many *ḥadīth* are introduced into his work which deal with the Day of Judgement, the *sirāṭ* (or Muslim Purgatory), the topography of Hell and Life in paradise.

In conclusion there was a strong case for the *miʿrāj* being known in Christian Spain.

(e) Turning his attention to Italy Asín noted that the aforesaid St Peter Paschal had resided in Rome between 1288 and 1292. This fact suggests itself as an example of the hidden channels through which the legend might have reached Dante, who was in touch with the papal court visited by St Peter Paschal.

(f) Also with reference to Italy Asín focused on the role of Brunetto Latini (d. *c.* 1294) who had been an influence on Dante in his early life. He was a Florentine scholar of encyclopaedic knowledge, who filled the highest offices of state. The affectionate discourse which Dante feigns to hold with him in circle iii of hell (canto XV, 30 "What, you here, Ser Brunetto? You!") is eloquent testimony of their spiritual tie. Thus it is in Brunetto's allegorical and didactic poem of the *Tesoretto* that scholars have sought the model and ideal that inspired the *Divine Comedy.* The *Tesoretto,* in fact, contains a biography of Muḥammad in which he shows knowledge of the doctrine and customs of Islam. It is not unlikely therefore that he was familiar with the *miʿrāj,* a conjecture which Asín bases intelligently on circumstantial evidence, for in 1260 Brunetto was sent as ambassador of Florence to the court of Alfonso the Wise (d. 1284).[36]

In support of his case as to the result of these "hidden channels of transmission" upon Dante, Asín pondered on the mentality of the man, suggesting somewhat dubiously "the attraction [he felt] towards Arabic culture".[37] Dante was in league with the ideas of Albertus Magnus (d. *c.* 1280; he was the founder of scholasticism and teacher of St Thomas Aquinas) who together with the Englishman, Roger Bacon (d. *c.* 1294), agreed on the superiority of the Arab philosophers. In a similar vein the fourteenth century Catalan, Raymond Llull, even recommended the imitation of Muslim methods in preaching to the people. However, the treatment of the Prophet Muḥammad in the *Divine Comedy* is anomalous to Asín's proposition of cultural attraction.

In fact, the placing of Muḥammad in Hell was in his perceived role as a sower of discord and an author of schism — an attitude perhaps formed in the wake of the recently disastrous Crusades, and born also of popular notions about Muḥammad that found circulation in Europe of the time.[38] In a variety of popular beliefs he was variously "a pagan; a Christian; given the names of Ocin, Pelagus, Nicholas and Mahomet. He was sometimes illiterate, other times a magician and even a scholar at Bologna; some confused him with his "mentor", the Nestorian monk Bahīra, hence he became a deacon aspiring to the Papacy who set out for Arabia from Constantinople". This is perhaps the background against which Dante chose the circle of the schismatics.

Contrarywise, one can argue that Dante, in identifying the important role of ʿAlī in Islam, placing him alongside Muḥammad, knew more about the Prophet than such popular, misguided beliefs would allow. Is, therefore, ʿAlī's role in the Inferno due to Dante's knowledge of the schism between Sunnī and Shiʿite Islam? Asín goes as far as equating the details of ʿAlī's affliction in the *Inferno* with traditions told of his death at the hands of the assassin Ibn Muljam (d. 661) — an unconvincing theory. Asín often pushed his material one stage beyond the borders of credulity.

Dante's suggested sympathies for Islamic sciences is based on the weak evidence of Averroes and Avicenna's placement in Limbo — this surely reflects no more than the fact that Dante was a man of learning. More importantly, however, Asín points to a curiosity that has been pondered by all scholars; namely the placing of St Thomas Aquinas next to the aforementioned Siger of Brabant in the circle of the souls of the wise; this circle of canto X of the *Paradiso* appears to Dante in the sphere of the sun:

> . . . this is the endless radiance of Siger,
> who lectured on the street of Straw, exposing
> invidiously logical beliefs.

Siger's role is a curiosity mentioned by Mark Musa in the notes to his translation.[39] He presents the standard view:

> [Siger was] a distinguished Averroist philosopher who taught at the University of Paris, which was located in the Rue de Fouarre (Street of

> Straw). His belief that the world had existed from eternity and doubt in the immortality of the soul involved him in lengthy dispute with his colleague Thomas Aquinas, and eventually led to the charge of heresy . . . Because of his questionable position with regard to the Church, Siger's presence in this canto has been a problem for commentators.

It is a problem which permits conjecture that Dante's preoccupations, represented as they are in his work, were abreast of the intellectual anxieties of his age. He was not as conservative — or willing to condemn — as one might be allowed to judge from a certain perspective — the perspective from which we behold, for example, the damnation of the heretic Fra Dolcino who stands alongside Mahoma in the circle of the schismatics.

The appearance of Asín's book attracted great interest and inevitably gave rise to a polemic which he himself summarised in *Historia y Critica de Una Polemica*, published in 1926. As Cantarino observes he did not budge an inch, publishing his apology as an appendix to the very same text of 1919. He rounded on his critics with a general survey of their views and answers to specific criticisms of both his method and conjectures. What is interesting to observe is that, as the polemic progressed in time, eminent scholars changed their minds *vis-à-vis* Asín's hypothesis; G. Gabrielli, the distinguished Italian Arabist at first welcomed the treatise, only to rescind and join "the other camp", adopting then the zeal of the converted. Whilst it is fair to say that Dantistas were those who most fervently opposed the thesis, the alignment of interested scholars was not necessarily one whereby Orientalists opposed Dantistas. The main anxiety among Asín's critics is that whilst the wealth of material he presented is at once convincing in the parallels drawn, one is left to ponder how all of this material could have had a direct influence on Dante.

The majority of scholars may have accepted Asín's presentation of the state of medieval European scholasticism, yet the case of Dante using such a vast corpus of disparate literature as inspiration for his own single work was artistically inconceivable. Repeatedly, therefore, opposing scholars suggested that literary parallels, especially those that existed between Ibn al-ʿArabī and Dante, were borne of archetypes of religious psychology; as to the channels of transmission posited by Asín, they also countered him on specific details, notably the importance which he attached to Brunetto Latini. Brunetto could not have spent long enough in Spain to have amassed such a wealth of material.

The polemic may have remained to this day much as it was in the twenties — unresolved — had it not been for a significant discovery made in 1949. Two scholars working independently published the text of a thirteenth-century translation into French and Latin of a version of the *miʿrāj* legend — *La Escala de Mahoma*[40] and *Il Libro della Scala*.[41] It was the type of text which Asín had intuitively thought to exist; indeed it is regrettable that he died before he could get a taste of its significance.

Both scholars, the Spaniard Muñoz Sendino and the Italian Enrico Cerulli, studied the text and its background in the light of Asín's hypothesis. Their respective analyses confirmed, yet significantly limited, the importance which Asín attached to the *miʿrāj* legend; at the same time it allowed one to discard Ibn al-ʿArabī *et al* as direct transmitters to the intellectual world of Dante. For by providing a fresh perspective and a single, concrete yet limited basis on which to reconstruct the original hypothesis, the final resolution of the debate (or what I perceive to be its most sensible resolution) became far more credible.

The text of the *La Escala de Mahoma* (the title of Muñoz's study) was originally translated into Castillian in the 1250s by the Jewish scholar Abraham al-Hakim at the behest of Alfonso the Wise. His rendering of the original Arabic text was then translated into Latin by an Italian notary called Bonaventura of Sienna, who was one of four or five Italian collaborators at Alfonso's court. It is not unlikely that his presence had something to do with the political ties between Alfonso and northern Italy (including Florence) during a time of Guelf domination; indeed, it was Florence which, as we observed above, sent Brunetto Latini to Spain as its ambassador.

Muñoz suggests cogently that *La Escala de Mahoma* chimed in with the anti-Islamic literature commissioned and collected by Peter the Venerable (d. *c*. 1156) in the middle of the twelfth century — it was he who had commissioned Robert of Ketton to translate the Qurʾān into Latin as an essential part of this literature of propaganda (the translation was completed in 1143). With this in mind we may conjecture that Alfonso shared the tendency of his contemporary Raymond Llull who recognised the mystical, allegorical element of Muslim literature and had the idea of absorbing and appropriating it into Catholic orthodoxy. Alfonso was no mere encyclopaedist who commissioned works in detachment. The prologue which survives in the French version of the *Escala* clarifies the intentions behind the translation: they are twofold: that people might know the life and doctrine of Muḥammad; and that they might compare the excesses and fables of the legend with the upright law of the Christians.

In defending Asín, Muñoz outlines five main objections common to his critics:

(a) Dante knew no Arabic.

(b) No contemporary Arabist would have had the wealth of erudition which Asín presumed for Dante.

(c) Dante never alluded to these Islamic models.

(d) Even if he knew them Dante could not have copied them due to his contempt for Islam.

(e) The Spanish literati, who were more familiar with this material, did not imitate it as Dante was presumed to have done.

Muñoz confronted these objections as follows:

(a) Since *La Escala de Mahoma* exists as a translated version, it does not matter that Dante knew no Arabic. Furthermore, two of the greatest scholastics of the age — Albertus Magnus and St Thomas Aquinas — knew no Arabic, yet this did not prevent them from studying Arabic material.

(b) Because of lack of modern communications we should not imagine that scholars in the thirteenth century were isolated; they absorbed a wealth of material which was made constantly available to them.

(c) and (d) The objection that Dante despised Islam and, furthermore, never alluded to his models is countered by the possibility, better explained by Cerulli, that the *Divine Comedy* was a Christian counter-text to the *miʿrāj*. He would have been more interested in transcending his model rather than paying lip-service to it.

Objection (e) is irrelevant; the Spanish Christians countered Islam by exposing its doctrines in translation; Dante, on the other hand, transformed an Islamic model; they were all engaged in the same polemic.

The text of *La Escala de Mahoma* itself is clearly more of a popular legend explaining the beginnings of Muḥammad's divine message than a mystical allegory. Quite apart from the distinct quality of the details of the text, the sequence of episodes (broadly speaking Heaven, Hell, Purgatory) is less well-ordered than the carefully assembled episodes of the *Divine Comedy*. Muñoz nevertheless points out those details which support Asín's original observations. These reminiscences, much akin to the ones already summarised above, together with the significance of the surviving text itself, allowed Muñoz, quite rightly, to disengage the direct relevance of Ibn al-ʿArabī and the other mass of Muslim material (some of which I haven't even mentioned) from the case of Dante and Islam.

Cerulli can be seen to have resolved the whole debate in a clear summary of the *Escala*'s significance.[42] First, Asín's reliance on the presumed role of Brunetto Latini in transmitting the text to Dante is vindicated by our knowledge that it was the Italian Bonaventura of Sienna who produced the French and Latin versions of the legend. Due to the apparent diffusion of Alfonso's commissioned text, which can be deduced from the provenance of the extant manuscripts, the question of whether Dante could have been familiar with such a text begs an affirmative response. Furthermore, *Il Libro della Scala* was believed to be one of the holy texts of Islam, a belief which led it to be added to the *Collectio Toletana* — namely those texts commissioned and collected by the aforesaid Peter the Venerable in an attempt to check the advance of Islam.

Cerulli lists references made to the *Libro* in various sources (both Italian and Spanish) from the thirteenth to the sixteenth century; all of these confirm the wide dissemination of the text. The legend was clearly a common reference-point in the anti-Islamic polemic. Hence Cerulli's credible belief that if Dante was at all influenced by the legend, it was in his antagonism to it. Problems arising from seeking details of reminiscence between Dante and the *miʿrāj* become redundant if one considers the *Divine Comedy* to have been inspired by this general spirit of antagonism.[43] Cerulli thus decries those whose objections to Asín's thesis misconstrued the use of the word "sources". They do not entail plagiarism; nor are they the use of material necessarily of the same artistic merit; nor even do reminiscences between two texts need have the same significance. A source may simply be an impulse or a point of departure.

Before concluding, attention should be drawn briefly to another text which sheds light on the problem at hand. In 1940–42 the French scholar Marie-Thérèse d'Alverny published an anonymous Latin manuscript dating from the end of the twelfth century, entitled *The Journey of the Soul in the Afterlife*. It contains a treatise on the nature of man and the destiny of his soul in the hereafter. Because of the text's unorthodox air, d'Alverny suspected it was derived from sources such as the metaphysics of Avicenna, al-Ghazālī, as well as the *miʿrāj* tradition and others. The manuscript is a good example of how the Ptolemaic system, clearly present in Dante's Paradiso, was absorbed into medieval Europe through Arab sources. Most scholars[44] seem to agree that it is precisely this kind of work, together with the *Escala de Mahoma*, which may have exerted influence on Dante; this is a particularly attractive assumption in view of the fact that it "was probably written in Bologna on the basis of a Spanish forerunner".[45]

Inasmuch as the case for the influence of Muslim sources, as we have seen, must be understood against the background of the cultural and intellectual interplay of medieval Europe, the *Divine Comedy* becomes a representation, in its own possibly limited way, of that interplay. The bottom line is this: the *Divine Comedy* was the product of a Europe engaged, anxiously at times, in the absorption, transformation and reappropriation of literary elements preserved in Arab sources. If during the course of this review we have limited Asín's original thesis to the possibility that Dante was familiar with at least one version of the *miʿrāj* tradition (*La Escala de Mahoma*), we have nevertheless come to an understanding of the kind of channels through which these texts were absorbed. Of course, firstly and ultimately the *Comedy* is the product of creative genius — it is indeed "the finest of Christian allegories"; we should understand, however, that the intellectually syncretic nature of Christian Europe in the twelfth–fourteenth centuries does not invalidate this claim.

Notes

1 The role which Dante played amongst Italian nationalists has been discussed in Charles T. Davis, "Dante and Italian Nationalism", *A Dante Symposium*, ed. De Sua and Rizzo (The University of North Carolina, 1965).

2 See the very clear review of the subject in Vincente Cantarino's "Dante and Islam: History and Analysis of a Controversy", *A Dante Symposium*, ed. De Sua and Rizzo (The University of North Carolina, 1965). Whilst the present essay covers much of the same material it attempts to give a greater sample of Asín Palacios' original thesis.

3 I paraphrase the title of Dorothee Metlitzki's *The Matter of Araby in Medieval England* (New Haven, 1977).

4 Maxime Rodinson, *Europe and the Mystique of Islam* (London, 1988) provides a clear summary of early perceptions which Christendom acquired of Islam; see pp. 3–40. See also the other essays collected in this volume.

5 Virgil's role appears to have been dual — both cultural and religious, for he was commonly thought to have presaged the coming of Christ in the 4th Eclogue; indeed Dante depicts the Silver Age poet Statius in *Purgatorio* XXII (pp. 64–73) expressing his thanks to Virgil for having guided him to Christianity:

> ". . . Thou first didst guide me when I trod
> Parnassus' cave to drink the waters bright,
> And thou wast first to lamp me up to God.
>
> Thou wast as one who, travelling, bears by night
> A lantern at his back, which cannot leaven
> His darkness yet he gives his followers light."

(Trans. Dorothy L. Sayers, *The Divine Comedy*, vol. 2 (London, n.d.; first published 1955), p. 242.

6 Averroes is mentioned also indirectly in Purgatory (XXV, pp. 62–3) where Dante belittles his own intellect before that of the Arab philosopher: ". . . twas at this point a mind wiser than thine was tripped by ignorance . . ."

7 This seminal work was translated into English in the twenties by Harold Sunderland, *Islam and the Divine Comedy* (London, 1926).

8 See J. Horovitz's "Miʿrāj", in *The Encyclopaedia of Islam*, 1st edn, vol. 3, pp. 505–8.

9 This order of events obtains in the most relevant version of the tradition, *La Escala de Mahoma* (Madrid, 1949), which was published only after Asín's death. See below.

10 Asín Palacios, p. 25.

11 For a fuller summary of comparisons see Asín Palacios, pp. 67–76.

12 *ibid.*, p. 68.

13 *ibid.*, p. 69.

14 *ibid.*, p. 69.

15 In *La Escala de Mahoma*, to be discussed below, this hag is in fact a beautiful maiden. This appears simply to be a variant of the same motif.

16 *ibid.*, p. 70.

17 *ibid.*, p. 70. In fact in the most relevant version of the *miʿrāj*, *La Escala de Mahoma*, the spheres of the heavens appear to be derived from the Qurʾānic Seven Heavens (*al-samawāt al-sabʿ*).

18 *ibid.*, p. 71.

19 *ibid.*, p. 71.

20 *ibid.*, p. 72. See *Inferno* canto XVIII, pp. 93–117.

Metlitzki in *The Matter of Araby in Medieval England* discusses how this feature of the legend may have been absorbed into the medieval Romance tradition of The Land of Cockayne – a sensuous paradise; see pp. 210–19. Speculating on the derivation of the place-name she states (p. 213): "there is . . . the obvious suggestiveness of the name as 'the land of the cock' and the strange coincidence, never noticed, by which a cock is the guardian of Paradise in the most popular account of Islamic paradisial abodes in medieval Europe — the *Liber Scalae* (*La Escala de Mahoma*)".

21 Asín Palacios, p. 112.

22 *ibid.*, p. 90, note 3.

23 *ibid.*, p. 44.

24 *ibid.*, p. 48.

25 *ibid.*, p. 49.

26 *ibid.*, p. 52. See *Purgatorio*, XVIII, pp. 46–8, where, in discussing Love and Free Will, Virgil claims that his instruction is limited; for the subject's fulfilment Virgil defers to Beatrice:

> "So much as reason here distinguisheth
> I can unfold," said he: "thereafter, sound
> Beatrice's mind alone, for that needs faith."

27 *ibid.*, p. 160.

28 These curious movements are explained within a purely Christian context, drawing its constructs from Aristotle, by the eminent Dantista John Freccero; see "Pilgrim in a Gyre", *Dante, The Poetics of Conversion* (Cambridge, Mass., 1986).

29 *ibid.*, p. 54.

30 *ibid.*, p. 55.

31 Trans. Dorothy L. Sayers, I, pp. 90–7.

32 See Lūīs ʿAwad's *ʿAlā hāmish al-ghufrān* (Cairo, 1966).

33 Both Asín and Lūīs ʿAwad overlook the fact that the spirit of al-Maʿarrī's work was probably derived from the Andalusian writer Ibn Shuhayd (d. 1035). His *Risālat al-tawābiʿ wa 'l-zawābiʿ* is a voyage into the realms of the *jinn* — the mystical, magical world of the mythical *Wādī 'l-ʿAbqar.*

34 Discussion of these sources as an alternative to Asín's propositions continued after 1919. See particularly Theodore Silverstein, "Dante and the legend of the *miʿraj*: the Problem of Islamic influence on the Christian literature of the other-world", *Journal of Near Eastern Studies*, (1952), pp. 89–110, 187–92. Consult also the well-researched bibliography in Cantarino's afore-mentioned article.

35 These points of contact, in any case, seem more reasonable than those posited by Blochet in his earlier work, "Sources Orientales de la Divine Comedie" (*Les littératures populaires de toutes les nations*, 41), (Paris, 1891). "To him the main channels (of communication) are the trade routes from Persia to the North-East of Europe via Byzance . . . Moslem Spain is hardly once mentioned as a means of communication. This appears to be due to the fact that in Blochet's opinion, the pre-Dante legends (such as the voyage of St Brandan, the Visions of St Paul, St Patrick *et al*) are derived rather from the Persian ascension of Arda Viraf than from Arabic and Islamic sources. He admits that the *miʿrāj* may also have influenced these legends but only as transmitted by the crusades from the East" (Asín, p. 246, n. 2). (It is interesting in this context that René Guenon in his *L'Esoterisme de Dante* suggested that Ibn al-ʿArabī's mystical allegory may have been transmitted to Dante via Rosicrucian crusaders, i.e. from the East; Asín himself rejects this thesis out of hand.)

36 In a footnote (p. 254) Asín adds: "Apart from the legend of the *miʿrāj* Brunetto may have obtained philosophical and theological information in Spain about the eschatology of Ibn al-ʿArabī, whose *ishrāqī* and mystical school of thought lived on in the works and teaching of other Murcian Ṣūfīs." Asín claims (p. 255) that Raymond Llull "had a vast knowledge of Islamic culture and knew and imitated the doctrines of Ibn ʿArabī". This needs to be confirmed.

37 These misconstrued, indeed unnecessary, ideas were disentangled sensibly by the Italian

scholar, Enrico Cerulli, who rightly concluded that Dante in fact showed no more knowledge of Arabic culture (in the whole corpus of his works) than would be expected of an educated man of his age.

38 Metlitzki speaks of these in detail, see pp. 197–210.
39 Mark Musa, *The Divine Comedy* (London, 1984), p. 132.
40 José Muñoz Sendino, *La Escala de Mahoma* (Madrid, 1949).
41 Enrico Cerulli, *Il Libro della Scala* (Vatican City, 1949).
42 See his own summary of ideas in "Dante e L'Islam", *Al-Andalus*, 21 (1956), pp. 227–53.
43 Maria Rosa Menocal reiterates these ideas in a stimulating chapter of her book, *The Arabic Role in Medieval Literary History* (Philadelphia, 1987); see "The Anxieties of Influence", pp. 115–35.
44 See Muñoz Sendino, *La Escala*, p. xvii–xviii, and Vicente Cantarino, *Il Libro della Scala.*
45 See Titus Burckhardt, *Alchemy* (Shaftesbury, 1987), p. 47; see also his essay on Dante in *The Mirror of the Intellect* (Cambridge, 1987).

Christian–Muslim Frontier in Al-Andalus: Idea and Reality

EDUARDO MANZANO MORENO*

Interpretations of the Iberian Middle Ages are usually centred on the long confrontation between Islam and Christendom in the Peninsula. Historians usually have in mind an ideal representation of this territory as a land dramatically divided in two parts by a thin line. North of this line lay the Christian kingdoms which expanded southwards at the expense of the Muslim land, al-Andalus, for almost eight centuries, until Islamic rule was completely defeated in 897/1492. At the epistemological level this graphic image is translated into broad conceptual categories which speak of two opposing faiths, of two different cultures, and of two divergent civilisations. "Islam" and "Christendom" have become in this context not just the names of two creeds, but abstract notions with a wider meaning.[1] This meaning is not defined in strict historical (and therefore changing) terms; instead, it is determined by apparent and immutable patterns such as religion, language or cultural tradition. In this way, these concepts have developed into explanatory categories in their own right, because it has not been deemed necessary to explain the "natural" opposition existing among two contending civilisations.

Spanish medieval historiography has suffered the consequences of this approach in many different ways. Theories and speculations on the impact and consequences of the sudden "orientalisation" (and gradual "rewesternisation") of the Iberian Peninsula have prevailed over lineal historical reconstruction. The recurrent dualism which

* I would like to express my gratitude to Derek Kennet who read and commented on a draft of this paper; his encouraging suggestions have contributed decisively to its final version.

pervades most of this historiography (even in works which analyse mutual contacts and influences), has entailed a fragmented perception of the past, in which the violent antinomy *western versus oriental* has been regarded as more relevant than the coherent analysis of historical processes.[2] From this perspective, the complex dialogue between change and continuity, always at the basis of such processes, has been persistently ignored and has been superseded by broad conceptual categories.

The limitations of this perspective become clearer when precise concepts are required for the study of complex issues. The example of the Christian–Muslim frontier illustrates very well the truth of this. The image and conceptualisation of two contending worlds in the Iberian Peninsula has made of their thin separating line no less than a frontier between civilisations. However, when it comes to defining its particular aspects, historians seem to be content with very general remarks, and their conclusions are usually drawn from literal interpretations of those sources which invariably speak of a perpetual conflict between Islam and Christianity throughout the Middle Ages.[3] Again this approach has made it difficult to see the wood for the trees. The obvious premises which built up the idea of "frontier" in the sources have attracted the attention of most scholars, whereas the information we have on its real existence has remained widely neglected. Despite being based on contemporary evidence, the resulting vision of this frontier is extremely superficial, mainly because it overlooks the role that ideology played in the definitions and perceptions elaborated by medieval writers.

The understanding of this ideology is essential in order to make intelligible the mechanisms which led to a very specific formulation of the Christian–Muslim frontier in the Iberian Peninsula.[4] The best "case-study" for this purpose is provided by the earliest accounts we have on the frontier on both sides of it. These accounts have two features which make them particularly remarkable. These are, firstly, the original adaptation of ideological premises to the concrete circumstances which prevailed in the Iberian Peninsula in the aftermath of the Muslim conquest of 92/711, and secondly, the persistence of some of these ideas throughout the whole Middle Ages.

A. The ideological frontier

Our first look is at the formulations that originated in the north. At the time of the third/ninth century a cleric in the city of Oviedo wrote a chronicle which has come to be known as *Crónica de Albelda*. The anonymous writer probably belonged to the palatine circle of King Alfonso III (866–911) who had become the undisputed ruler of the kingdom of Asturias: a territory well defended by chains of craggy mountains, and which had successfully resisted the Andalusian attacks for more than a century. By the time our chronicler was writing, the kingdom was well consolidated and had expanded beyond its wild original land, stretching to Galicia in the west and to the upper part of the Iberian Plateau or Meseta in the south.

Our anonymous chronicler undertook a difficult task; apart from a series of brief "Annals" (not all of which are extant nowadays), there was no well-established historiographical tradition in the buoyant kingdom. This was a real breakthrough. His historical account did not begin with a list of the kings of Asturias, as might have been expected, but with an abridged and sketchy history of Rome, starting with Romulus and ending with the Byzantine emperor Tiberius (610–41).[5] As is well known, the fall of the Roman Empire led the way in the Iberian Peninsula to the rule of the Visigoths and our author went on to write a chapter arranged chronologically on the German kings, starting with Atanaricus (366–81).[6] When he came to the reign of the last king a usurper named Rodrigo (709–11), he tersely stated that in his time the Arabs had conquered the Iberian Peninsula and added a significant paragraph which it is worth quoting:

> [The Saracens] took over the kingdom of the Goths which even nowadays they persistently possess in part. And the Christians have battles with them day and night, though they cannot turn them out of all Spania, until Divine Predestination orders their cruel expulsion. Amen.[7]

It was at this point that our chronicler started the historical account of those Christians fighting "day and night" against the Muslims: the kings of Asturias who were struggling to recover the lost kingdom of the Visigoths.[8]

The encyclopaedic perspective chosen by our writer had a very distinctive aim. Through this representation of the past in the Iberian Peninsula an important concept was born: the idea of Reconquista, a sustained holy struggle aimed at recovering a land which had been lost by its legitimate rulers after the Muslim conquest. Other writers also working at Alfonso III's court, held similar views. The author of the *Crónica de Alfonso III* went even further, stating explicitly in his account that the kings of Asturias were descendants of the Visigothic kings.[9] Consistent with the same idea of "loss" and "recovery" he mentions all the predecessors of King Alfonso III, always stressing the kind of relationships that each of them held with the southern enemies. The writer is at his best portraying those warlike kings who fought continuous combats against the Muslims, and seems to be more uncomfortable describing the reigns of kings like a certain Aurelius (who "did not engage in battles and had peace with the Chaldeans") or his successor Silo (who "had peace with the Ishmaelites").[10]

The necessity of throwing back the intruders became, therefore, an unavoidable duty for any Christian ruler and this idea gave way to the formulation of a "frontier" which was mainly polemical.[11] The most sophisticated representation of this conceptual "frontier" was elaborated at that time under the guise of a religious prophecy. A piece known as *Crónica Profética* relates that God had announced to the Prophet Ezekiel that Ishmael would subdue Gog and make a tributary of him; however, after 170 ages Ishmael would abandon God and Gog would finally defeat him. The interpretation of the prophecy was that Gog represented the people of the Goths whose land was Spania; because of their sins God had delivered them to their enemies, the Ishmaelites, who had conquered the land and made them tributaries. All this had already happened at the time the author was writing in 883, but he claims that the completion of the period of 170 ages was still to come; even among the Ishmaelites, he says, there were prophecies announcing the end of the rule of the Arabs, the restitution of the peace for the Church, and the restoration of the Gothic kingdom in just a few months.[12]

The year 883 passed and the prophecy was not fulfilled. Nonetheless the idea that Gog dominated the north, and the intruder Ishmael occupied the rest of the country remained — one way or another; besides, the idea that the Christian kings who resisted the Muslims were descendants of the Visigothic sovereigns was destined to be a recurrent topic in later medieval historiography.[13]

We know for certain that the authors of these early chronicles were clerics of Mozarab origin: their ancestors had remained in al-Andalus at the time of the Arab conquest, keeping their religion and preserving the Visigothic cultural tradition. During the third/ninth century the status of these Mozarabs worsened considerably due to the hardening of fiscal conditions in al-Andalus. Some of them chose to emigrate to the north, taking with them the Gothic legacy which pervades all their writings. However, it is obvious that they were also very well acquainted with the situation in al-Andalus. When, for instance, the author of the *Crónica Profética* refers to prophecies which were similar to the ones mentioned before, he is giving very accurate information. In the *Kitāb al-bida*ʿ by the Andalusian Muḥammad b. Waḍḍāḥ (d. 287/900) there are also references to eschatological prophecies based on the Islamic tradition. Other indications seem to suggest that in the second half of the third/ninth century on both sides of our frontier there was a feeling that a new era was just about to begin.[14]

Nevertheless despite their very good knowledge of al-Andalus, the Mozarab writers of our chronicles were only interested in highlighting the idea of "loss" and the necessary "recovery". When these writers referred to the enemy, to the people who stood beyond the line of the frontier, they never called them Muslims; instead, they used names drawn from the classical or biblical tradition such as Ishmaelites, Saracens, Chaldeans or Babylonians.[15] The creed of the opponents did not matter so much as their classification according to the previous cultural legacy.[16]

If we look at the Andalusian side, the picture we get is very similar. Most of the authors of the extant Arab chronicles of this early period lived in third/ninth or fourth/tenth century Córdoba, the seat of the Umayyad dynasty which ruled al-Andalus until 422/1031. Also, most of them (or at least most of those whose works have been preserved) were *mawālī* or clients of the Umayyad family and had strong personal links with the members of the dynasty who claimed to rule the whole country.[17] This circumstance influenced their writings significantly. The reality portrayed by these chroniclers is only justified by and for their masters. This obsessive bias implies that their historical accounts are only concerned with gathering information on the deeds and glorious actions of Umayyad rulers. Anything which did not affect them directly or indirectly was simply left out. The idea, (or the deception, if one prefers to put it this way) works very well because the Umayyads are always identified with the Muslims.

Andalusian chroniclers had a particular word for the divisory line which separated the two worlds: *thaghr* (pl. *thughūr*). This is a very interesting word which occurs not only in Arabic but in other Semitic languages as well, with an original meaning of "pass" or "opening".[18] The Arabic classical dictionaries give a definition of this word as the strip of land which separates the "dwelling place of Islam" (*dār al-islām*) and the "dwelling place of the war" (*dār al-ḥarb*).[19] Therefore, after going through the *thaghr*, the "Holy War", the *jihād*, becomes an unavoidable duty for any Muslim ruler. Islamic political theory of the classical period put strong emphasis on this point, and it also stressed that one of the main tasks of the ruler was to defend the *thughūr* and to provision them with troops.[20]

Andalusian writers, obsessed as they were with the religious and political legitimacy of their masters, did not miss any chance to remark how faithfully the Umayyad rulers were observing this duty. The founder of the dynasty, ʿAbd al-Raḥmān I (138–72/756–88) is praised in the chronicles for his tireless efforts in subduing the *thughūr*.[21] His successor, Hishām I (172–80/788–96) is portrayed as a ruler who led countless expeditions in order to safeguard the frontiers and to protect his subjects.[22]

> Ask one of my frontiers if there is any breach in them today/ and I shall run there holding my sword and with my cuirass on.

The third Umayyad amir, al-Ḥakam I (180–206/796–822), allegedly wrote in a poem.[23]

The keynote is identical in the accounts of the rest of the Umayyad rulers and in this way the "defence of the frontiers" became a recurrent topic which justified the political aspirations of the dynasty.

B. The real frontier

The graphic and conceptual division of the Iberian Peninsula mentioned above seems to be well justified. As we have seen, both Arabic and Latin texts build up a seemingly coherent idea of the frontier: Gog or the polytheists in the north, Ishmael or the believers in the south. In fact, this idea became the accepted traditional view of the Iberian Peninsula for a very long time. The trouble is, however, that the historian may have the somewhat disturbing feeling that he is merely reproducing ideas and schemes which were bred ten centuries ago.

If we want to grasp historical reality and not merely historical ideology which is obvious, we need to trace historical processes. In the northern part of the Iberian Peninsula, where the kingdom of Asturias originally emerged, these processes go back to a period long before the Muslim conquest, and more particularly to the time of the late Roman Empire. At that time, the Romans were compelled to set up a *limes* to face the Asturians who posed a serious external threat. Despite the fact that Hispania had been conquered well before the beginning of the Christian era, the testimony of different Latin texts is clear and very precise. In the fourth century AD there was a frontier in the north of the Peninsula. This frontier comprised a number of fortifications in the Upper Ebro valley and in the northern parts of the Iberian Plateau, according to a list of military posts known as the *Notitia Dignitatum*, which was written at the end of the fourth century or the beginning of the fifth century AD. However, this *limes* was not a temporary response to a definitive situation. It was firmly established because the problems in the north of the Peninsula were very serious indeed. When the Visigoths took over the Iberian Peninsula, they had no choice but to keep the defensive line built by their predecessors. We have a good deal of evidence which shows that the Visigothic kings had to face continuous troubles in the north and to send military expeditions. They also fortified strategic sites in those regions.[24]

The source of all these troubles were groups of peoples known as Vasconi, Cantabri and Asturi who occupied the inaccessible high lands of the northern strip. We have some information about them provided by Roman authors, particularly Strabo (d. after AD 23), and from epigraphic evidence. These people practised a very primitive economy; their tribal structures were still prevalent in a society characterised by the existence of a matriarchate. Despite eventual submissions first to the Roman armies and later to the Visigoths, these peoples preserved their independence throughout the whole period. In these circumstances there is no wonder that paganism was widespread among them. Christianisation of these regions began at a late date; monks and hermits only started to convert these peoples at the end of the sixth century AD.[25]

The interesting thing about these peoples and the reasons why they are mentioned here, is that they occupied the northern parts of the Iberian Peninsula from where the Reconquista is said to have begun. The Asturi in particular, dwelt in the same mountainous regions where a place called Covadonga is located. In this spot an Arab army was defeated around the year 107/725, a battle which has been commonly regarded as the starting-point of the Reconquista.[26] But here the fantastic paradox emerges. The same peoples who had opposed the Roman rule, who had been a continuous source of trouble for the Visigothic kings until the very eve of the Arab conquest, and who only began to become Christians at a very late date, were precisely those who started the Reconquista of the Iberian Peninsula in the name of Christianity and of the restoration of the Visigothic kingdom. The trouble is, of course, that they simply could never reconquer this land because in fact they had never possessed it.

What the Arabs found in the north of the Peninsula was a very similar situation to that which their predecessors had had to face. The itinerary followed by the conquering armies in the aftermath of their victory against the Visigoths in 92/711 shows very clearly that they avoided advancing in the northern strip. The victorious expedition led by Mūsā b. Nusayr (d. 98/716–17) in 93/712 took over the main defensive posts of the Visigothic *limes* but its commander did not dare to penetrate the high lands which stood beyond.[27] A few years later, the new rulers could verify for themselves the reasons which had compelled their predecessors to keep those fortifications. Clashes with the unsubdued northern peoples became as frequent as they had been before, with the exception that what happened at Covadonga achieved a disproportionate notoriety.

When the Mozarab chroniclers of King Alfonso III had to write the history of these events, they tried by every means to disguise this flagrant paradox. Thus, the Asturi became "Christians" (though it may be suggested that the Christianisation of these regions was not fully completed at the beginning of the second/eighth century), and their chieftains became descendants of the Visigothic kings. To some extent they succeeded but a close scrutiny of their accounts, as

Barbero and Vigil have demonstrated, reveals a number of inconsistencies which allow us to conclude that the leader of the "Christian" forces in the battle of Covadonga, and founder of the dynasty, a man named Pelayo, was not a Visigoth but a local chieftain. Pelayo (718–37) fought the intruders in the same way as his ancestors had repelled the Romans and Visigoths. It is most probable that he had not the slightest religious motive in his struggle. The dynasty which he founded was an Asturian one, and was not a Gothic lineage. As a reminiscence of the old matriarchate of the Asturi, the transmission of power in this dynasty was still ruled by matrilineal descent.[28] Therefore, it was not Gog who dwelt in the north of the Iberian Peninsula, but a bunch of primitive peoples; it was not a dynasty of kings descended from the Goths who was struggling to recover the land of their ancestors, but a family of local chieftains continuing the tradition of reluctance to assimilate; and, finally, it was not the aim of these peoples to defend Christianity but rather to preserve their independence. Under these circumstances the rigid definition of the Christian–Islamic frontier begins to blur.

It was not true either that al-Andalus was occupied by a monolithic community with religion as its only obsession. As we have seen before, the frontiers, the *thughūr*, have a very special meaning in Islamic political and religious theory. In the east, where these ideas had been originally formulated, this meaning was associated with the practice of *jihād*, or Holy War, and with the duty of protecting these frontiers by means of *ribāṭs*. These *ribāṭs* were fortifications which lodged Muslim warriors who combined their military tasks with a strict religious observance.[29] The ideological framework expressed in the Andalusian chronicles suggests that construction of *ribāṭs* would have been undertaken by the Umayyads, had they had the opportunity of doing so. However, the fact is that there is an almost absolute lack of evidence for *ribāṭ* foundations in the *thughūr al-andalus* by the Umayyads during this period. It is true that the rulers of Córdoba sent expeditions against the north, that they fortified some places, and that there are occasional references in biographical dictionaries to individuals who are described as *murābiṭ*;[30] but *ribāṭ* foundations fostered by the Umayyads are notably absent from our sources during this period.[31] The most logical conclusion seems to be that, despite the rhetorical expressions of the chronicles, the *thughūr* were not the defensive line of the *umma*. Instead, the frontiers of al-Andalus were a farrago of contradictions. Paradoxical though it may seem, their boundaries were not defined on the basis of religious allegiances. In fact, there is a good deal of evidence which shows that at the core of the *thughūr*, in their very first line, Christian communities were living under Islamic rule. An unusual Latin document dated in AD 987 reflects this state of affairs. In that year, the inhabitants of Aguinaliu and Juseu (two tiny little villages near one of the rivers which sprang from the Pyrenees) held a litigation over the ownership of a well. From the document in which are assembled the proceedings of the trial, we learn that these people were Christians and that they referred the dispute to the Christian judge of Lérida.[32] This city was the main centre of the region and is described in the sources as one of the more important sites of the *thughūr* in the area.[33] It is significant that Aguinaliu and Juseu were only thirty or forty miles south of Roda de Isabena, an important episcopal see which was in the hands of the Christian counts of Ribagorza.

The Christians who dwelt in these two little villages were not an exception in the area. In his geographical description Aḥmad al-Rāzī (274–344/887–955) tells us that in the district of Lérida there were many places inhabited by Christians, because at the time of the Muslim conquest, pacts were covenanted with the natives by means of which these natives "would stand by the Muslims and the Muslims would stand by them without disagreement."[34]

The crack that this case reveals in the ideological building of the Christian–Muslim frontier widens in other places. Political events and social conditions in the area contributed decisively to shape a very unstable situation in the *thughūr al-Andalus.* Despite all of their efforts the Umayyads had to face a double enemy up in the north. On the one hand, there were the emerging kingdoms to which I have referred before, and on the other, aristocratic families which occupied whole sectors of the frontier, ruling them independently, despite the best efforts of the rulers in Córdoba to control them. Some of these families were of Arab origin, some of them were Berbers and some of them were descendants of the indigenous stock, but their dominating role in their fiefs came to be the same in the course of time.

One of the most prominent and best-known lineages is the family of the Banū Qasī (714–924). Their ancestor, Casius (d. after 715), was the Visigothic dux of the frontier against the Vasconi in the upper valley of the River Ebro at the time of the Muslim conquest. By that time he had probably become a feudal lord who combined military and fiscal duties in his district.[35] The Arab conquest of the Peninsula did not bother him too much. He converted to Islam and kept the same territories that he had been dominating in the past. When he died, these lands were inherited by his descendants who were eventually able to extend them to other parts of the frontier until the decline of the family in the first half of the fourth/tenth century.[36] The major role played by the Banū Qasī in the affairs of the frontier of the Ebro valley was very much helped by their ability in building alliances with other powers of the region. Soon after the Arab conquest they became related by marriages with a family of Vasooni who ended up ruling one of the emergent kingdoms of the north, the kingdom of Navarra. Throughout the whole period the alliance between the Banū Qasī and the Arista dynasty interfered with Umayyad pretensions to hegemonical sovereignty in the *thaghr*. The dismayed amirs of Córdoba had to deal with constant rebellions by this turbulent family and their allies with very little results. Latin and Arab chronicles eventually refer to them as *reges* or *mulūk*, kings.[37]

Absence of neat religious boundaries and political fragmentation belie the Umayyad chronicles' pretensions of uniformity in the *thughūr*. This critical area lacked the necessary homogeneity to become a frontier because many times it turned out to be a frontier itself against the rulers of Córdoba.[38] Nothing tells us more about complexities of this frontier than the brief analysis of another sector which is particularly obscure. This is the area of the Duero valley, a territory which from the middle of the second/eighth century lay between Gog and Ishmael, apparently undisputed by both the northern and the southern rulers of the Peninsula. It was only from the beginning of the fourth/tenth century onwards that this region increasingly became the actual borderline betwen al-Andalus and the northern kingdoms. The obvious question is: what had been going on there before that date?

For a long time the prevalent view has been that these areas became a depopulated no-man's-land, a strategical desert consciously created by the kings of Asturias in order to protect their territories. According to this view, only when this kingdom became more consolidated in the fourth/tenth century, did its rulers repopulate the area with settlers brought from the north. This transfer of population produced a very peculiar society, dominated by free men and small landholders who were granted liberties and lands in order to encourage their migration.[39]

These ideas, however, are inconsistent. Again, a literal interpretation of the sources has produced a distorted historical image which lacks coherence and solid grounds.[40] Apart from the practical infeasibility of consciously depopulating such a vast area by the feeble kings of a tiny kingdom, there is archaeological and toponimical evidence which shows that the population of the Duero valley remained in place.[41] This would suggest that the Latin scribes who from the fourth/tenth century onwards depicted this region as "deserted by its inhabitants" were only trying to justify the appropriation of the land by the aristocracy and the religious orders. The fiction of a depopulated area, a no-man's-land, allowed the expansion of the kingdom and its ruling classes in an unrestrained frontier.[42]

From this perspective the whole picture changes radically. It might be argued that for more than a century and a half the remaining peoples of the Duero Valley enjoyed the enviable privilege of living without any central administration. Both the rulers of al-Andalus and the kings of Asturias were not powerful enough to control them. Unfortunately for historians this meant their literal erasure from the written sources. However, it is perhaps possible to pick up some evidence of their living conditions from information included in late texts which may reflect a very peculiar frontier life. Particularly intriguing in this regard is the local code of law (*fuero*) of the village of Sepúlveda written down in the second half of the fifth/eleventh century but which perhaps included consuetudinary law. Some of the rules of this code are particularly striking. Killers coming from the north were safe in Sepúlveda because the village community was prepared to defend them against their persecutors; anybody arriving with a concubine or with stolen goods was also welcome in the village; and, finally, there was a "blood-price" which was much higher if the assassinated person was a member of the village of Sepúlveda.[43]

All these rules have traditionally been regarded as special

privileges granted to the new settlers of the village, but this interpretation is only based on the assumption that Sepúlveda had previously been a deserted spot. However, there are some indications which suggest that this might not have been the case.[44] This would lead us to consider the possibility that the local legal code of Sepúlveda encapsulated legal customs which had prevailed among populations lacking any central administration. Though the evidence is very scarce, it would be tempting to think these rules bring us more the "taste of the frontier" than the elaborations made up under the shadow of the Holy War.

When the people of the Duero valley appear again in Latin documents of the fourth/tenth and early fifth/eleventh centuries they have indeed a very remarkable feature; many of them bear Arabic names such as Tareq, Zaher or Abolmaluc and many of them dwell in villages whose place names are unmistakably Arabic such as Muhummud, Alcozer, Villa Mesquina or Zahara.[45] That they were Christians is clear because their names occur in documents of monasteries witnessing transactions or even being described as priests. More striking still is the fact that this feature occurs in many places along the Duero valley; places which are never mentioned by the Andalusian chroniclers as held by the Umayyads or by any other Andalusian ruler.[46]

It has commonly been considered that these populations were Mozarabs coming from the south who emigrated to the Duero valley in order to fill the human gap in a deserted area. However, we have to bear in mind that this feature pervades the whole valley and that it would reveal a huge and large movement of people which is not testified by any source. The only possibility that remains then is to consider that these peoples at some time and somehow had become at least partially arabised. There is a tiny piece of evidence which might support this view. A text by a late Muslim writer of the sixth/twelfth century named Muḥammad b. Ibrāhīm al-Muwāʿinī perhaps reflects this pattern of arabisation. Describing two castles of the Duero Valley in the north of modern Portugal, called al-Ikhwān, he states that their inhabitants were Christians who had lived there since the time of the Muslim conquest. At that time they made a pact with Mūsā b. Nuṣayr; some of them, the chronicler adds, could speak Arabic and they even pretended to have an Arab origin despite being Christians.[47]

It is difficult to know why and how this arabisation happened. It might be suggested that a similar phenomenon occurred in other parts of close contact, such as Sicily for instance. Perhaps this remarkable feature has much to do with the strength shown by the Arabic language during this early period as a result of it being the language of military expansion. Be that as it may, what seems to be clear is that these ignored peoples of the Duero valley reflect a complicated pattern of assimilation. Boundaries are not as clear as one would have expected and conceptual categories do not always work as well as they do when they are formulated in theory. We may conclude that the quest for a clear and well-defined "frontier" turns out to be an unsuccessful enterprise; in fact it is important always to bear in mind that the whole medieval territory was itself a "frontier".

Notes

1 See particularly the works by C. Sánchez Albornoz who openly speaks of "two Spains" in the Middle Ages in his "El Islam de España y el Occidente", *Settimane di Studio dell Centro Italiano di Studi sull 'alto Medioevo, XII: L'Occidente e Islam nell 'Alto Medioevo* (Spoleto, 1965), p. 225.

2 As is the case of A. Castro, *The Structure of Spanish History*, (Princeton, 1954).

3 C. Sánchez Albornoz, "The frontier and Castilian liberties", *The New World looks at its History. Proceedings of the Second International Congress of Historians of the United States and Mexico* (Austin, 1962), pp. 27–46.

4 It is important to bear in mind the fact that the very notion of "frontier" may have very different meanings in diverse contexts and in changing historical circumstances, see R.I. Burns, "The significance of the frontier in the Middle Ages", *Mediaeval Frontier Societies*, ed. R. Bartlett and A. Mackay (Oxford, 1989), pp. 307–30.

5 The chapter is headed "Incipit Ordo Romanorum Gentium"; see *Crónica de Albelda, España Sagrada*, ed. E. Flórez (Madrid, 1753), pp. 438–44. This chapter was not included in the more modern edition of this chronicle undertaken by M. Gómez Moreno, "Las primeras crónicas de la Reconquista, el ciclo de Alfonso III", *Boletín de la Real Academia de la Historia* (1932), pp. 600–9.

6 "Incipit Ordo Gentis Gotorum", *Crónica de Albelda*, ed. Flórez, pp. 445–9; *Crónica de Albelda*, ed. Gómez Moreno, pp. 600–1.

7 "Regnumque gotorum capiunt. quod adhuc usque ex parte pertinaciter possident. et cum eis xpistiani die noctuque bella iniunt. et quotidie confligunt. sed eis ex toto Spaniam auferre non possunt. dum predestinatio usque diuina dehinc eos expelli crudeliter. Amen", *ibid.*, p. 601.

8 "Item Ordo Gottorum Obetensium Regum", *ibid.*, p. 601.

9 *Crónica de Alfonso III*, ed. Gómez Moreno, pp. 609–22.

10 *ibid.*, p. 617.

11 Neither the *Crónica de Albelda* nor the *Crónica de Alfonso III* give concrete details on the actual frontiers of the kingdom of Asturias.

12 *Crónica Profética*, ed. E. Gómez Moreno, pp. 622–4. The identification of Magog with the Goths goes back to the works of Isidore of Seville (d. 636): "Gothorum antiquissimam esse gentem quorum originem quidem de Magog lafeth filio suspicatur a similitudine ultime syllabae", C. Rodríguez Alonso (ed.), *La historia de los Godos, Vándalos y Suevos de Isidoro de Sevilla* (León, 1975), p. 172.

13 When King Alfonso VI conquered Toledo in 478/1085 he proclaimed in a document that he had recaptured the capital of his ancestors, the Gothic kings; the document is quoted in J. Fernández Conde (ed.), *Historia de la Iglesia en España*, vol. II (Madrid, 1982), p. 239. Five centuries later the Catholic kings justified their attack against the Naṣrid kingdom of Granada on the grounds the "Moors" held that land "tyrannically". The ancestors of the Christian kings had possessed the whole country in the ancient times, see Fernándo del Pulgar, *Crónicas de los Reyes Católicos*, ed. J.M. Carriazo, vol. II (Madrid, 1943), pp. 396–7.

14 Compare "Quod etiam ipsi sarrazeni quosdam prodigiis uel austrorum signis interitum suum adpropinquare predicunt, et gotorum regnum restaurari per hunc nostrum principem dicunt", (*Crónica Profética*, ed. Gómez Moreno, p. 623) with the series of eschatological traditions included by Muḥammad b. Waḍḍāḥ, *Kitāb al-bidaʿ* (*Tratado contra las innovaciones*), ed. and trans. M.I. Fierro (Madrid, 1988), pp. 206–7 and 330–1. See also the interesting remarks by this scholar on the eschatological prophecies in Islam, *ibid.*, p. 98. It is also worth mentioning here that in 267/881 a formidable internal rebellion against the Umayyads was begun by a *muwallad* named ʿUmar b. Ḥafṣūn. In his account of this event, the Andalusian chronicler Ibn al-Qūṭiyya mentions an earlier episode in which ʿUmar is recognised by an old man as the character who will destroy the power of the Umayyads in al-Andalus. This fictitious anecdote fits in extremely well with other such prophecies; see Ibn al-Qūṭiyya, *Taʾrīkh iftitāh al-Andalus* (*Historia de la conquista de España de Abenalcotía el cordobés*) ed. and trans. J. Ribera (Madrid, 1920), pp. 91 and 76–7.

15 N. Barbour, "The significance of the word 'Maurus' and its derivates 'Moro' and 'Moor' and of other terms used by Mediaeval writers in Latin to describe the inhabitants of Muslim Spain", *Actas do IV Congresso de Estudios Arabas e Islamicos. Coimbra-Lisboa, 1968* (Leyde, 1971), pp. 253–66.

16 Only the *Crónica Profética* includes an account of the life of Muḥammad, who is portrayed as *nephandus propheta*; several motifs of this account seem to be inspired in Byzantine polemic texts; see M.T. d'Alverny, "La connaissance de l'Islam en Occident du IXe au milieu du XIIe siècle", *Settimane di Studio dell Centro Italiano di Studi sull'alto Medioevo, XII L'Occidente e Islam nell 'Alto Medioevo* (Spoleto, 1965), pp. 586–8. There is an excellent edition of the above-mentioned text by M. Díaz y Díaz, "Los textos antimahomatenos más antiguos en códices españoles", *Archives d'Histoire Doctrinale et Littéraire du Moyen Âge* (1970), pp. 157–9.

17 This circumstance was already perceived by R. Dozy, *Histoire de l'Afrique et de l'Espagne intitulé Al-Bayano-l-Mogrib par Ibn Adharí (de Maroc) et fragments de la chronique d'Arib (de Cordoue)*, vol. I (Leyde, 1848–51), p. 19.

18 R. Blachère, M. Choiuemi and C. Denizeau, *Dictionnaire Arabe-Français-Anglais* (Paris, 1967), s.v. *thaghr.*

19 Ibn Manẓūr, *Lisān al-ʿarab*, vol. IV (Beirut, 1935), pp. 103–4.

20 A.K.S. Lambton, *State and Government in Mediaeval Islam. An Introduction to Islamic Political Theory: The Jurists* (Oxford, 1981), pp. 18–19 and 91.

21 Ibn ʿIdhārī, *Al-bayān al-mughrib*, ed. G.S. Colin and E. Lévi-Provençal, vol. II (Leyde, 1948–1951), p. 60. There is an identical account in Ibn al-Khaṭīb, *Kitāb ʿamāl al-aʿlām*, ed. E. Lévi-Provençal (Beirut, 1956), pp. 9–10. The former lived in seventh/thirteenth century, whereas Ibn al-Khaṭīb died in 776/1332; the fact that both of them compiled the same account suggests that they based it on the Umayyad models which we know they utilised at length.

22 *Akhbār majmūʿa*, ed. and trans. E. Lafuente Alcántara (Madrid, 1867), pp. 120 and 109.

23 The same poem is found in *Akhbār majmūʿa*, pp. 132–3 and Ibn ʿIdhārī, II, pp. 71–2, among other chronicles.

24 A. Barbero and M. Vigil, *Sobre los orígenes sociales de la Reconquista* (Barcelona, 1974), pp. 14–98.

25 *Ibid.*, pp. 146–94.

26 The battle of Covadonga is summarily described by the *Crónica de Albelda*, ed. Gómez Moreno, p. 601; a more elaborated and rich description in *Crónica de Alfonso III* ed. Gómez Moreno, pp. 613–14. A different account of the first clashes between the invaders and the Asturi in *Akhbār majmūʿa*, pp. 28 and 38–9. On the importance of the name "Covadonga" (cova dominica) see the illuminating remarks by A. Barbero and M. Vigil, pp. 193–4.

27 C. Sánchez Albornoz, "Itinerario de la conquista de España por los musulmanes", *Orígenes de la nación española. Estudios críticos sobre el reino de Asturias*, vol. I (Oviedo, 1972), pp. 450–4.

28 A. Barbero and M. Vigil, *La formación del feudalismo en la Península Ibérica* (Barcelona, 1978), pp. 232–78 and 327–53.

29 See, for instance, the descriptions on fourth/tenth century *ribāts* in Tarsus in M. Canard, "Quelques observations sur l'introduction géographique de la Bughyat at-taʿalab de Kamāl ad-Dīn ibn al-ʿAdīm d'Alep", *Annales de l'Institut d'Etudes Orientales de l'Université d'Alger*, 15 (1957), pp. 41–53.

30 Ibn al-Faraḍī, *Taʾrīkh ʿulamāʾ al-andalus*, (Bibliotheca Arabico-Hispana, VII–VIII), ed. F. Codera, and J. Ribera (Madrid, 1891–1892), n. 432, 532, 1464 ff.

31 This can be seen in the study by J. Oliver Asín, "Orígen árabe de rebato, arrobda y sus homónimos. Contribución al estudio de la historia medieval de la táctica militar y de su léxico peninsular", *Boletín de la Real Academia de la Historia*, 15 (1928), pp. 347–95, 496–542.

32 R. D'Abadal, *Catalunya Carolingia. El orígen dels comtats de Pallars i Ribagorza* (Barcelona, 1954), p. 427.

33 E. Lévi-Provençal, "La description de l'Espagne d'Ahmad al-Razi. Essai de reconstitution de l'original arabe et traduction française", *Al-Andalus*, 18 (1953), pp. 73–4.

34 *Ibid.*, p. 74.

35 Ibn Hazm (d. 456/1064) mentions him as *qūmis al-thaghr*, see *Jamharat ansāb al-ʿarab*, ed. A.S.M. Harūn (Cairo, 1982), p. 502.

36 Ibn al-Qūṭiyya, 114; as this chronicler points out the beginning of the decline coincided with a change of dynasty in Navarra.

37 Ibn al-Hayyān, *al-Muqtabas (V)*, ed. P. Chalmeta (Madrid, 1979), p. 125. *Crónica de Albelda*, ed. Gómez Moreno, p. 603.

38 The case of the former capital of the Visigothic kingdom, Toledo, is particularly revealing in this regard; until its conquest by ʿAbd al-Raḥmān III in 320/932, this city led continuous rebellions against the Umayyads.

39 C. Sánchez Albornoz, *Despoblación y repoblación del valle del Duero* (Buenos Aires, 1966). Readers acquainted with F.J. Turner's ideas on the significance of America's

western frontier in the nineteenth century will find Sánchez Albornoz's ideas extremely familiar.

40 The whole plan of deliberate depopulation is attributed by the sources to King Alfonso I who ruled Asturias during the middle of the second/eighth century, "Campos quos dicunt Gothicos usque ad flumen Durium eremauit et xpistianorum regnum extendit", *Crónica de Albelda*, ed. Gómez Moreno, p. 602; *Crónica de Alfonso III*, ed. Gómez Moreno, p. 616, mentions several cities in the Duero valley and adds: "Omnes quoque arabes gladio interficiens, xpistianos autem secum ad patriam ducens." An excellent criticism of the literal interpretation of these texts by C. Sánchez Albornoz can be found in R. Menéndez Pidal, "Repoblación y tradición en la cuenca del Duero", *Enciclopedia Lingüística Hispana*, vol. I (Madrid, 1960), pp. XXIX–LVII.

41 A. Barrios Garcia, "Toponomástica e Historia. Notas sobre la despoblación en la zona meridional del Duero", *En la España Mediaeval. Estudios en memorai del Pfr. D. Salvador de Moxo*, vol. I (Madrid, 1982), pp. 115–34. T. Mañanes, *Arqueología vallisoletana* (Valladolid, 1979–83), p. 127.

42 A. Barbero and M. Vigil, *La formación*, pp. 224–8.

43 *Fuero de Sepúlveda*, ed. E. Sáez (Madrid, 1952), pp. 46–8.

44 The Romanesque church of Sepúlveda is located near a Visigothic necropolis. This shows an impressive continuity in patterns of spatial functions which is difficult to explain. We have the memorial to a local hermit, St Frutos, who lived in the area in the second half of the seventh century. Four centuries later a monastery dedicated to him was founded there; see Marqués de Lozoya, "La Iglesia de Nuestra Señora de las Vegas de Pedraza y el romance de los Siete Infantes de Lara", *Boletín de la Real Acadamia de la Historia*, 158 (1963), p. 10. M.S. Martín Postigo, *S. Frutos de Duratón. Historia de un proirato benedictino* (Segovia, 1907), pp. 19–21. The whole question, however, remains debatable as can be seen in A. Linage Conde, "La donación de Alfonso VI a Silos del futuro priorato de San Frutos y el problema de la despoblación", *Anuario de Historia del Derecho Español*, 41 (1971), pp. 973–1011.

45 *Cartulario de San Pedro de Arlanza*, ed. L. Serrano (Madrid, 1925), pp. 34–5; 45–6; *Becerro Gótico de Cardeña*, ed. L. Serrano (Valladolid, 1910), pp. 13, 42, 47^{ff}.

46 *Colección Diplomática del Monasterio de Sahagún* (Siglos IX y X), ed. J.M. Mínguez Fernández (Léon, 1976), pp. 37, 47, 48, 64^{ff}. The same feature occurs in northern lands of present day Portugal; see *Portugaliae Monumenta Historica*, II, *Diplomata et Chartae*, docs. I–VII and XII.

47 R. Dozy, *Scriptorum arabum loci de Abbadidis*, vol. 2 (Leyde, 1843–56), p. 7. "al-Ikhwān" has been identified with modern "Alafoes", near Viseu; see D. Lopes, "Toponimia árabe de Portugal", *Revue Hispanique*, 9 (1902), p. 45.

An Islamic Divinatory Technique in Medieval Spain

CHARLES BURNETT

The map of the Iberian Peninsula looks rather similar to the shoulder-blade of a sheep. Both have a "neck" or isthmus, below which a large flat area spreads out. One would, therefore, be forgiven for mistaking a schematic diagram of a shoulder-blade (Figure 1) for a primitive map of medieval Spain, especially since several Spanish towns are mentioned on this diagram. Figure 1 illustrates a text on how to divine the future and discover hidden things from various marks on a shoulder-blade. The texts describing this form of divination — known as scapulimancy — came into Europe via Islamic Spain. But unlike the majority of works on medicine, mathematics and astronomy that were translated from Spanish Arabic copies which in turn had come from the East, the extant texts in Arabic and Latin appear to have originated in Spain. They refer frequently to Spanish towns and to situations specific to al-Andalus. As such they provide an interesting insight into the society of medieval Spain.[1]

The art of scapulimancy involves choosing a sheep either from one's own fold or from a trustworthy merchant. Having kept it in one's house for three days, one has it slain and boiled in water. As the meat starts to fall off the carcass one extracts the shoulder-blade and reads the message that is conveyed on it. This is signified by the marks, such as scratches, grooves, hollows, and pieces of meat sticking to the bone, which are discerned in the different "places" on the shoulder-blade. These places are marked out on the diagrams in the Arabic and Latin manuscripts. Each place is relevant to a different subject, but over and above this some places have proper names of their own — such as "money box" (*pixis*), "nose" (*nasum*),

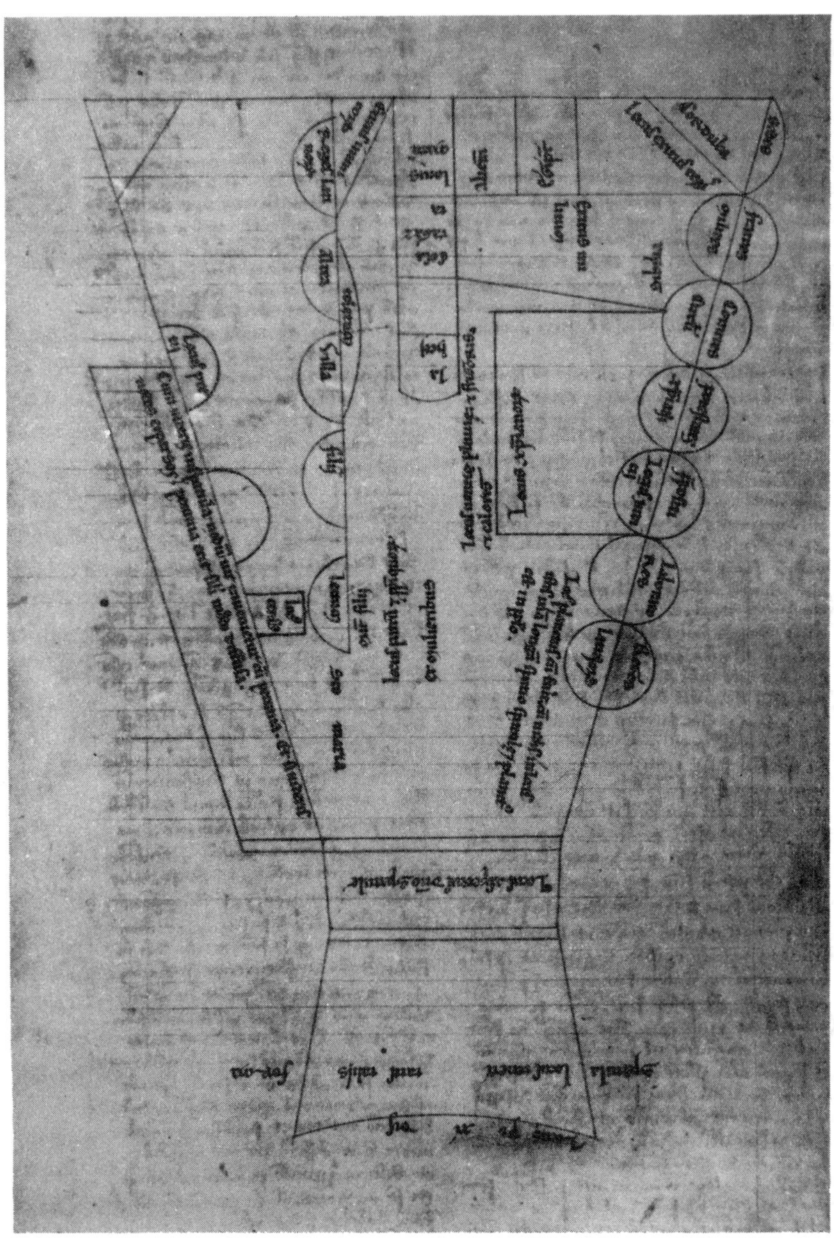

Figure 1 The right shoulder-blade, MS Oxford, Bodleian Library, Canon. Misc. 396, fol. 112r.

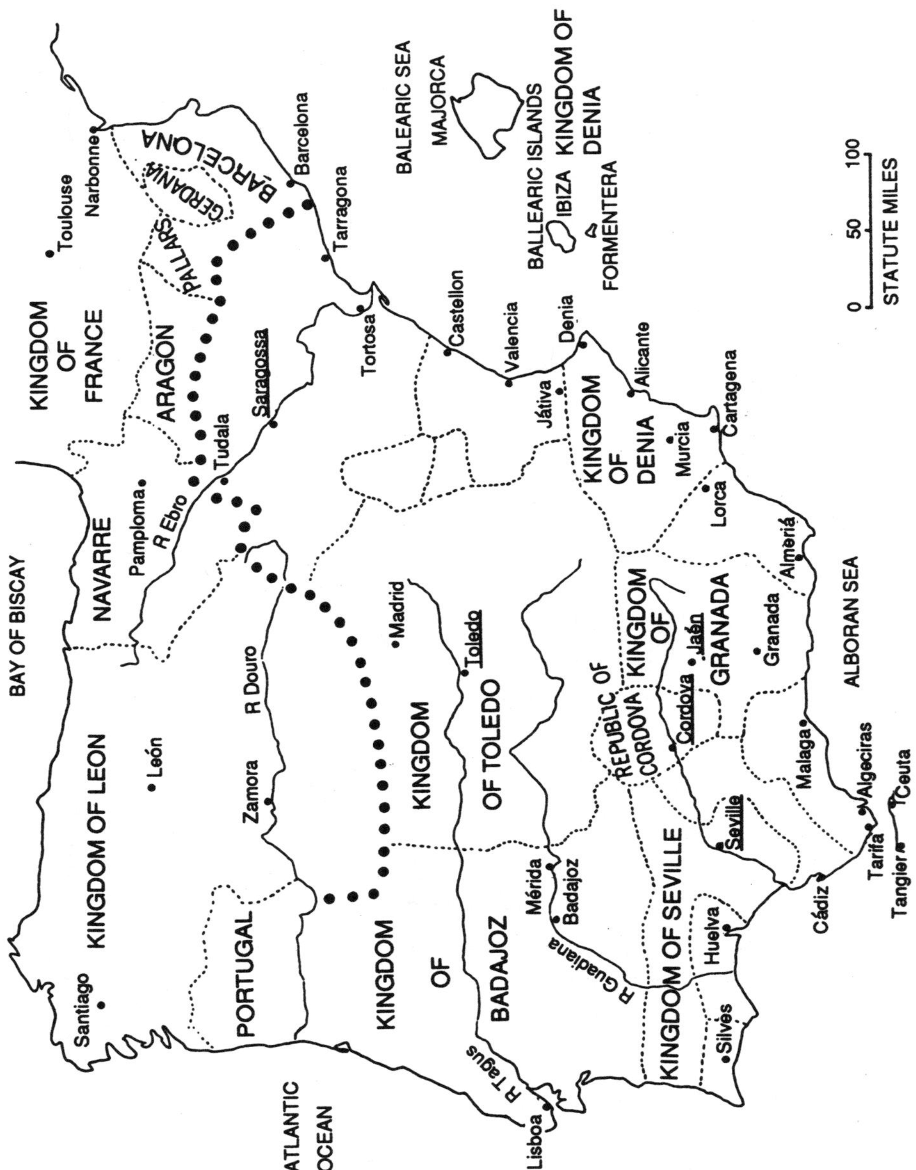

Figure 2 Spain after the Fall of the Umayyad Caliphate in the eleventh century. The plates marked on the shoulder-blade in Figure 1 are underlined. The map has been reproduced from A. G. Cheyne, *Muslim Spain*, p. 54.

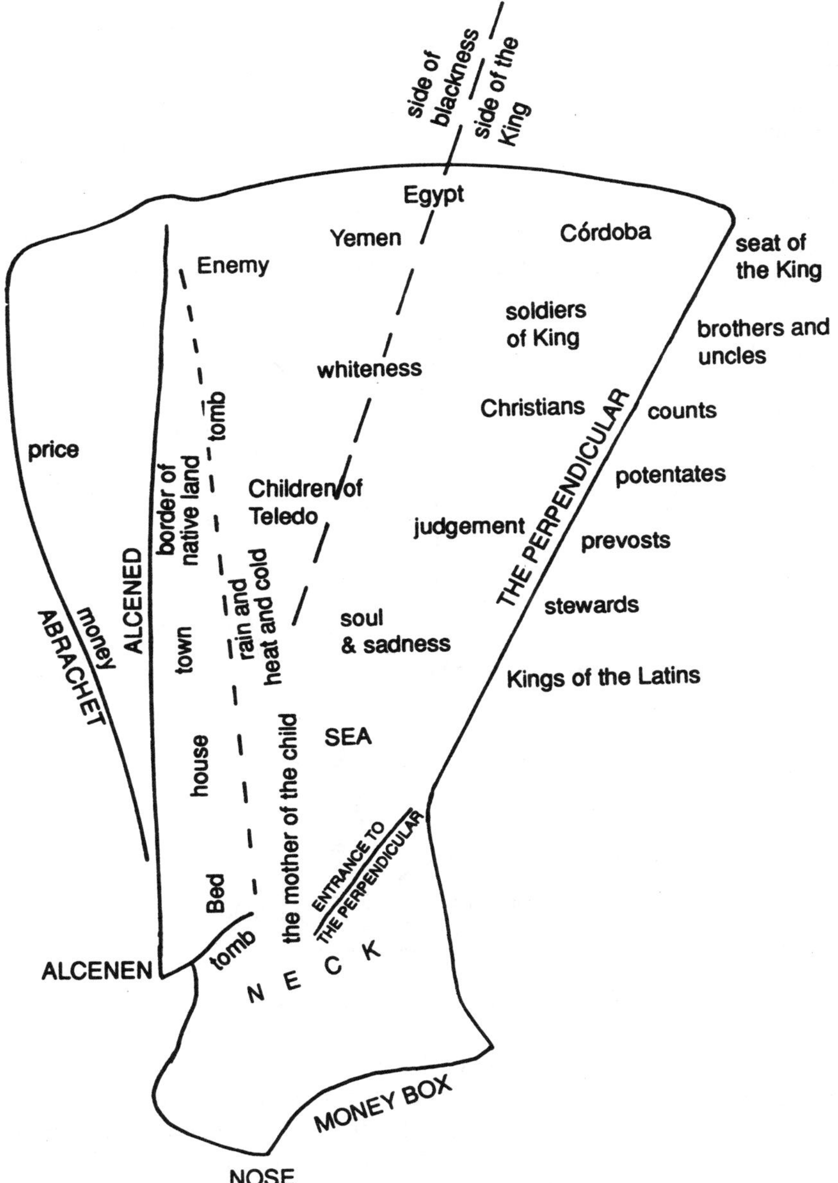

Figure 3 The "places" on the shoulder-blade described in the text and diagram in Oxford, Bodleian Library, Canon. Misc. 396, fols. 108r–112r. The parts of the shoulder-blade are indicated by capital letters; for all other words one must understand "the place of". The back of the shoulder-blade.

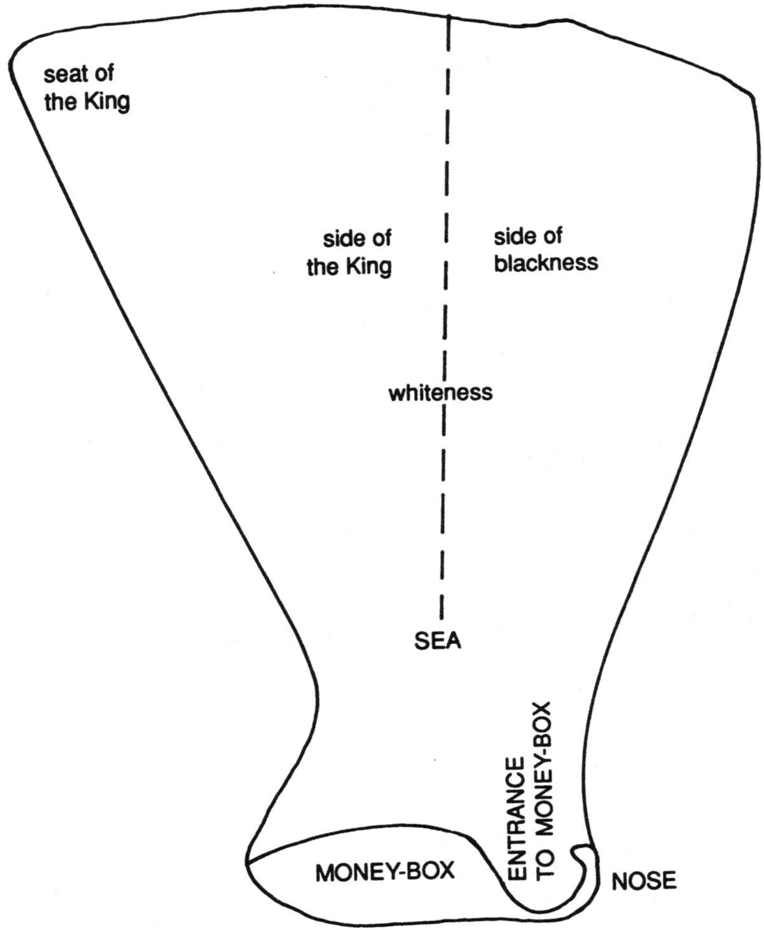

Figure 4 The front of the shoulder-blade

"sea" (*mare*), etc. The fact that one of these places is called "the place of Córdoba" (Ar.46) gives the clue to the Spanish context of the chart. This clue is substantiated by the further point that at least two of the Latin translations were made by *magister* Hugo of Santalla for Michael, Bishop of Tarazona in the 1140s. For the translation of another work Hugo used a manuscript which his patron had probably found in the library of the last stronghold of the Islamic rulers of Zaragoza, Rueda de Jalón, which was captured in

1141. Indeed the place adjacent to the place of Córdoba is called "the place of the frontier province and of Zaragoza" (Ar.45). The other Spanish towns marked on the diagrams are Jaén, Seville and Toledo.

The shoulder-blade reveals both affairs of the family whose sheep has been slain and affairs of state. Two of the places are described respectively as "the place of the family of Fihr and what happens to them" (Ar.9), and "the place of the family of Marwān and what happens to them" (Ar.10). The Fihr and the Marwān were the two most important Arabic tribal divisions in Spain. The Muslims landed in Spain in AD 711 and very quickly overcame the Visigoths and overran the peninsula, calling the land they acquired "al-Andalus". Until 756 al-Andalus was ruled by a governor under the political and religious supremacy of the caliphs of Damascus. The last of these governors was called Yūsuf al-Fihrī (i.e. Yūsuf of the Fihr tribe). In 750 the Umayyad caliphate was overthrown by the ʿAbbāsids who relocated their capital in Baghdād. Most of the Umayyad family were killed, but one of their number — ʿAbd al-Raḥmān — fled to the West and, in 756, founded an independent amirate in al-Andalus. The Umayyads traced their descent from Hishām ibn ʿAbd al-Malik ibn Marwān, and hence were known as the family of Marwān. The disputes between the Fihrites and the Marwānids continued throughout Andalusian history. The Marwānids received the support of Arabs who had originally come from the Yemen, whereas the Fihrites were supported by the Muḍarī and the Syrians. Two places on the Arabic diagram are described respectively as "the place of Yemen and the tribe of Quḍāʿa" (Ar.52) and "the place of the Muḍarī" (Ar.53). The Umayyads were also known as the descendants of the eastern caliphs, and to them perhaps belongs "the place of the family of the Caliphate" (Ar.11).

Pure Arabs, however, formed only a very small part of the population of al-Andalus. Much greater were the numbers of Berbers from the adjacent regions of North Africa. These came over with the first Muslim invaders and are said to have settled the higher and less fertile areas, but they were also prominent in Valencia. After the collapse of the emirate in al-Andalus (AD 1031) there were two further Berber invasions, the first of the Almoravids in the late eleventh century, the second of the Almohads in the second half of the twelfth century. The Almoravids are implied in the name

Moabitae given to the enemies of the Christians in one of the Latin texts.[2] More significantly, the main tribal divisions of the Berbers — the Butr and the Barānis — are mentioned both in one of the Latin texts (IV.78–83), and also on the Arabic diagram, where, opposite the places of Yemen and Muḍarī, one finds: "The place of the Butr, and these are the Berbers, and what happens to them" (Ar.55), and "the place of the Barānis, and these are the negroes, and their region, and what happens to them" (Ar.56). These two clans of Berbers are frequently mentioned in the histories of al-Andalus. They are found taking sides with one or other of the Arabic tribal divisions. Thus in AD 889 Kurayb ibn Khaldūn of Seville led a confederacy of Barānis Berbers and Yemeni Arabs against another alliance of Butr Berbers and Muḍarī Arabs.[3] It would be interesting to know whether he consulted a shoulder-blade before going into battle.

A third component of Andalusian society does *not* seem to be mentioned in the texts of scapulimancy: this is the *muwallads* or neo-Muslims, i.e. the indigenous Spaniards who converted to Islam in great numbers. However, through intermarriage and deliberate fabrication of Arabic genealogies, they attempted to assimilate themselves into the Arabic ruling minority, and the success of this assimilation might explain the lack of reference to them.

The fourth element were the Christians, who were for most of Andalusian history freely allowed to practise their religion. Many adopted the Arabic language and Arabic customs. At least two translations of the Psalms, the Gospels and the Epistles of Paul were made from Latin into Arabic.[4] A Christian is mentioned in an Arabic text on scapulimancy. The Jews on the other hand, who formed an important part of the mercantile and intellectual class of Andalusian society, are mentioned in one of the Latin texts (I.44). Finally there are frequent references to slaves (Ar.5, IV.23).

The texts on scapulimancy reflect the racial mix of the society: the wife of the owner of the sheep may be a desert Arab (*badawiyya*), the mother of the child or concubine (*umm walad*) may be black, a Christian may have cooked the shoulder-blade.

Down the "big column" (*al-ʿamūd al-kabīr*) of the shoulder-blade we may see the structure of the Andalusian political hierarchy at the time when it was centred round the person of the amir (756–1031). The head of the column "pertains to the Emir and his companions and his jurisdiction" (Ar.1). After this, in turn, one finds his family and his bed (i.e. his concubines) (Ar.3), his children (Ar.4), and his slaves (Ar.5). Then come his closest advisers — his viziers (Ar.6), his provincial governors (Ar.7), and his secretaries and administrators (Ar.8). The viziers were in charge of different administrative departments and used to communicate with the emir through a chief minister or chamberlain (*ḥājib*).[5] The "place of the chamberlain" is also marked on the shoulder-blade (Ar.40). Further state officials are referred to in the Arabic text: the chief of the city (*ṣāḥib al-madīna*), the chief of the police (*ṣāḥib al-shurṭa*), and the chief of the postal service (*ṣāḥib al-barīd*). At the end of the tenth century the notorious al-Manṣūr (Almanzor) had worked his way up through several of these grades, having become successively chief of police, vizier, and chamberlain, until he was effectively the ruler of al-Andalus.[6]

One of the principal functions of scapulimancy was to determine the outcome of battles and conflict. The enemies in the Arabic texts are usually described simply as *mushrikūn*, i.e. "polytheists", but it is clear that in most contexts this term refers specifically to Christians. This was the inference of the Latin translator who rendered "Arabs and *mushrikūn*" as "Sarraceni et Christiani" (I.43). While the "big column", as we have seen, belongs to the amir and his companions, the "slender column" is described as "the place of the polytheists and their companions" (Ar.13). The flat part of the shoulder-blade between the two columns is described as the "sea", and in it the outcome of conflicts between Muslims and polytheists (or Christians) can be ascertained (Ar.29). The spine on the back of this flat part makes one side of the flat part opaque, whereas light can pass through the other side. Thus the two sides are called "the dark sea" and "the light sea" respectively. It may be no coincidence that "the sea of darkness" (*baḥr al-ẓulma*) is also the Arabic for the Atlantic Ocean; on this ocean their enemies held sway. Vikings raided al-Andalus from this direction several times during the amirate, and there may be a reference to the Viking practice of burying their dead at sea in the description of "the place of the tombs of the polytheists on the sea" (Ar.35). This is next to "the place of the sea of the polytheists and their boats and fleets and their going to the Muslims and their wars and what happens between them" (Ar.34).

Land battles are indicated in a different part of the shoulder-blade.

We read on the Arabic diagram "the place of the path of calvary and armies and soldiers and their departure to the polytheists and what happens between them of wars and harmful calamity, and this is the place of Córdoba" (Ar.46). The significance of the adjacent place is more sinister: "The place of the frontier province and of Zaragoza and those who beguile [others] away from the amir, and what happens between them" (Ar.45). Another place is described as "the place of the spies, the wayfarers and enemies, and these are inside the country" (Ar.22).

Contacts between Christians and Arabs were not always hostile. Ambassadors were sent back and forth, trade was brisk. By the eleventh century French shoemakers were called "cordoainers" because their raw materials and their technique of preparing the leather had been imported from Córdoba.[7] The political situation became complicated after the collapse of the amirate and the rise of the "party states". For Christian kings sided now with one petty Muslim ruler, now with another, in their attempts to manipulate power. One way they did this was through the extraction of protection money (*parias*) from weak Muslim rulers. The *Cantar de Mío Cid* illustrates one aspect of this relation between the party states. In 1079 El Cid was sent by Alfonso VI of Castile to collect the *parias* due from the ruler of Seville. However, soon after this, he had an argument with the king, and was sent into exile. He took his retinue of soldiers into the service of Muslim rulers, such as al-Muʾtamin of Zaragoza, and Christian princes, until finally he became lord and independent ruler of Muslim Valencia.[8]

At least one of the Latin texts on scapulimancy probably reflects the situation in al-Andalus after the establishment of the party kingdoms. For the diagram in Figure 1 includes Seville, Jaén, and Toledo which were capitals of these kingdoms.[9] Each of these cities became important cultural centres. Astronomical tables were composed for the meridian of Jaén in the eleventh century.[10] Seville was the home of one of the best known translators (and one of the most shadowy) of the twelfth century, John of Seville.[11] And Toledo, having always been the ecclesiastical capital of Spain, was to become, after the reconquest in 1085, the foremost centre for the transmission of Arabic learning to the west.[12]

Hugo of Santalla, the only named translator of texts on scapulimancy, does not belong to the group of translators working in Toledo. Rather, he can be associated with other scholars working in the valley of the Ebro. Hermann of Carinthia and he appear to have joined forces in translating texts for a compendium of judicial astrology, known in its first version as *The Book of the Three Judges*, but in its most complete version as *The Book of the Nine Judges.*[13] Hermann in turn collaborated with an archdeacon of Pamplona, Robert of Ketton, in translating astronomical and astrological texts, as well as in fulfilling a commission from Peter the Venerable of Cluny to translate the Qurʾān and other texts concerning the Muslim religion. Hugo, however, was the translator most interested in mantic texts. He introduced "sand-divination" (*ʿilm al-raml*) into the West and seems to have been responsible for giving it the name by which it became best known: "geomancy". He found the term *geomantia* alongside *hydromantia*, *aeromantia*, and *pyromantia*, in a quotation from Varro preserved by Isidore of Seville. In the preface to one text he promises to write about each of these "mancies".[14]

The history of scapulimancy in the West does not end with the two translations by Hugo and the two anonymous translations, one of which (Latin III) follows Hugo's texts in the only manuscript in which it occurs. Some time in the first half of the fifteenth century a professor of medicine in the University of Parma called Giorgio Anselmi (d. *c.* 1440–3) wrote a substantial work on magic in five tractates entitled *Divinum opus de magia disciplina.* He dedicated two chapters of the first tractate to a full account of scapulimancy.[15] He started off by explaining that the sheep was the preferred animal because its shoulder-blade was the most susceptible to receiving impressions. When the answer to a question was sought a sheep was sacrificed and the shoulder-blade was consulted. The priest held the bone in his right hand and made his acolytes (*pueri*) face him. He then looked into the blade and read its message. After this hieratic opening, Anselmi's text coincides quite closely in content (though not in arrangement of material or terminology) with Latin IV. As such it makes frequent mention of the *Saraceni.* It is no coincidence that Latin IV is the only text to occur in a manuscript of Italian provenance. Latin IV is the text which is closest to an Arabic original, preserving Arabic syntax and use of words. Moreover, since the only manuscript to preserve Latin IV is also the oldest known

Latin manuscript of a scapulimantic work it seems worthwhile to conclude this short account of the technique of shoulder-blade divination with an edition and translation of this text.

Notes

1 This article draws on the more detailed information given in C. Burnett, "Arabic divinatory texts and Celtic folklore: a comment on the theory and practice of scapulimancy in Western Europe", *Cambridge Medieval Celtic Studies*, 6 (1983), pp. 31–42, and *ibid.*, "Divination from sheep's shoulder blades: a reflection on Andalusian society", *Cultures in Contact in Medieval Spain: Historical and Literary Essays presented to L.P. Harvey*, ed. D. Hook and B. Taylor (London, 1990), pp. 29–45. References in the form "Ar.1, Ar.2" etc. are to the descriptions of the "places" on the Arabic diagram of the shoulder-blade in MS Tunis, National Library, 18848, which are translated in the Appendix to "Divination from sheep's shoulder-blades". Numbers preceded by the capital Roman numerals I, II, III, or IV refer to the four unpublished Latin works described in "Arabic divinatory texts", pp. 40–41. Latin IV, which is the richest source of references to Andalusian society and probably the earliest text among the extant Latin works on scapulimancy is edited and translated in full in the Appendix. I am currently preparing editions of Arabic and Latin texts on scapulimancy.

2 Latin III.2: Erit exercitus Christianorum qui ingreditur terras Moabitarum.

3 É. Levi-Provençal, *Histoire de l'Espagne musulmane*, 1 (Leiden, 1950), p. 360.

4 P.S. Van Koningsveld, *The Latin–Arabic Glossary of the Leiden University Library* (Leiden, 1977), pp. 52–6.

5 S.M. Imamuddin, *Muslim Spain: 711–1492 A.D.* (Leiden, 1981), p. 4.

6 A.G. Cheyne, *Muslim Spain* (Minneapolis, 1974), pp. 38–42.

7 Imamuddin, p. 110.

8 A. Mackay, *Spain in the Middle Ages* (London, 1977), p. 18.

9 D. Wasserstein, *The Rise and Fall of the Party-Kings* (Princeton, 1985), p. 89 (Jaén), p. 95 (Sevilla), and p. 96 (Toledo). See Figure 2.

10 H. Hermelink, "Tabulae Jahen", *Archives for the History of Exact Sciences*, 2 (1964), pp. 108–12.

11 L. Thorndike, "John of Seville", *Speculum*, 34 (1959), pp. 20–38.

12 M.T. d'Alverny, "Translations and translators", in *Renaissance and Renewal in the Twelfth Century*, ed. R.L. Benson and G. Constable (Oxford, 1982), pp. 421–62 (see pp. 444–7).

13 C. Burnett, "A group of Arabic–Latin translators in Northern Spain in the mid-twelfth century", *Journal of the Royal Asiatic Society* (1977), pp. 62–108 (see pp. 65–70).

14 C.H. Haskins, *Studies in the History of Medieval Science*, 2nd edn. (New York, 1960), pp. 78–9.

15 MS Florence, Bibliotheca Laurenziana, Plut. 45, cod. 35, fols. 32r–37r. On Anselmi, see L. Thorndike, *A History of Magic and Experimental Science*, vol. 4 (New York, 1934), pp. 243–5, and *Dizionario biografico degli Italiani*, vol. 3 (Rome, 1961), pp. 377–8. Neither of these works mention the scapulimancy. Anselmi is best known for his dialogue on music — *De harmonia* — which is the only work of his to be published (ed. G. Massera, Florence, 1961).

An edition of the earliest latin Scapulimancy
(Oxford, Bodleian Library, MS Canon. Misc. 396, fols 108r–112r).[1]

Editorial additions are placed in pointed brackets, deletions in square brackets. \ / indicates words or letters added by the corrector of the manuscript. The scribe has added pointing hands next to sentences 28, 147, 164, 198, 215 and 221. I have omitted to include the scribe's frequent writing of double consonants instead of single (e.g. *accutum, occulus, peccunia, fertillis, allia, gracillis,* etc.), and his substitution of *ci* for *ti* (e.g. *tercius, nuncium, negociosus, tristicia, fabricacio, concucio, precium, spacium* etc.). Whereas the scribe regularly joins the preposition and *si* to the words following them (*excursu, admare, sivideris,* etc.), I have divided the words; modern punctuation has been added. I have not corrected grammatical errors, no matter how blatant (e.g., 65 "viam vadens").

fol. 108ra

1 Rememoratio spatule et expositio eius adiutorio dei.

2 <I>ncipiam adiutorio dei de ratione spatule ex modo spatule.

3 Tres digiti sunt ex cursu pixidis ad mare. 4 Cum videris sepulturam in primo digito qui sequitur pixidem, morietur infirmus usque ad .xii. menses. 5 Et cum videris sepulturam in digito secundo, morietur usque ad octo menses. 6 Et cum videris sepulturam in digito tertio, morietur infirmus usque ad .iiii. menses. 7 Et cum videris sepulturam nigram, tunc morietur procul dubio. 8 Et cum videris sepulturam albam, est angustia quam pertransiet dominus rei. 9 Et sepultura viri est longa, et mulieris est quasi foramen. 10 Et cum videris iter nigrum continens cursum pixidis, est obsessio civitatis ex civitatibus Saracenorum. 11 Et cum videris nasum pixidis iam detortum, tunc coctrix carnis menstruata est. 12 Et cum videris in cursu pixidis nodum a parte qua super perpendicularis annexum pixidi, mulier dominatur virum suum. 13 Et nodus in via perpendicularis a parte qua <. . .>, super eam est vir. 14 Et cum delebitur nodus ab illo loco, est separatio mulieris a viro suo. 15 Et cum videris in loco lecti viri signum album, est mulier pregnata, tenens in utero mulierem. 16 Et si videris iter nigrum trahens ad rubedinem ingrediens palatium caste, tunc vir contrarius erit progeniei sue. 17 Et cum videris iter nigrum cum rubedine ad

nodum procedens matris filii, tunc adul [fol. 108rb] teratur mulier. 18 Et non est adulterationi signum aliud preter istud.

19 Secunda pars

20 <Q>uum consideraveris in parte interiori scapule[2] a parte abrachet[3] <manum> in cuius medio \sit/ rotunditas similis denario quadrato vadens ad medium spatule, tunc illud denotat exercitum exeuntem. 21 Si autem videris ad partem regis — ab ea scilicet parte qua sequitur abrachet[4] — quiddam exiens semper multum, dic itaque iste est exercitus exiens, et est rex per se ipsum. 22 Si non fuerit ex exercitu,[5] proba ex parte regis ad partem nigredinis, et ibi dupla filum, et incipiens experiri ex parte regis ad locum exercitus, et si concesserit tibi experientia, regis est exercitus et ille exercitus est exiens. 23 Et si videris in spatula lineas multas albas et vias diversas, inquietudo est in servis. 24 Et si videris viam illam longam \in/longitudine spatule, planctus est in hominibus. 25 Si fuerit a parte qua super regem, est super eum. 26 Et si fuerit a parte qua super nigredinem, trahit ad nigredinem. 27 Et si videris a parte abrachet,[6] in eo viam descendentem ad locum exercitus, sunt homines incarcerati. 28 Et scias numerum linearum, quia tot trabes elevabuntur. 29 Et si videris viam transeuntem ad abrachet,[7] victoria erit super Christianos. 30 Et si videris viam illam albam ex parte regis et plures nigredines ex parte nigredinis, gaudium est regi et eis qui cum eo[8] sunt. 31 Et si videris iter album a parte nigredinis et nigredo \sit/ ex parte regis, gaudium indicat regi et eis qui cum eo sunt.

32 Pars tertia

33 <M>emoratio[9] loci cathedri regis. 34 Cum videris simile lentis quod sit lene, album, [fol. 108va] tunc rex exit. 35 Si vero quasi lens non[10] affuerit, tunc innuit nuntium missum a rege.

36 <C>um videris in interiori parte spatule a parte abrachet quasi manum in cuius medio sit quasi circulus similis denario vadens versus medium spatule, tunc illud demonstrat exercitum exeuntem. 37 Et si videris ad partem regis — ab ea scilicet qua super abrachet — quiddam exiens communiter et multum, dic igitur iste est exercitus exiens et est regalis proprie. 38 Et si non fuerit exercitus, tunc experire ex parte regis ad partem nigredinis. 39 Demum dupla filum[11] et incipies probando ex parte regis ad locum exercitus et si concesserit tibi experientia, tunc scias exercitum esse regalem

exeuntem in proximo. 40 Et si non comprehenderis experientia, nigredinis est exercitus. 41 Et si videris in spatula plures lineas albas et diversas, tunc inquietudo erit in servis. 42 Et si fuerit via longa spatio spatule, tunc planctus erit in hominibus. 43 Et si fuerit a parte qua super regem, est pro eo. 44 Et si fuerit a parte qua super nigredinem, est infortunium. 45 Et si videris in inferiori[12] parte abrachet viam descendentem ad locum exercitus, denotat homines incarceratos. 46 Scias tunc numerum linearum, quoniam tot trabes ad suspendendum homines erigentur.[13] 47 Et si videris iter transiens ad abrachet, devictos indicat Christianos. 48 Et cum videris iter illud[14] album ex parte regis et plures nigredines ex parte nigredinis, tunc gaudebit rex et qui cum eo sunt. 49 Et si videris albam ex parte nigredinis et nigredo ex parte regis, gaudium igitur est in nigredine.

50 Pars quarta

[fol. 108vb] 51 <M>emoratio[15] loci regis: cum videris in collo cathedre simile lenti leni album, tunc rex exit. 52 Si vero non fuerit ibi lens, innuit nuntium a rege legatum. 53 Et si tibi apparuerit in cathedra fovea parva, lacrime in regno regis effunduntur. 54 Et si videris ab inferiori parte palatii regis \tumbam procedentem ad partem exteriorem, tumba regis/[16] indicatur. 55 Et si ex ea aliquid diminutum fuerit, filii regis est. 56 Et si videris fossam ex parte nigredinis et fenestra apud regem, tunc capita sunt apud regem amputata. 57 Et si videris sepulturam ex parte regis et foramen ex parte nigredinis, victoria est nigredinis. 58 Et si videris ex parte abrachet viam in capite itineris, tunc trahit ad nigredinem. 59 Et si videris citrinum colorem sub palatio regis aut aliquid egrediens,[17] rex est negotiosus et in angustia positus. 60 Et considerantur hec in interiori parte spatule.

61 Pars quinta

62 <C>onsidera in medio pixidis, et si videris punctum nigrum aut viam egredientem ab ostio[18] pixidis ad punctum nigrum, tunc adulterium esse infra ostium[19] domus indicat. 63 Si autem inveneris viam ex parte[20] rubedinis, tunc adulter ingreditur per parietem aut per fenestram domus. 64 Et si inveneris in capite pixidis membrum album grossum ex carne, tunc illud bestia<m> que emetur et est ingrediens significat signum.[21] 65 Et si consideraveris in medio pixidis fenestram citrinam aut viam vadens ex ostio[22] pixidis ad

aliam partem, significat egrotum in lecto [fol. 109ra] suo. 66 Et si non videris in medio pixidis punctum citrinum et videris iter ingrediens ostium[23] aut aliam partem, tunc homines attrahunt pecudes[24] suas in domos suas. 67 Cum consideraveris punctum viride in medio pixidis que est in concavitate eius et pixidis concavitas apparuerit, filia mechabitur hominis. 68 Et si fuerit punctum rubeum aut circa ipsum simile itineri,[25] domui conexum est alicuius animalium caro fetida quam corrodunt aves. 69 Et cum videris extra ostium[26] pixidis punctum nigrum, canem significat nigrum. 70 Et si fuerit minimum punctum, catulus parvus est. 71 Et si videris in collo spatule interius[27] lineam que pertransit collum et fuerit alba, viri \uxorem/ ab aliquo visam et dilectam veruntamen non habitam ab aliquo portendit. 72 Et si consideraveris in corde spatule a parte[28] crassitudinis in directo colli, proba[29] in circuitu colli a fovea colli usque ad sepulturam, et si concesserit experientia, est domini domus. 73 Et si non invenitur in eo experientia, filius suspendetur.[30] 74 Et si non advenerit filio, filio filii aut filio filie sue. 75 Et si videris ante crassitudinem — scilicet ante sepulturam quam domino domus vidisti — simile sepulcris pluribus rubeis aut nigris aut citrinis, incarcerati sunt quos rex incarceravit. 76 Et si videris sub pixide carnem que non potest auferri, dominum domus significat novas induere vestes.

77 Pars sexta

78 <B>ellorum rememoratio inter Albutr[31] et [fol. 109rb] Christianos. 79 Experire pollice ex parte nigredinis ab exteriori parte ad interiorem et quod fuerit ex sepultura sub duobus pollicibus <. . .> 80 Que sunt ex sepultura[32] a parte qua super pixidem sunt Christiani, et quod fuerit a parte pollicis inferioris — scilicet a parte abrachet[33] — sunt Albutr.[34] 81 Et si videris in nigredine albedinem nubibus similem, tunc in gentibus erit controversia. 82 Et si videris sepulturam obliquam, interfectio et mors precipue in eis. 83 Et nota quod locus Albutr est Saracenorum, et locus Albaraniz est Christianorum. 84 Et si videris a parte nigredinis lineas a parte regis, sunt exploratores. 85 Et si fuerit linea una, est unus explorator. 86 Et si fuerint due, sunt duo exploratores. 87 Et cum videris sepulturam in inferior parte spatule ubi est albedo, domino domus signum attribuitur.

88 <C>ommemoratio perpendicularis.[35]

89 Perpendicularis autem digitis[36] experiendus est. 90 Primus digitus cathedra regis dicitur; si autem sepultura ibi inveniatur, regis filii indicatur.[37] 91 Secundus digitus fratrum et patruorum eius dicitur, tertius digitus comitibus attribuitur,[38] et quartus potestatibus, et quintus prepositis, sextus maioribusdomus,[39] septimus regibus Latinorum ascribitur.

92 Locus iudicii.

93 Cum videris in introitu perpendicularis in collo eius a parte perpendicularis lineam aut lineas, si fuerint exeuntes a collo, notat depositum. 94 Et si fuerit ingrediens collum, tunc nuntius est venturus cum digni [fol. 109va] tate sua. 95 Et nota in perpendiculari in facie spatule quod primus digitus est Cordube. 96 Secundus, militum regis. 97 Tertius, locus Christianorum. 98 Quartus, locus iudicii. 99 Quintus, locus anime et coniugis — scilicet viri — et gaudii[40] et tristitie et angustie inpetuose. 100 Et cum videris in medio spatule — in albedine scilicet — quasi nubem albam concavam, argentum et pecunia furabitur domino spatule. 101 Et si eam inveneris in loco anime, est angustia fortis aut census aufertur ab eo. 102 Si autem volueris scire[41] qualis est pecunia, si fuerit punctum nigrum minimum, sunt nummi. 103 Et si fuerit punctum maximum, sunt vestes. 104 Et si videris circum sepulturam punctum album, sunt cilicia linea. 105 Et quod fuerit inferius spatule extrinsecus ubi est abrachet, est Saracenorum et Christianorum. 106 Ex parte \regis/, Saracenorum, et ex parte nigredinis,[42] Christianorum. 107 Et cum videris lineam accidentalem ex transverso positam, denotat erectas trabes. 108 Et si fuerit longa, sunt vexilla. 109 Et si trabes fuerint magne, sunt Saracenorum. 110 Et si parve, dicimus Christianorum.

111 Septima pars[43]

112 <S>i videris viam ex parte faciei spatule et videris in fovea pixidis simile faciei triangule, si diverterit ad nigredinem, tunc erit \vir/ contrarius sue coniügi. 113 Et si non pervenerit ad lectum, est fur nocturnus veniens ad domum. 114 Et si videris punctum rubeum aut citrinum iuxta lectum et diverterit pernix[44] ad ipsum et declinaverit a lecto, puellam indicat in domo que ducetur a sene in uxorem. 115 Et si videris in pixide albedinem, gaudium significat. 116 Et si nigredinem videris, tristitiam et [fol. 109vb] planctum portendit. 117 Et si videris albedinem et rubedinem et citrinitatem in cacumine capitis pixidis trahentes foras ad faciem spatule, hominem

habentem vestes in domo sua et pecuniam remotam de loco ad locum portendit. 118 Et si videris foveam pixidis iam declinantem extrinsecus, tunc dominus spatule est debitor, et accidit ei detrimentum in pecunia sua. 119 Et si videris secundum exiens a vertice pixidis, fortiter angustiam et cogitationem domino spatule innuit. 120 Et si videris rectum non tortuosum, gaudium domino spatule portendit venturum. 121 Et si videris in eo rubedinem, tunc coctrix spatule est rubea, varios habens oculos. 122 Et si videris in eo punctum[45] minimum rubeum, coctrici spatule accidunt variole aut in eius facie sunt lentigines aut cicatrices. 123 Et si videris sub pixidis fovea a parte qua sequitur cacumen punctum nigrum, carnem a cacabo fuisse furatam significat, et furtum frustorum[46] secundum numerum punctorum.[47] 124 Et si videris in loco illo rem exeuntem, tunc dominus spatule aut frater aut soror eius aut filius eius aut eius propinquus penetrabitur. 125 Et si videris in eo fenestram rotundam, fabricationem indicat.

126 Et si videris in interiori parte spatule quasi nubem albam spatulam totam continentem, pluviam et bonam proportionem[48] iudica.[49] 127 Et si videris in medio spatule in albedine quasi formam cacabi in qua si fuerit albedo, est pluvia et aquarum decursus.

[fol. 110ra] 128 Et si videris in albedine — in medio scilicet spatule — quasi circuli formam et in circuitu eius quasi capillorum formam, domino spatule mortem significat. 129 Et si perpendicularis super quam est rex videatur inclinari ad tergum spatule, regis depositionem denotare nullus dubitet. 130 Et cum videris locum sedis eius album ac si recessisset medulla eius, tunc rex abiit. 131 \Et/ si videatur super aulam eius fovea fenestram, planctus et nenias in domo regis portendit.[50] 132 Et si videris in eo tumbam secundum trium digitorum longitudinem et ad nasum perveniens, si fregerit ipsum super regis cathedram, aliud quam supradictum iudicium significare nullus meditetur.

133 Et cum visum fuerit quiddam locum Cordube ingrediens secundum trium digitorum spatium, destruentur homines a manibus regis. 134 Et si nigredinem extensam videris exeuntem a loco regis versus albedinem spatule et sit in ea punctum album, timorem in exercitu et conturbationem procul dubio denotat. 135 Et cum videris illam nigredinem, rex est exiens procul dubio. 136 Et cum videris a parte sinistra nigredinem et a \con/traria parte nulla alia fuerit apparens, regem ad venatum vel exire[51] spatiatum significat. 137 Et

cum videris nigredinem econtra apparentem, et castra regis exierint et rex exierit et societas \eius/ apparuerit. 138 Considera igitur quem exercitum[52] albedo ingreditur et quorum turba dispergitur et in manipulos dividitur, ipsis victoria attribuitur, et nichil aliud quam hec significare dicitur. 139 Et cum videris in exercitu regis signa ista, prospice itaque si in eo [fol. 110rb] fuerit albedo, et <cum> locum militum eius videris candere, nichil aliud quam super eos fore victoriam iudica. 140 Et cum videris sepulturam a parte regis et capita in loco Cordube, capita militum illius exercitus amputata \et/ ad Cordubam portata significat. 141 Et si videris in opposito illius loci infra spatulam foramina, illa prelatorum regis capita et plures homines de exercitu eius indicat interfectos. 142 Et cum videris in loco nodorum quasi cancerem, equi regis invenientur post exercitum factum. 143 Et si videris sepulturas tenues,[53] destructionem exercitus et mortem hominum[54] significat. 144 Et cum videris eudaha[55] — scilicent locum iudicii — gracilibus sepulturis rubeis \et/ nigris et citrinis, similem inventionem regis equorum portendit. 145 Et si videris puncta alba, pecuniam quam habebit a rege[56] a maioribusdomus eius significat. 146 Et cum videris a parte perpendicularis in introitu eius — scilicet in collo[57] — rubedinem fortem, tunc ovem cuius est spatula diminutam aut confractam innuit. 147 Et cum videris in loco iudicii punctum nigrum, equi regis fugiunt. 148 Quere igitur vestigia et invenies eos a parte regis. 149 Et cum videris nigredinem exeuntem a parte regis continuam loco domini, hoc exercitum regis procul dubio significat.

150 Probanda est igitur hic spatule latitudo a loco Cordube, et attribuendus hic idem locus Cordube. 151 Et digitus secundus est Egipto, et tertius digitus Iemen, et quartus loco inimici, qui est in loco sepulture coram inimico, et locus natorum Toleti. 152 Et cum videris spatulam iam dimin\ui/ deorsum in loco maris [fol. 110va] apertam, non potest esse quin naves veniant super Yspaniam. 153 Et cum videris punctum magnum exiens a loco maris et terminans apud regem et apud generationem contrarietatis, hoc denotat regem exire a mari. 154 Et cum videris spatulam iam diminui in inferiori parte in loco inimici, carnem a spatula illa distractam significat esse caprinam. 155 Et cum videris lineas in \lo/co Cordube plures, populo Cordube annum fertilem significat. 156 Et cum videris in \lo/co Cordube aquarum decursum in quo non sint lineature, carestiam in Corduba denotat. 157 Et cum videris exercitus exeuntes

et albedinem exeuntem a parte qua sequitur milites, tunc exercitus insurgens super regem superabitur. 158 Et cum videris nigredinem exeuntem a loco regis a parte faciei spatule ad albedinem eius tendere, deinde spargitus in su<m>mitate eius, milites regis coniunctos fore nullus dubitet. 159 Et cum videris nigredinem illam coadunatam et non diffusam ita quod non ingreditur ipsam albedo aliqua, militum regis est victoria.[58] 160 Et cum videris in dorso spatule quiddam supereminens versus partem colli, et coram eo nubem nigram et non est preter ipsam in perpendiculari, denotat inimicos reverti ad quasdam civitates regis. 161 Et cum videris coram nube quiddam supereminens et altum, et pervenerit ad illud nigredo, denotat inimicos capere civitatem.

162 Octava pars[59]

[fol. 110vb] 163 <E>t cum videris deorsum a spatula in loco cathedre regis nigredinem, tunc ovis nigra fuit. 164 Et si fuerit rubedo aut albedo, est secundum illum colorem. 165 Et cum videris spatulam iam denigratam totam, tunc ovis iugulator fuit polutus. 166 Et si pars sinistra denigrata fuerit et dextra pura, tunc ovem iugulatam fore in loco immundo denotat. 167 Et cum videris spatulam citrinam trahentem ad rubedinem, coctrix spatule est fetida. 168 Et cum videris eam nodosam, proficuum magnum evenire domino spatule significat. 169 Et cum videris spatule summitatem a parte colli tortuosam multum, angustiam domino spatule magnam portendit. \170 Et si videris ipsam rectam, gaudium domino spatule significat./[60] 171 Et si videris albedinem spatulam excedere, multitudinem nivis et frigoris in anno illo denotat. 172 Et cum videris spatulam albam excoriatam, si sciveris dominum spatule fore ex consortio domus, carnem spatule missam fuisse in exennio iudica.[61]

173 <R>ememoratio[62] alcened.[63]

174 Alcened autem reperitur cum digito. 175 Digitus primus a parte qua sequitur caput domus viri est. 176 Secundus digitus secundum qui[64] est in eo. 177 Et tertius aliquis tertiorum ville, et quartus extremitas patrie.[65]

178 Et cum nasum spatule videris eminere super pixidem, planctum in domo significat. 179 Et cum videris ipsum inclinatum iuxta collum, tunc mulierem habentem nates magnas [fol. 111ra] denotat.[66] 180 Et si videris nasum spatule tortuosum in parte, ovem

vi captam fore et iugulatam portendit. 181 Et cum videris sub naso illo tortuositatem magnam, coctrix spatule aut domina ovis dolebit dorsum aut in eius utero infirmitatem habet antiquam aut pregnans est. 182 Et si videris ad radicem cacuminis quasi similitudinem dentis eminentis, coctrix iacet cum serviente nigro. 183 Et si videris nasum nimis acutum, fornicatur cum serviente albo. 184 Et cum videris in loco lecti quiddam longum, tunc coctor spatule est vir et non est mulier. 185 Et cum nasum illum videris confractum, est pregnans mulierem tenens. 186 Et cum videris medium cacuminis iam detortum, vir est infirmus. 187 Et si incurvetur extremitas, coctor spatule stultizat aut in domo eius est contractus aut qui iugulavit ovem \est/ loripes aut sinister. 188 Et cum videris ultimum cacuminis non album, tunc mulieri accessit aliquis. 189 Et cum in latitudine cacuminis videris iter nigrum ad rubedinem trahens et ad lectum iens, aliquem ad uxorem suam accedere significat. 190 Et si videris viam in domo rubeam, exiens ad alterius domus, et <. . .> duas vias exeuntes <aut> plures, latronem significat. 191 Et si videris esse in interiori vestigii surgentis punctum rubeum aut nigrum, recuperationem furti significat. 192 Et si non videris in eminentiori loco eius punctum, fur ingredietur domum et non revocabitur furtum.

193 Et si videris viam venientem a patria et ingredientem domum, exen [fol. 111rb] nium quod presentatur significat. 194 Et si videris in loco lecti rubedinem fortem loco lecti adhibentem,[67] ignem in domo cadere denotat. 195 Et cum videris eam in digito secundo ex cacumine, cadet ignis in villam. 196 Et si in tertio videris eam digito, cadet ignis in termino ville.

197 Et si videris locum in quo est mater filii — et est radix perpendicularis — nodum exeuntem, matrem filii honoratam fore a viro suo significat. 198 Et si videris in eo punctum rubeum, frater filii conburetur ab igne aut his similia.[68]

199 Et si videris perpendicularem dilatatum, dominus spatule est invidiosus propter multam pecuniam quam habet. 200 Et si videris rubedinem et nigredinem, dampnum accidere segeti significat. 201 Et si videris in eo fracturam, nigredo est in segete. 202 Et si videris eam in secundo, magnum[69] da<m>pnum in frugibus significat. 203 Et cum videris rubedinem illam in extremitate et fuerit in rubedine nodus eminens, est carestia[70] in oleo. 204 Et quanto diminuitur nodus, tanto pretium minoratur, et quanto crescit nodus, tanto pretium eius augmentatur.

205 Et cum videris sepulturam in primo digito infra inimicum loco domus adhibentem, in tuorum mercatorum coadunatione amicorum iudicatur. 206 Et si in digito secundo apparet, propinquis tuis ex lege tua attribuitur. 207 Et si videris in tertio digito, tuis procul dubio vicinis iudicatur. 208 Et si videris in primo digito a parte qua sequitur domum inter perpendicularem et inimicum sepulturas duas, [fol. 111va] ipse sunt in mercatorum coadunatione Saracenorum. 209 Et si in digito secundo fuerit, proximorum tuorum ex Saracenis. 210 Et si fuerit in tertio, Latinorum regibus attribui iudicatur.

211 Et cum videris in tumba punctum nigrum, febres significat. 212 Et si fuerit rubeum, mortem. 213 Et si citrinum, variolas, et si album, papulam[71] portendit. 214 Et si summitatem eius iam denigratam videris et ponderosam et ex alia parte rubeam, egrotus peribit usque ad duos menses. 215 Et si videris eam dealbari, significat mortalia vestimenta. 216 Et si volueris scire huius rei veritatem et mortis eius propinquitatem, considera sepulturam egroti et videbis eam albam in spatula fossam, et hoc est iudicium ut fertur cilicii. 217 Et si videris in interiori parte \albedinis spatule a parte/[72] qua sequitur dorsum eius, spatio duorum digitorum a coniunctione duorum perpendicularium puncta varii coloris[73] que sint brevis longitudinis, ploratrices in domo viri super mortuum significat. 218 Et si in extremitate extrinseca spatule visum fuerit quiddam longum, planctum significat.

219 Et cum videris in loco alcenen — in loco scilicet domus — simile sepulture gracili in latitudine, ovis est in domo. 220 Et si fuerit exiens de domo in digito secundo, exploratorem in patria ibi[74] explorantem denotat. 221 Sepulture locus ita reperiendus est. 222 Non enim sepulture in latitudine patrie inveniuntur sed in radice alcenen. 223 Exploratores quidem in latitudine alcenen ante sepulturas. 224 Si autem fuerint albe aut rubee aut nigre, eiusdem coloris erunt explorato [fol. 111vb] ris vestimenta. 225 Et cum videris albedinem ad populum[75] ingredientem, rancuram portendit in eo. 226 Sed si nigredo ingrediatur, gloriam et honorem significat. 227 Et si videris in spatula milites declarari, exercitum impetuosus concutiet timor. 228 Et si videris inter perpendicularem et collum in perpendicularis introitu — scilicet in oculo extra perpendicularem — est hominis ex domo. 229 Et si videris caput sepulture elevatum, virum de Arabia significat. 230 Et si sepulturam videris ad similitudinem duorum capitum, Barbarum portendit. 231 Et si videris

eam albam et nullum fuerit in ea caput nec signum aliquod, Latinum indicat virum. 232 Et si fuerit tumba aliquantulum longa, dominum significat potentem.

233 Et si fuerit nigredo diffusa a loco iudicii, iudicia ex inproviso veruntamen te obtinere[76] in ultimo nullus dubitet. 234 Et si videris in loco iudicii subter perpendicularem sepulturas strictas, albas vel nigras aut citrinas, incarceratos a rege captos portendunt. 235 Et cum videris citrinitatem claram in loco cacuminis in ostio[77] domus et fuerit citrinitas a dextris et a sinistris apparuerit obscura, ovem sine pretio habitam et raptam fore aut furatam procul dubio significat.

236 Deus autem est absentium cognitor et occultantium revelator. AMIN.

Notes

1 This is a manuscript written entirely in one hand of the thirteenth century (not "s.xiv[ex]" as the catalogue gives). The MS containing the *De spatula* follows *Liber Messeballa de receptione interpretatus a Iohanne Ypsalensi* (i.e. Hispalensi) *ex Arabico in Latinum*, beginning *Invenit quidam vir ex sapientibus librum ex libris secretorum.*

2 In margin: al<iter> spatule

3 Written above: id est locus teneritatis

4 Written above: id est teneritatis

5 exercitū MS

6 Written above: id est locus teneritatis

7 Written above: id est teneritatis

8 Changed from "eos"

9 In margin: al<iter> Comemoratio

10 "fuerit" added and then lined out

11 Changed from "filium"

12 Changed from "inferiore"

13 Changed from "cur-"

14 Changed from "illum"

15 In margin: al<iter> Comemoratio

16 tumbam . . . regis] added in margin

17 Changed from "ingrediens"

18 hostio MS

19 hostium MS

20 "nigredin" added and then expunged (see below)

21 Cf. Giorgio Anselmi, fol. 34r: Cum vero fuerit in eius capite vermis magnus et grossus ex carne, bestiam notat emendam et domum ingredientem.

22 hostio MS

23 hostium MS

24 pecunias MS; cf. Giorgio Anselmi, fol. 34r: At si <non est> punctus citrinus eius tenens medium et fuerit eadem via, pecus e domo trahendum est.

25 "simile" added and then expunged

26 hostium MS
27 "spatulam" added and then expunged
28 apparte MS
29 propria MS
30 suspendatur MS
31 Written above: id est Saracenos
32 extra sepulturam MS
33 Written above: id est locus teneritatis
34 Written above: id est Saraceni
35 In margin: puto quod hec sit .7. pars
36 In margin: al<iter> digitus
37 In margin: al<iter> fillius, vel indicantur
38 attrubuitur MS
39 maioridomus MS
40 guadii MS
41 Changed from "scire volueris"
42 "Sara . . ." added and then expunged
43 In margin: Puto quod si pars aliqua tantum sit hic, sit 8a
44 pernox MS, changed from "per noctem"
45 "rubedinem" added and then expunged
46 frustrorum MS
47 In margin: id est tot quot
48 "significat" added and then expunged
49 Cf. Giorgio Anselmi, fol. 36v: Intervallum pallę nebulosum omne spatium vel fere comprehendens, uberem pluviam et anni fertilitatem portendit.
50 Cf. Giorgio Anselmi, fol. 36r: Foramen item vel veluti fovea loco hoc apparens, graves planctus in domo regia futuros ostendit.
51 exiere MS
52 "ab eo" added and then expunged
53 Changed from "sepulturam tenuem"
54 Changed from "hominem"
55 Written above: id est locus iudicii
56 "a maioribus" added and then expunged
57 loco MS
58 MS adds: ē
59 In margin: Puto quod si pars aliqua tantum sit hic, sit 9a
60 Et . . . significat] added in the margin
61 Cf. Giorgio Anselmi, fols 33v–34r: Siquidem alba sit et squamosa, sunt carnes donate domino.
62 In margin: Co<memoratio>
63 In margin: Puto quod hec sit .9. pars
64 Changed from (or to) "quod"
65 Cf. *De scapula II*, Paris, Bibliothèque nationale, lat. 4161, fol. 74r: In lato itaque cartilagine et filiarum loco quid simile fovee si forte constat reperiri, is explorator domum ingreditur; in secundo namque, atrium; in tertia, regionem et villam ingressus est.
66 Cf. Giorgio Anselmi, fol. 35r: Et si ad collum reclinat, coquens mulier grandes habet nates (natos MS).
67 adhabentem MS
68 In margin: scilicet sequentur ei
69 magno MS, in margin: al<iter> magnum

70 carastia MS
71 ppłm MS
72 albedine . . . parte] added in the margin
73 Changed from "colores"
74 Changed from "tibi"
75 ppłm MS
76 obptinere MS
77 hostio MS

A translation of the earliest latin scapulimancy.[1]

1 Description of the shoulder-blade and explanation of it, with the help of God.

2 With the help of God I will begin the account of the shoulder-blade from the shape of the blade.

3 There are three fingers from the rim of the money-box to the sea. 4 When you see a tomb in the first finger which follows the money-box the ill man will die within twelve months. 5 And when you see a tomb in the second finger, he will die within eight months. 6 And when you see a tomb in the third finger, the ill man will die within four months. 7 And when you see a black tomb, then he will die without doubt. 8 And when you see a white tomb, there are difficulties which the master of the affair will pass through. 9 And the tomb of the husband is long, and the tomb of the wife is like a hole. 10 And when you see a black path including the rim of the money-box, it is the siege of one of the cities of the Saracens. 11 And when you see the nose of the money-box now turned back, then the woman who cooked the meat has menstruated. 12 And when you see on the rim of the money-box a protuberance in the part of the perpendicular next to the money-box, the wife dominates her husband. 13 And a protuberance on the path of the perpendicular in the part of <. . . means> the husband is over her. 14 And when the protuberance is erased from that place, there is a separation of the wife from her husband. 15 And when you see in the place of the bed of the husband a white sign, his wife is pregnant, having a female child in her womb. 16 And if you see a black path verging towards red entering the palace of the chaste woman, then the husband will be against his offspring. 17 And

when you see a black path with redness proceeding to the protuberance of the mother of his son, then the wife is committing adultery. 18 And there is no sign of adultery other than this.

19 The second part[2]

When you see on the inner part of the shoulder-blade in the area of the *abrachet* (i.e., the place of tenderness)[3] <a hand> in whose centre is a round shape similar to a fourpence piece, going towards the middle of the shoulder-blade, then that shows an army going out. 21 But if you see on the side of the king — that is, in the area which is next to the *abrachet* — something going out always in a great amount (?), then say that it is the army going out, and the king is by himself. 22 If there is no army, investigate from the side of the king to the side of blackness, and double the size there (?), and beginning your investigation from the side of the king to the place of the army, if your investigation discovers something for you, it is the army of the king and that army is going out. 23 And if you see in the shoulder-blade many white lines and different paths, there is unrest among the slaves. 24 And if you see that path stretching along the length of the shoulder-blade, there is grief among men. 25 And if it is from the part which is over the king, then <that grief> is for him. 26 And if it is from the part which is over the blackness, it is for the blackness. 27 And if you see in the area of the *abrachet* a path in it descending to the place of the army, there are imprisoned men. 28 And you should know the number of lines, because the same number of stakes will be erected. 29 And if you see a path going across to the *abrachet*, there will be victory over the Christians. 30 And if you see that path white on the side of the king and many blacknesses on the side of the blackness, there is joy to the king and those who are with him. 31 And if you see a white path on the side of the blackness and blackness is on the side of the king, that indicates joy to the king and to those who are with him.

32 The third part

33 Description of the place of the seat of the king. 34 When you see something like a lentil which is smooth and white, then the king goes out. 35 But if something like a lentil is not present, then it indicates a messenger sent by the king.

36 When you see on the inner part of the shoulder-blade in the

area of the *abrachet* something like a hand in whose centre is a circle similar to a penny, going towards the middle of the shoulder-blade, then that shows an army going out. 37 But if you see on the side of the king — that is, in the area which is next to the *abrachet* — something going out together and extensively, then say: it is the army going out and it is properly the king's <army>. 38 And if there is no army, then investigate from the side of the king to the side of blackness. 39 Then double the size (?), and you should begin by investigating from the side of the king to the place of the army, and if your investigation discovers something for you, then you should know that the army belonging to the king is going out very soon. 40 And if you have no success, the army belongs to the blackness. 41 And if you see in the shoulder-blade many different white lines, then there will be unrest among the slaves. 42 And if that path stretches along the area of the shoulder-blade, then there will be grief among men. 43 And if it is from the part which is over the king, <that grief> is for him. 44 And if it is from the part which is over the blackness, it is a misfortune. 45 And if you see in the lower part of the *abrachet* a path descending to the place of the army, that denotes imprisoned men. 46 You should then know the number of lines, because the same number of stakes are erected for hanging men. 47 And if you see a path going across to the *abrachet*, it indicates defeated Christians. 48 And if you see that path white on the side of the king, and many blacknesses on the side of the blackness, then the king and those who are with him will rejoice. 49 And if you see a white path on the side of the blackness and blackness on the side of the king, then there is joy among the <people of> blackness.

50 The fourth part.

51 Description of the place of the king. When you see in the neck of the seat something white like a smooth lentil, then the king goes out. 52 But if there is no lentil there, it indicates a messenger sent by the king. 53 And if there appears to you in the seat a small pit, tears are shed in the kingdom of the king. 54 And if you see in the lower part of the palace of the king a tomb proceeding to the outer part, the tomb of the king is indicated. 55 And if in that part there is anything made smaller, it is <the tomb> of the son of the king. 56 And if you see a groove on the side of blackness and an opening in front of the king, then there are heads cut off in front of the king.

57 And if you see a tomb on the side of the king and a perforation on the side of blackness, it is the victory of the blackness. 58 And if you see in the area of the *abrachet* a path on the top of the way (?), then it is for <the people of> blackness. 59 And if you see a yellow colour under the palace of the king or something going out, the king is full of cares and placed in difficulty. 60 And these things are considered in the inner part of the shoulder-blade.

61 The fifth part

62 Look in the middle of the money-box, and if you see a black point or a path going out from the entrance of the money-box towards a black point, then it indicates that adultery is within the entrance of the house. 63 But if you find the path on the red side, then the adulterer enters through the wall or through the window of the house. 64 And if you find at the head of the money-box a thick white piece of meat, then that sign signifies an animal which is bought and is entering <the house>. 65 And if you see a yellow window in the middle of the money-box or a path going from the entrance of the money-box to another part, it signifies an ill man in his bed. 66 And if you do not see a yellow point in the middle of the money-box and you see a path entering the entrance or another part, then men bring their animals into their houses. 67 When you see a green point in the middle of the money-box which is in its hollow and the hollow of the money-box is clear to view, the daughter of the man will commit adultery. 68 And if it is a red point or there is something like a path round it, connected to the house is the stinking meat of one of the animals, which birds are devouring. 69 And when you see outside the entrance of the money-box a black point, it signifies a black dog. 70 And if the point is very small, it is a small puppy. 71 And if you see in the neck of the shoulder-blade on the inside a line which passes through the neck and it is white, it portends that the wife of the man is seen and loved by someone, but not taken (i.e. raped) by anyone. 72 And if you look in the heart of the shoulder-blade in the area of the thick part in the direction of the neck, investigate round the circuit of the neck from the pit of the neck as far as the tomb, and if the investigation finds something, it refers to the master of the house. 73 And if the investigation is not found in him (?), his son will be hanged. 74 And if it does not arrive at his son, then <it refers> to his son's son or his

daughter's son. 75 And if you see in front of the thickness — i.e. in front of the tomb which you looked at for the master of the house — something similar to many red or black or yellow tombs, those who the king imprisoned are imprisoned. 76 And if you see under the money-box a piece of meat which cannot be removed, it signifies that the master of the house puts on new clothing.

77 The sixth part

78 Description of the wars between the Butr (i.e., the Saracens) and the Christians. 79 Investigate with the thumb from the side of blackness from the outer side to the inner and <find> any tomb under the <first> two thumbs. 80 Anything of a tomb in the part which is above the money-box belongs to the Christians, and what is in the area of the lower thumb — i.e. in the area of the *abrachet* — belongs to the Butr. 81 And if you see in the blackness whiteness similar to clouds, then there will be argument among the races. 82 And if you see a slanting tomb, there is killing and death especially among them. 83 And note that the place of Butr belongs to the Saracens, and the place of Baraniz belongs to the Christians. 84 And if you see on the side of blackness lines on the side of the king, there are spies. 85 And if there is one line, there is one spy. 86 And if there are two, there are two spies. 87 And when you see a tomb in the lower part of the shoulder-blade, where it is white, the sign is attributed to the master of the house.

88 Description of the perpendicular.

89 The perpendicular should be investigated with the fingers. 90 The first finger is called the seat of the king; if a tomb is found there, the son(s) of the king are indicated. 91 The second finger is called that of his brothers and uncles, the third finger is attributed to counts, and the fourth is ascribed to potentates, the fifth to prevosts, the sixth to stewards, the seventh to the kings of the Latins.

92 The place of judgement.

93 When you see in the entrance to the perpendicular, in its neck in the area of the perpendicular, a line or lines, if they are coming out from the neck, it indicates deposition. 94 And if it is entering the neck, then a messenger will come with his retinue (?). 95 And note that on the perpendicular on the face of the shoulder-blade the first finger is <the place> of Córdoba. 96 The second, of the soldiers of the king. 97 The third, the place of the Christians. 98 The fourth, the

place of judgement. 99 The fifth, the place of the soul and the spouse — i.e. of the man — and of joy and sadness and vehement suffering. 100 And when you see in the middle of the shoulder-blade — i.e. in the white part — something like a hollow white cloud, silver and money will be stolen from the master of the shoulder-blade. 101 And if you find it in the place of the soul, it is severe suffering or money is taken from him. 102 And if you want to know what kind of money, if it is a very small black point, they are coins. 103 And if it is a very large point, they are clothes. 104 And if you see round the tomb a white point, they are flaxen cloths. 105 And what is lower on the outside of the shoulder-blade where the *abrachet* is, belongs to the Saracens and Christians. 106 The side of the king belongs to the Saracens, the side of blackness to the Christians. 107 And when you see an accidental* line placed obliquely, it denotes stakes that have been erected. 108 And if it is long, they are banners. 109 And if the stakes are large, they are of the Saracens. 110 And if they are small, we say <that they are> of the Christians.

111 The seventh part

112 If you see a path in the area of the face of the shoulder-blade and you see in the pit of the money-box something like the face of a triangle, if it turns to the blackness, then the husband will be against his wife. 113 And if it does not arrive as far as the bed, there is a thief entering the house by night. 114 And if you see a red or yellow point by the bed, and it turns persistently (?) towards it and turns away from the bed, it indicates a girl in the house who will get married to an old man. 115 And if you see whiteness in the money-box, it signifies joy. 116 And if you see blackness, it portends sadness and grieving. 117 And if you see whiteness and redness and yellowness on the top of the head of the money-box leading outwards towards the face of the shoulder-blade, it portends a man having clothes in his house and money removed from place to place. 118 And if you see the pit of the money-box now turned outwards, then the master of the shoulder-blade is in debt, and there happens to him a loss in his money. 119 And if you see something (?) going out from the top of the money-box, it hints strongly at

* The Latin translator may have confused "ʿarḍī" ("transverse") and "ʿaraḍī" ("accidental").

suffering and mental stress for the master of the shoulder-blade. 120 And if you see it straight, not twisted, it portends happiness about to come to the master of the shoulder-blade. 121 And if you see redness in it, then the female cook of the shoulder-blade is red, having eyes of different colours. 122 And if you see a very small red point in it, the female cook of the shoulder-blade has smallpox or there are on her face moles or scars. 123 And if you see under the pit of the money-box in the part which is next to the summit a black point, it signifies that the meat has been stolen from the pot, and the number of pieces stolen is according to the number of points. 124 And if you see in that place something going out, then the master of the shoulder-blade or his brother or his sister or his son or his relative will be pierced. 125 And if you see a round opening in it, it indicates construction.

126 And if you see on the inner part of the shoulder-blade a kind of white cloud spreading over the whole shoulder-blade, judge rain and good weather (?). 127 And if you see in the middle of the shoulder-blade in the whiteness something looking like a cooking pot, if there is whiteness in it, there is rain and the flowing of water.

128 And if you see in the whiteness — i.e., in the middle of the blade — something like a circle and on its perimeter something like hairs, it signifies death for the master of the shoulder-blade. 129 And if the perpendicular where <the place of> the king is seems to bend towards the back of the shoulder-blade, no one should doubt that it denotes the deposition of the king. 130 And when you see the place of his seat is white and if its marrow has come out, then the king has gone away. 131 And if a pit <or> a window (?) is seen above his palace, it portends grieving and wailing in the house of the king. 132 And if you see in it a tomb of three fingers' length, and it reaches the nose, if it breaks the <nose> above the seat of the king, no one should consider that it signifies anything other than the above-mentioned judgement.

133 And when something is seen entering the place of Córdoba the space of three fingers, men will be killed at the hands of the king. 134 And if you see an extensive blackness going out from the place of the king towards the whiteness of the shoulder-blade, and if there is a white point in it, it denotes without doubt fear and conturbation in the army. 135 And when you see that blackness, the king is going out without doubt. 136 And when you see blackness

on the left side and no other <blackness> appears on the opposite side, it signifies the king is going out hunting or walking. 137 On the other hand, when you see blackness appearing, the camps of the king will go out and the king will go out and his company will appear. 138 Consider, then, which army the whiteness enters and whose host is scattered, and is divided into companies — to them is the victory attributed, and it is said that it signifies nothing other than this. 139 And when you see in the army of the king these signs, then notice if there is whiteness in it, and <when> you see the place of his soldiers whiten, judge nothing other than that there will be a victory over them. 140 And when you see a tomb on the side of the king and heads in the place of Córdoba, it signifies the heads of the soldiers of that army are cut off and carried to Córdoba. 141 And if you see opposite that place below the shoulder-blade perforations, that indicates the heads of the prelates of the king and many men from his army are killed. 142 And when you see instead of protuberances a kind of cancer, the horses of the king will be found after the army has been defeated (?). 143 And if you see slender tombs, that signifies the destruction of the army and the death of men. 144 And when you see the *eudaha* — i.e. the place of judgement[4] — with graceful red or black or yellow tombs, it portends a similar discovery of the horses of the king. 145 And if you see white points, it signifies the money which he will have from the king, from his stewards. 146 And when you see in the area of the perpendicular, at its entrance — i.e. on the neck — a strong redness, then it hints that the sheep to which the shoulder-blade belongs is deficient or broken. 147 And when you see in the place of judgement a black point, the horses of the king run away. 148 Seek, then, their tracks and you will find them on the side of the king. 149 And when you see blackness going out from the side of the king continuous with the place of the master <of the shoulder-blade>, this signifies the army of the king without doubt.

150 The breadth of the shoulder-blade, therefore, should be investigated here from the place of Córdoba, and this first place should be attributed to Córdoba. 151 And the second finger is to Egypt, and the third finger is to the Yemen, and the fourth is to the place of the enemy, which is in the place of the tomb before the enemy (?), and the place of the children of Toledo. 152 And when you see the shoulder-blade now diminished on the lower side and

open in the place of the sea, it must be that ships come against Spain. 153 And when you see a large point going out from the place of the sea and ending in front of the king and the "generation of contrariety",[5] this denotes the king going out from the sea. 154 And when you see the shoulder-blade now diminished in the lower part in the place of the enemy, it signifies that the meat taken from that shoulder-blade is goat's meat. 155 And when you see several lines in the place of Córdoba, it signifies a fertile year for the people of Córdoba. 156 And when you see in the place of Córdoba a flowing of water in which there are no lineations, it denotes a scarcity in Córdoba. 157 And when you see armies going out and whiteness going out from the part which follows <the place of> the soldiers, then an army rising up against the king will be defeated. 158 And when you see blackness going out from the place of the king in the area of the face of the shoulder-blade <and> tending towards its whiteness and then being dispersed in its highest part, no one will doubt that the soldiers of the king will be united. 159 And when you see that blackness joined together and not diffused in such a way that no whiteness enters it, this is the victory of the soldiers of the king. 160 And when you see on the back of the shoulder-blade something rising up near the area of the neck, and in front of it a black cloud and there is nothing except this on the perpendicular, it denotes enemies returning to some of the cities of the king. 161 And when you see in front of the cloud something rising up and high, and blackness reaches it, it denotes that enemies capture the city.

162 The eighth part

163 And when you see in the lower part of the shoulder-blade in the place of the seat of the king blackness, then the sheep was black. 164 And if there is redness or whiteness, it is according to that colour. 165 And when you see the shoulder-blade now completely blackened, then the person who cut the throat of the sheep was polluted. 166 And if the left-hand side is blackened and the right-hand pure, then it denotes that the sheep had its throat cut in a dirty place. 167 And when you see the shoulder-blade yellow verging on red, the female cook of the shoulder-blade has a bad smell. 168 And when you see it covered with protuberances, it signifies that a great profit comes to the master of the shoulder-blade. 169 And when you see the top of the shoulder-blade in the area of the neck very

twisted, it portends great hardship for the master of the shoulder-blade. 170 And if you see that it is straight, it signifies joy for the master of the shoulder-blade. 171 And if you see whiteness dominating the shoulder-blade, it denotes a great amount of snow and cold weather in that year. 172 And when you see the shoulder-blade white with its surface scraped off, if you know the master of the shoulder-blade will be from the company of the house, judge that the meat of the shoulder-blade has been sent as a present.

173 The description of the *alcened*.[6]

174 The *alcened* is measured with the finger. 175 The first finger of the part which follows the head belongs to the husband of the house. 176 The second finger is <one> of the "seconds" who is in <the house> (?). 177 And the third is one of the "thirds" belonging to the town (*villa*), and the fourth is the border of his native land.

178 And when you see the nose of the shoulder-blade rise above the money-box, it signifies grieving in the house. 179 And when you see it bent against the neck, then it denotes a woman having large buttocks. 180 And if you see the nose of the shoulder-blade twisted on <one> side, it portends that the sheep will have been captured by force and will have had its throat cut. 181 And when you see under that nose great twistedness, the female cook of the shoulder-blade or the mistress of the sheep will have a pain in her back or has an old illness in her womb or is pregnant. 182 And if you see at the root of the tip something like a tooth rising up, the female cook lies with a black servant. 183 And if you see that the nose is very sharp, she fornicates with a white servant. 184 And when you see in the place of the bed something long, then the cook of the shoulder-blade is a man and not a woman. 185 And when you see that nose shattered, it is a woman pregnant with a female child. 186 And when you see the middle of the tip now turned back, the husband is ill. 187 And if the tip is curved in, the male cook of the shoulder-blade is a fool or lies at home as a cripple, or the man who cut the throat of the sheep is club-footed or left-handed. 188 And when you see the last part of the top not white, then someone has approached his wife. 189 And when you see in the breadth of the top a black path verging on red and going to the bed <of the man>, it signifies that someone is approaching his wife. 190 And if you see a red path in the house, <he is> going out to the house of the other one, and <if you see> two or more paths going it, it signifies a thief. 191 And if

you see that there is on the inside of the rising footsteps (?) a red or a black point, it signifies the recovery of the stolen goods. 192 And if you do not see a point in its more elevated place, the thief will enter the house and the stolen goods will not be recalled.

193 And if you see a path coming from the native land and entering the house, it signifies a gift which is being presented. 194 And if you see in the place of the bed a strong redness touching the place of the bed, it denotes fire falling on the house. 195 And when you see it in the second finger from the top, fire will fall on the town. 197 And if you see it in the third finger, fire will fall on the edge of the town.

197 And if you see <in> the place in which is the mother of his son — and this is the root of the perpendicular — a protuberance going out, it signifies that the mother of his son will be honoured by her husband. 198 And if you see in it a red point, the brother of his son will be burnt by fire or things similar to these.

199 And if you see the perpendicular spreading out, the master of the shoulder-blade is envied because of the large amount of money that he has. 200 And if you see redness and blackness, it signifies harm happening to the crop. 201 And if you see a crack in it, there is blackness in the crop. 202 And if you see it in the second <finger?>, it signifies great harm in the fruit. 203 And when you see that redness in the extremity and there is a protuberance rising up in the redness, there is scarcity in oil. 204 And the price is lowered by the amount that the protuberance becomes smaller, and the price rises by the amount that the protuberance grows.

205 And when you see a tomb in the first finger below <the place of> the enemy, touching the place of the house, in the meeting of your merchants <an agreement> among friends is judged. 206 And if it appears in the second finger, it is attributed to the closest people to you of your own religion. 207 And if you see it in the third finger, it is judged without doubt to your neighbours. 208 And if you see in the first finger from the part which follows the house between the perpendicular and the <place of> the enemy two tombs, they are in the meeting of the merchants of the Saracens. 209 And if it is in the second <finger>, it will be <one of> your closest <colleagues> on the side of the Saracens. 210 And if it is in the third <finger>, it is judged to be attributed to the kings of the Latins.

211 And when you see in the tomb a black point, it signifies

fevers. 212 And if it is red, death. 213 And if it is yellow, it portends smallpox, and if it is white, pustules (?). 214 And if you see its tip now blackened and heavy and red in any part, the ill man will die within two months. 215 And if you see it whitened, it signifies funeral vestments. 216 And if you wish to know the truth of this affair, and the nearness of his death, consider the tomb of the ill man, and you will see that white groove on the shoulder-blade, and this is the judgement — as it is said — of the hair shirt. 217 And if you see on the inner part of the whiteness of the shoulder-blade in the part which is next to its back, at a distance of two fingers from the junction of the two perpendiculars, points of various colours which are not long, it signifies women in the house of the man mourning over a dead man. 218 And if something long is seen on the outer tip of shoulder-blade, it signifies grieving.

219 And when you see in the place of the *alcenen*[7] — i.e., in the place of the house — something like a slender tomb on the breadth <of the *alcenen*>, the sheep is in the house. 220 And if it is going out from the house in the second finger, it denotes a spy spying there in the native land. 221 And the place of the tomb should be discovered in this way. 222 For tombs are not found in the breadth of the native land, but in the root of the *alcenen*. 223 Spies indeed <are> in the breadth of the *alcenen* in front of the tombs. 224 But if they are white or red or black, the clothes of the spy will be of the same colour. 225 And when you see whiteness entering the *populum* (?), it portends bitterness in him. 226 But if the blackness enters, it signifies glory and honour. 227 And if you see on the shoulder-blade soldiers becoming manifest, sudden fear will strike the army. 228 And if you see between the perpendicular and the neck, at the entrance to the perpendicular — i.e. in the "eye" outside the perpendicular — it belongs to the man from the house. 229 And if you see the head of the tomb raised, it signifies a man from Arabia. 230 And if you see the tomb is like two heads, it portends a Berber. 231 And if you see it white and there is no head in it nor any sign, it indicates a Latin man. 232 And if the tomb is somewhat long, it signifies a powerful master.

233 And if the black spreads out from the place of judgement, no one will doubt that you obtain judgements unexpectedly, but nevertheless in the end (?). 234 And if you see in the place of judgement under the perpendicular narrow white or black or yellow

tombs, they portend prisoners captured by the king. 235 And when you see clear yellowness in the place of the tip in the entrance of the house and there is yellowness on the right and obscurity appears on the left, it signifies without doubt that the sheep will be taken without payment and seized or stolen.

236 But God makes known what is absent and reveals what is hidden. AMEN.

Notes

1 Note that this translation is only provisionary; much remains obscure because of the state of the Latin text in this single manuscript and the impenetrability of the subject-matter. In Figure 3 I have attempted to locate the "places" mentioned in this text.

2 20–35 are repeated in slightly more idiomatic Latin in 36–52.

3 i.e., *al-raqīq*, "the slender/tender (column)"; *abrachet* appears to be marked in the wrong place in Figure 1.

4 It is unclear which Arabic term is rendered by *eudaha*.

5 This is presumably a literal translation of *ahl al-khilāf*, "the people of disparity", referring to the enemies of Islam.

6 *al-sanad*, "the support, prop", i.e. the protruding spine of the shoulder-blade.

7 *al-sanām*, "the hump", i.e. the tip of the spine of the shoulder-blade.

Boys, Women and Drunkards: Hispano–Mauresque Influences on European Song?

DAVID WULSTAN

Introductory notes

The *zajal* is written in vulgar Arabic (*laḥn*), whereas the *muwashshaḥ* is typically written in Classical Arabic or in Hebrew, though there are many examples in *laḥn* which follow the symmetrical pattern of the *muwashshaḥ*.

Anatomy

(simple examples — more elaborate rhymes often found, especially for the *muwashshaḥ*)

zajal **(plural *azjāl*):**

M M	=	*maṭlaʿ* or refrain
a	=	*ghuṣn* — independent line — there
a		may be more or less than three *aghṣān*
a		
m		*simṭ* or link with refrain — only *partial* in the typical *zajal* i.e. ASYMMETRICAL

muwashshaḥ **(plural *muwashshaḥ āt*):**

M M	*maṭlaʿ*
a	
a	*ghuṣn* (as before)
a	
m m	*simṭ*: here the link is same length as the *maṭlaʿ* i.e. SYMMETRICAL

aghṣān + *simṭ* = *dawr*

The last *simṭ* of the *muwashshaḥ* is called the *kharja* — sometimes Arabic, but sometimes Romance (*ajāmiʿ*)

Alternative terms

qufl (=*simṭ*), *bayt* (=*dawr* though according to the Ibn Sanāʾ al-Mulk (d. 608/1211) *bayt* applies to the *aghṣān* alone: this is doubtless an error).

M	(N O)	=	refrain rhymes
a	(b c)	=	independent stanza rhymes
m	(n o)	=	stanza rhymes linked with the refrain rhymes
x		=	rhymeless lines

muʿāraḍa = contrafaction, imitation of pre-existent model (cf. *ʿarūḍ* = metre) with its music: *matlaʿ* of model becomes *kharja* of *muʿāraḍa*, or a popular *kharja* (also sometimes called *markaz*, a musical term denoting "base") is quoted by more than one imitation.

In the following paper, I have used, with some reluctance, the word "Mauresque" to denote the Iberian Arabic and Hebrew writers and their milieu; this at least avoids the problem of "Arab" having to subsume Berbers, "Arabic" having sometimes to include Hebrew writers, and so forth. Accordingly, "Hispano–Mauresque" denotes the Christian, Jewish and Islamic cultures and their languages. Also for convenience, "Galician" and *gallego* subsume Portuguese. Ibn Quzmān's d. 555/1160 *azjāl* are numbered according to the edition of García Gómez (1972).

*   *   *

Ibn Maymūn, known as Maimonides (d. 600/1203–4), the Jewish contemporary of Ibn Sanāʾ al-Mulk, wrote a tract entitled "On listening to music" (Farmer 1942, 15) in which he rehearsed a topic, much discussed by Arab writers, as to whether music was a legitimate pastime. "Is it lawful," he asks, "to listen to the singing of the *muwashshaḥāt* of the Arabs?" In his answer, he echoes Ibn Gabirol (d. *c.*450/1058), himself an author of Hebrew *muwashshaḥāt*: it is not music or singing *per se* which is reprehensible, but the indecent words with which it might be associated. Nevertheless, he also echoes al-Ghazālī (d. 505/1111–12) in adding that a woman singing or playing is offensive, as is the presence of wine at the performance. Since the singing girls were associated with the *muwashshaḥāt*, whose words were frequently to do with sensual pleasure of all kinds, it seems that Maimonides would have abjured many of the songs which his contemporary Ibn Sanā' al-Mulk describes in his *Dār al-ṭirāz*. Ibn Sanā' speaks of the *kharja*, or parting shot of the *muwashshaḥ*, saying that it should be introduced by "I, he, or she said (or sang)" or some such expression, and is usually put into the mouth of "boys, women or drunkards" (cf. Stern, 1974, 33). Although the *kharja* may be in the classical language, he says, it may be in the vernacular (*laḥn*).

The vernacular, especially the *'ajamī* dialect of the Mozarabic Christians, would rule such songs further out of court. Indeed, it was these vulgar elements (often in both senses of the word) which gave the *muwashshaḥ* its racy appeal. But why boys? There is a passage in the ninth century *Kitāb al-malāhī* of Ibn Salama (d. 293/905) (Robson and Farmer, 1938, 19) which speaks of the first musicians in various categories, including the first to sing a camel song (*ḥudā'*). Ibn Salama goes on to describe the *naṣb*, a more cultured version of the camel-driver's song, which was sung, he says, by youths (*fityān*). This seems to have been based on a standard piece of mythology about the origins of music, since its substance is found elsewhere (e.g. the *Mustaṭraf* of al-Ibshihī (d. after 850/1446) (see Robson and Farmer, 1938, 19, n. 3). A variant version appears in the *Kitāb al-'iqd al-farīd* of Ibn 'Abd Rabbihi (d. 328/939–40) (see Farmer 1942, 4) where *fityān* is changed to *qiyān*: youths have become singing girls. Perhaps a later author combined the alternatives and was followed by Ibn Sanā' al-Mulk. Tifashī (see García Gómez 1952, p. 523) is probably half referring to a similar passage when he says that the old Arabic songs of al-Andalus were "either in the style of the Christians or in the style of the Arab camel-drivers".

Epithets such as these are intended, when used derogatorily, to put such lyrics beyond the pale; more often than not, however, they are used in mock censure, taking a prurient delight in low life. And, in common with the goliards, the poet's apparent espousal of debauchery of all kinds was doubtless largely a pose. This having been said, the connection with the "songs of the Christians" and with singing girls is undoubted: many *kharajāt* are put into the mouth of a girl (or indeed a youth or a drunkard), as Ibn Sanā' al-

Mulk says; and, as we know, these lines are not infrequently in Romance, if sometimes in a considerably fractured dialect. The recorded language may sometimes have been accurate, sometimes corrupted, and sometimes perhaps intentional gibberish (a sort of Mozarabic precursion of Lewis Carroll). There is no need to agonise too much over the supposed dialectal inconsistencies and grammatical solecisms of the *kharajāt*: they were a conceit, not a literary text for posterity.

The possibility of a Hispano–Mauresque influence on European lyric has been discussed often enough. Most recent writers are dismissive, and after the excessive claims of Ribera and others, this is understandable; but it is unwise to forget the obvious fact that the rebec, nakers and lute were three common European instruments of the Middle Ages, and not only their forms, but their names, are direct borrowings from Arabic (or Persian) sources. Nor has the occurrence of the word "gazel" (= *ghazal*) in the Occitan lyric "Mei amic e mei fiel" been explained away. Although much of Dante's knowledge of Arabic literature may stem from Sicilian sources, his friend Brunetto Latini, who spent some time at the court of Alfonso the Wise, may have been an equally important link with oriental culture. It is also striking that Dante, in his *De Vulgari Eloquentia, II, x* mentions elements such as *syrma* which are highly suggestive of the *muwashshaḥ* terms, as is his use of *stantia* > *stanza*, which looks remarkably akin to *dawr* or *bayt* (going back to an ancient equivalent, since congruent terms are found in Egyptian hieroglyphic *he*, Syriac *bayit*, Greek *oikos*, and the like). None of these things can be pressed too far, but it does seem inconceivable that when Arab instruments were imported into Europe, the gramophone came without any discs.

A fruitful line of enquiry in regard to possible influence concerns the form and rhyme schemes of the *muwashshaḥ* and *zajal* on the one hand, and of the cantiga and kindred lyrics on the other. Similarities in rhyme schemes have been noted for a long time: unfortunately the apparent identity between *zajal* and cantiga rhyme schemes often hides a fundamental difference in musical form. As a result, the technical term *zejel* used of Spanish lyric is chimerical. The *aaam bbbm* scheme is indeed typical of the *cantiga de amigo*, and seems to resemble that of the *zajal;* but in the cantiga the *m* is the typical end-refrain, whereas the *zajal* refrain (*matlaʿ*)

comes at the beginning, e.g. *MM* (refrain) *aaam* (stanza) *bbbm* (stanza). This latter scheme, however, looks much the same as that of a typical Alfonsine Cantiga (the use of a capital letter henceforward assumes the *Cantigas de Santa Maria* of Alfonso el Sabio). Yet here again, the similarity is illusory. In this kind of Cantiga (what is now generally known, from later French, as a *virelai*), the first two elements of the stanza (*aa*) are typically sung to an independent but repeated musical phrase, whereas the third and the fourth elements (*am*) were typically sung to the same music as that of the refrain: thus, although the second part of the stanza presaged the refrain musically, only the last line of the stanza introduced the link rhyme. The typical *zajal* had a different musical structure, although examples of it, too, are to be found in the Alfonsine Cantigas. We know something of the musical form of the *zajal* because of many instances where a poet composed a contrafaction (*muʾāradḍa*) on a pre-existing model, but which differed in having one line extra, or less: the music of the model must therefore have been capable of expansion or contraction, but because some *azjāl* were heterometric (as *muwashshaḥāt* commonly are) as between, say, the *m* and *a* lines, it follows that the music for the *aaa* lines was the same, sung thrice (or more, or less, should the *muʿāraḍa* require it).

A closer look at the question of rhyme reveals further curiosities; but first the notorious museum exhibit purporting to show the liturgical origins of vernacular poetry must be dusted down once more for a reluctant viewing. Despite its being no more than a literary Piltdown skull, the hymn is still paraded as a species of missing link from whence Romance and other poetic systems emerged onto two feet. The typical features of Romance lyric, especially of the *cantigas de amor* (refrains, rhyme and its musical structures) are conspicuously absent in the earlier Latin hymn. The few processional refrain hymns such as "Gloria laus" are exceptional, but these serve only to prove the point, for their initial refrains are quite different from those found in Romance lyric. Similarly, the *prosae* with a rhyming final vowel (on a melisma) display a technique which was never transplanted to the hymn, in which systematic rhyme is absent until comparatively late: exceptions such as "Ad coenam agni", which *very nearly* rhymes throughout, simply prove the rule; if anything, they can be seen as attempts to imitate a substrate vernacular rhyme convention (on the question of the relationship of vernacular and Latin rhyme, see Wright, 1982). Then again, musical repetition in the hymn, if it occurs, does not accord with the patterns found in secular song (not to mention the question of tonality) so the paternity of the vernacular lyric cannot seriously be foisted upon a celibate liturgy. No elaborate blood testing or genetic fingerprinting is necessary: the child is patently of different stock. Furthermore, though vernacular song is first noted in literary records at a fairly late date, many previous generations of its forebears, though unregistered, must have existed. Cousins appear in Latin contrafactions (such as the Carolingian "Ut quid jubes" of Gottshalk); they can be recognised by the family likeness of refrain, rhyme and musical form. The supposed Aquitaĩnian "models" for troubadour lyric are also manifest contrafactions: the vernacular song was the seed, the later Latin lyric was merely its progeny.

Gottshalk's lyric is monorhymed in *-e* throughout, though he also achieves a double rhyme (or at least assonance) in several stanzas. His difficulty is, of course, that the Latin accent cannot be properly oxytonic (only by monosyllabic line ends or by secondary accent can an acute rhyme normally be achieved in Latin). As elsewhere, Gottshalk is obviously attempting to imitate a vernacular model in which no such difficulty existed. Nonetheless, the earliest evidence of Romance lyric betrays fairly primitive rhyme schemes: indeed, Alvarus of Córdoba expresses amazement at the rhymes of the Arab poets (see below). Yet, the *qaṣīda* lyrics rhyme *xaxa* throughout, apart from the opening distich, rhyming *aaxa*. From whence, then, do the virtuoso rhyme schemes of some of the *muwashshaḥāt* stem? Moreover, the schemes of the Alfonsine Cantigas, if less elaborate, are also more complex than those of earlier lyrics, and thus pose a similar question.

By a fortunate chance a *nasīb*, the opening of a *qaṣīda*, is preserved in a couple of early manuscripts in unequivocal notation. According to al-Jāḥiẓ (d. 255/868–9: see Beeston, 1980, 18ff) the songs of the *qaynāt* consisted only of two to four *abyāt* (i.e. lines): his quotations bear this out, showing, as in the example given below, that the typical distich *nasīb* had an independent life of its own. I have transcribed the piece in Example 1 with its drum rhythm accompaniment (i.e. *ḍarb:* its rhythm is *ramal* — though doubtless originally related, this is not the metrical pattern of the same name). The original notation of the tune is in unequivocal letter-notation, given here in Roman equivalents: since they indicate the frets of the lute, the letters therefore represent precise pitch relationships. Similarly, the rhythm of the tune is exactly indicated by numbers, also recorded here. I have appended the metrical scheme (*ṭawīl*) of these lines. It will immediately be seen that the "feet" of the metre do not correspond with the beats of the rhythm, nor are the quantities necessarily echoed in the note values. Furthermore, the article is not really elided, the *-l-* being given a separate note (in two instances, at least: this is what happens often today in Arabic, especially Maghribine, song). All of these features show that the musical element vastly alters the argument about the metric of the *muwashshaḥ* (*pace* Alan Jones, 1988 — see Example 1 below). On paper, Romance metric seems wholly incompatible with the classical *ʿarūḍ*: when the musical dimension restores the perspective, however, the two seem to be nearer together, even down to the use of paragogic letters:

Example 1

(London, B.L. MS. Or. 2361, collated: see Farmer 1957, p. 454, for references and for a slightly different transcription.)

The musical structure is formulistic, employing variant melodic cells; and the two lines of music are repeated to form the second half of the tune, with the rhymes falling thus:

a *a*
(repeated music) *x* *a*

Or, if the music is regarded as monothematic with variants, the structure is:

a
a'
x
a'

Compare this with a Galician *cantiga de amor* by the thirteenth-century Martin Codax (see facsimile in Ferreira 1986):

Example 2

Here the musical structure is repeated for each of the six stanzas, and there is also some internal repetition. The form, in relation to the rhyme (or rather assonance) scheme, is as follows:

a
(variant repeat) *a*
(independent music) .... *A* (refrain)

The melodic motive indicated by the star is an important thumbprint. It occurs in several of Alfonso's decadal Cantigas: these (i.e. nos. 10, 20, 30 and so on) are set apart from the others in several ways. Most obviously they are identified in one of the manuscripts by beautiful vignettes of instrumentalists in ravishing colours; also they are called *cantigas de loor*, cantigas of praise. Although all the others are in honour of the Virgin, they are narrative in form, recounting miracles wrought by her. The decadal songs, on the other hand, are paeans without a narrative element. Formally, they are also quite different from the narrative "virelai" type with initial refrain: the *cantigas de loor* are often very close to the *cantiga de amigo* in their rhyme scheme and end-refrain, and frequently carry the melodic thumbprint already identified. Cantiga 250, for example, has these features and, as Anglés (1958) pointed out, is a parallel of the *cantiga de amigo* of the twelfth-century King Dinis (Alfonso's grandfather) beginning "Pois que diz meu amigo". We can be fairly certain, then, that many of the decadal songs stem from a peculiarly *gallego* tradition, perhaps remembered by Alfonso from his youth at his tutor's house in Orense, in Galicia (cf. Ballesteros, 1963, pp. 50–1), and possibly heard from the mouth of his nurse. That is why he often seems to have modelled the *cantigas de loor* on the female *cantiga de amigo* not, as would more logically be expected, on the *cantiga de amor*, sung by a man of his lady. Apart from a sole surviving lyric in Castilian, he used Galician for all of his Cantigas (and for his secular songs, some of which are startlingly crapulous): the use of this well-established poetic language was further reinforced by its closer resemblance to Occitan and the languages on the periphery of the Iberian Peninsula which would therefore more easily enter into a poetic *koinê* than Castilian. This feature also has some bearing on the curiously promiscuous, often peripheral, forms of the Romance *kharajāt*.

The Galician women who might have sung to the youthful Alfonso would have had at least some passing knowledge of Arabic music (indeed, their beauty and voices were much favoured by the Muslim conquerors — cf. Stern, 1979, p. 52): *gallego* lyrics mention the *adufe*, *alaude* and other instruments, and one has the refrain *leilia doura*. A particular four-note melodic element is found in Galician song which recurs in a Maghribine Arabic version of a *muwashshaḥ* by Ibn Sahl (see d'Erlanger 1941, p. 625, and Wulstan 1982, p. 258). The same melodic figure may be seen in the Codax cantiga entitled "Quantas sabedes" (see Wulstan 1982, p. 247) and in a decadal Cantiga (230) which in turn seems to resemble a *cantiga* de amor by Roi Paes di Ribela ("Par deus ai dona Leonor" — see below). The same four-note element is found in Alfonso's Cantiga number 47, given at Example 3, where this melodic figure is identified by an asterisk. Instead of Alfonso's words, however, I have given those of a *zajal* by Ibn Quzmān with identical rhythm:

Example 3

(see García Gómez No. 17, and Anglés No. 47. Note the word *layla* [pronounced *leila* in al-Andalus] and note also that the *zajal* shares its typical rhyme scheme with the Cantiga):

M	*M* (refrain)
	a
	a
a	*m*
M	*M* (refrain)

As already indicated, this pattern is not that of the "virelai" Cantiga: instead, it resembles more that of the French rondel. The double bar marks off the two strains of the music, so it can be seen that the majority of the piece is sung to the second strain, represented by the right hand of the diagram. The Occitan rondel "Tuit cil qui sunt enamorat" (Gennrich, 1921, No. 54) has much the same form. The rondel type better known in the French repertory, however, is the "left-handed" variety: metrical evidence (i.e. the majority of lines being isosyllabic, but others being heterosyllabic) shows that many of Ibn Quzmān's *azjāl* could have employed now one, now the other musical structure, or either indifferently: these types also occur fairly commonly in the Cantigas.

Some of the earliest "virelais" are extremely primitive in regard to their musical form, e.g. "Onque an ameir" (Gennrich 1921, No. 251):

M	*M*
a	
a	
a	
m	

(In this instance the rhyme letters indicate little more than assonance.)

Now this structure does not differ musically from the rondels found in the Cantigas (many, but not all, of which occur in the decadal songs); the difference is in the refrain structure, which employs the truncated refrain characteristic of the rondel:

M	*N*
m	
M	
m	*n*
M	*N*

Another observation should be added: the two strains of music, separated in these examples by the double bar, are sometimes so similar that the whole song is virtually monothematic.

These structures are perhaps similar to those of the "songs of the Christians" on which the *zajal* may have been modelled. Although the literature appears to indicate that the *muwashshaḥ* preceded the *zajal* (for much the same reasons as the primacy of Latin liturgical music and poetry seems at first sight to be supported by their earlier appearance in the sources) there is evidence (see Wulstan 1982, p. 259, and Corriente 1982) that a "prehistoric" *zajal* existed, as suspected by Nykl (1946, p. 339). Furthermore, Ibn ʿAbd Rabbihi (cf. Farmer, 1942, p. 8) quoted from Ibn Waḥshiyya (fl. end of third/ninth century), of a century earlier, to the effect that bees are delighted with singing and that their young will alight for love of a "noise" (*zajal*). Ibn ʿAbd Rabbihi is mentioned by Ibn Bassām d. 543/1147 as being the inventor of the *muwashshaḥ* and though he may have been only an innovator of some of its refinements, or possibly merely a *washshaḥ* (see Stern, 1974, p. 93), it is extremely unlikely that his use of the word *zajal* is coincidental. In addition, by quoting from a *rajaz* poet immediately afterwards, the connection with popular song is obvious. Poems of the *rajaz* type were unintelligible according to the rules of Classical Arabic metric. As Rabbihi says (cf. Farmer, 1942, p. 11), music was needed to establish its metre (*wazn*). This reflects what Ibn Sanā' al-Mulk says (*Dār*, paras. 20–1) that the *muwashshaḥāt* did not conform to classical rules, but their rhythm was ruled by musical considerations: Safī al-Dīn Ḥillī (d. 750/1349) (*apud* Hoernerbach, 1956) says the same in regard to the *zajal*.

If the *zajal* was current in the time of Ibn ʿAbd Rabbihi, or earlier, this would make sense of a comment by Alvarus of Córdoba (d. third/ninth century). In his *Indiculus Luminosus* of AD 854, Alvarus speaks of the lascivious songs by which the Muslims affronted the piety of the Christian priests, and upbraids some of his fellow Christians for knowing nothing of the beauty of the Church's literature, but looking instead to the "grandiloquent lines in the Chaldean (*sc* Arabic) language. They compose songs with more metrical assurance than the Gentiles, displaying lofty heights of elegance, every line ending with the same letter" (Migne, *P.L., Tom.* 121, cols. 521 and 555–6: "qui erudite Chaldaria verborum explicet pompus. Ita ut metrice eruditiori ab ipsis gentibus carmine, et sublimi pulchritudine finales clausas unius litterae coarctationes decorent"). It is not entirely clear what called forth this display of jealous admiration: was it rhyme as opposed to assonance; or was it the monorhyme of the *qaṣīda* of Classical Arabic, so difficult to imitate in Latin, which excited his attention? Either way, it is obvious that Arabic poetry was known to Romance speakers, and surely exerted some influence on their own lyrics: certainly Alvarus attempts rhyme in one of his own Latin verses (*Versus IV*, *ibid.*, col. 557: Wright 1982, pp. 156–9, using a slightly differing text of the obscure passage quoted above, glosses it as a possible reference to the *muwashshaḥ* and to its Romance *kharja*, an interpretation which in my view is difficult to sustain).

Crossed rhyme (*abab*) is a feature of more complex *azjāl* and *muwashshaḥāt*, and is found in later Romance poetry, being also plentiful in the Cantigas of Alfonso. There are, however, particular rhyme schemes which show how difficult the question of supposed relationships must be accounted. Ibn Quzmān, in *zajal* No. 4, only once uses the extremely unusual pattern *aabb* (see Example 1). This scheme is also surprisingly rare in Romance, though it does occur a century or so later in virtually the earliest written *gallego* lyric, a *cantiga de amor* attributed to Sancho I, King of Portugal, beginning "Ai eu coitada como vivo". At first, the *cantigas de amor* make sparing use of chiastic rhyme *abba*, a wholly un-Arabic pattern never found, so far as I am aware, in *muwashshaḥāt* or *azjāl* either in Hebrew or Arabic (but see Excursus 1). It is extremely rare in the Cantigas, outside the decadal songs, but much more common in Catalan or Occitan lyric.

The chiastic pattern *abba* is probably a hallmark of the *cantiga de amor*, rather than of the usually shorter *cantiga de amigo*: the appearance of chiastic rhyme in a few Cantigas could therefore be taken to suggest, perhaps, that Alfonso used one or two *cantigas de amor* as models for some of his decadal songs. He also used popular songs (rondels, carols and the like, which may be identified by their differing forms) and probably songs from a wide geographical area (one is a contrafaction of music by the Occitan Cadenet); most striking, however, is his use of Galician song, as shown by the clear parallels identified by Anglés (1958) and others. Although Alfonso's contrafaction of the *cantigas de amigo*, women's songs, is doubtless a reflection of the singing of the female servants of his youth, this line of influence is by no means unique: the practice of sending boys of the nobility to be educated in the country was widespread in Spain (see Ballesteros, 1963, p. 50). The female *cantigas* (apart, perhaps, from some Castilian examples in the later *cancioneros*) survive only as echoes in the literary *cantigas de amigo*, all written by men, in which the woman's point of view was a literary conceit. The same is true of the *kharja*; often, as we have seen, it was put into the mouth of a girl, and not infrequently was couched in the Romance dialect (often strangely resembling, moreover, the word forms of Galician). The *zajal* already quoted as Example 3 has the curious melodic ornament which may be Arabic, or may be Galician, or again may be a Mozarabic trait of the native singing girls. Whatever the truth of this, it crops up in several *cantigas de loor*, and notably in Cantiga 230, mentioned earlier. As Ferreira (1986) has pointed out, this Cantiga closely resembles in scheme a *cantiga de amor* by Roi Ṗaes de Ribela. What makes the resemblance so striking, however, is that this *gallego* cantiga is the only one discovered, outside the Alfonsine Cantigas, with an initial refrain. It is also structurally very similar to the kind of monothematic *zajal* discussed previously:

M ‖ *M*
a ‖ *a*
a ‖ *m*
M ‖ *M*

The transcription which follows identifies the melodic flourish of Example 3 with an asterisk, as before. The words underlaid are those of the opening stanzas of (i) Alfonso's Cantiga 230 as in the source, together with, conjecturally, that of (ii) the cantiga of Roi Paes de Ribela and of (iii) Ibn Quzmān's *zajal* No. 10, of which more will be said below.

Example 4

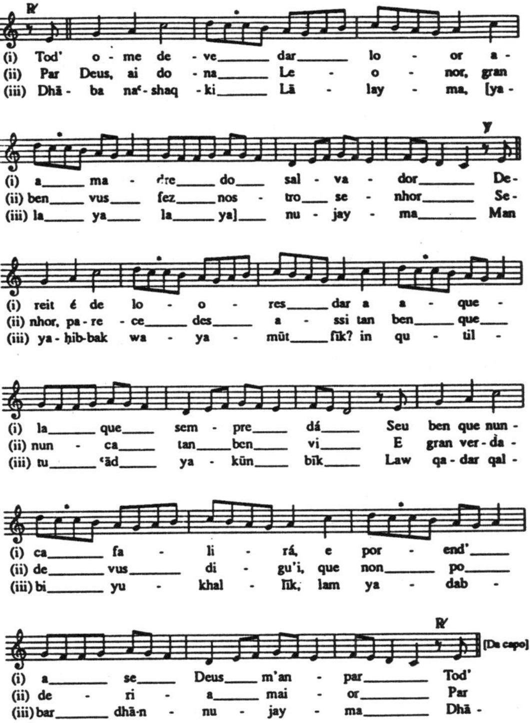

Is this a representative of the interchange between the culture of the Galician singing girl and the Arabic *qayna*? Remarkably, the

Cantiga resembles the musical structure of the *qaṣida* more than any of its Alfonsine companions: on the other hand, it also resembles the structure of the earliest, somewhat undifferentiated "virelais" from east of the Iberian Peninsula. Here perhaps is a late Romance equivalent of the earliest proto-*zajal*, with its initial refrain, a feature which was not to achieve any status in *gallego* courtly lyric until comparatively late and most typically in the Cantigas. As to the conjectural Quzmānian equivalent, the duple rhythm does not conflict with the prosody any more, indeed rather less, than the uncompromising rhythmic pattern of Example 1.

The principle of the refrain is at the heart of the *kharja*. In many songs an Arabic refrain (*matlaʿ*) from a well-known *muwashshaḥ* is borrowed as the *kharja* of the contrafaction, written either in Arabic or in Hebrew. This is what Ibn Sanāʾ al-Mulk meant by the *kharja* being the "starting point" of the *muwashshaḥ*, its "pepper . . . its sugar, its musk, its ambergris . . . will have laid the foundations, and have grasped the tail on which to fix its head" (cf. Stern, 1974, p. 34). From the point of view of the audience, there would be the pleasure of anticipating the punch-line. For although a new refrain (*matlaʿ*) was added at the beginning, to be repeated (chorally, as we know from various sources) after every stanza, its music was that of the *kharja*, so the listeners would know what was coming: the singing girls' parting shot would be sung to the theme song of the whole *muwashshaḥ*.

The idea of a quotation was perfectly reconcilable with the *musammaṭ* style, for the last line of the *murabbaʿ* scheme (*aaab*) for example, could incorporate a quotation. Thus, a *zajal* of the form *MM aaam* (asymmetrical *simṭ*) could incorporate such a quotation as the final *m* (*kharja*) element. This is precisely what Ibn Quzmān does in the *zajal* beginning *law jā shawwāl kannafiq* (No. 16), imitating Ibn Baqī (d. 540/1145–6). The *kharja* is the same as Ibn Baqī's which begins

al-ghazāl shaqqa-l-ḥarīq

The same line occurs, however, in another *zajal*, No. 56, (with symmetrical *simṭ*) which Ibn Quzmān says imitates the same *muwashshaḥ* by Ibn Baqī. Here, nonetheless, the syllable pattern is quite different. Ibn Quzmān's *zajal* 56 has a more or less uniform count of 7:7 throughout, whereas the Ibn Baqī model has 7:7:9:4 in the refrain and corresponding *simṭ*, and 9:4 in the *ghuṣn*. This latter scheme is followed in Ibn Quzmān's *zajal* 16, though it has only three *aghṣān*.

Two things are striking here: in these contrafactions it is the *kharja* which is quoted, not, apparently, a *matlaᶜ*. The obvious explanation is that the *kharja* is already a quotation, a refrain from a popular song. The other peculiarity is that the line quoted appears in the wrong place in *zajal* 56: it is in the last line, whereas it begins Ibn Baqī's *kharja*, as also that of Ibn Quzmān's *zajal* 16. The only way to bring order to this apparent jumble is to posit a pre-existing popular song of 7:7 metre sung to a repeated musical phrase. Because the first and second elements would then have the same music, this would explain how the even element could bear the *al-ghazal* line in the *zajal*, the odd element in the other: it would make no difference. This theory would also explain why Ibn Quzmān twice refers to his model as *al-ghazal* rather than Ibn Baqī's first line, *bi abī aḥwā rashīq*, as would be expected. Thus, Ibn Quzmān's *zajal* 56 more than probably had a structure akin to that of Cantiga 288, which has an identical rhyme and syllable scheme:

7	: 7
X	*M*
X	*M*
x'	*a''*
x'	*a*
x	*a*
x	*m**

(NB: syllable counts employed here are real throughout, and do not accord with the notional system of Spanish prosody.)

In the Cantiga, both strains are virtually identical (dashes indicate further slight variants: the star marks the *kharja* line in Ibn Quzmān's *zajal* 56. Represented as being entirely monothematic, but with slight variants, the structure is as follows:

7
X
M'
X
M'

x''
$a'\,''$
x''
a'
x
m'^{*}

If this structural argument be accepted, then Ibn Quzmān's complete *kharja* (*xm**) represents the refrain of what was originally a popular song, taken up by Ibn Baqī (and in turn by Ibn ʿEzra [d. 561/1165], in Hebrew) in a more elaborate format, whereby he extended the tune with an additional melodic strain for his (heterometric) *simṭ;* but the *aghṣān* and *matlaʿ* preserved the popular tune:

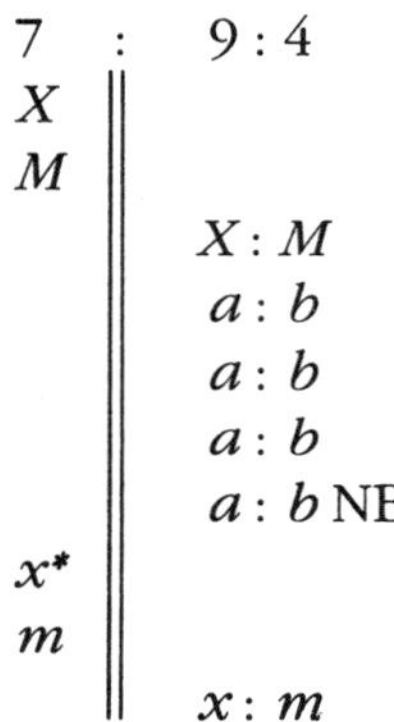

Here, Ibn Baqī's non-rhyming *x** is Ibn Quzmān's *m** element. In *zajal* 16, however, Ibn Quzmān imitated Ibn Baqī's version exactly (as to rhyme and metre) apart from omitting the fourth *ghuṣn* marked NB.

This, to my mind, is the only explanation which fits the facts of the apparent *muʿāraḍa* poems in question. It might be argued, as to *zajal* 56, that Ibn Quzmān says merely that "I have written this in the metre (*fi-ʿarūḍ*) of *al-ghazal* . . ." and therefore the imitation is metrical, not musical. Yet, if this means anything, the metrical congruence must refer to a lyric of the same metre. Then again, *muʿāraḍa* means, as we know, that the tune was used as the model: moreover, the word *ʿarūḍ* itself includes a musical connotation, and does not simply mean "metre"; indeed *ʿarūḍ* is given as *melodia* in a medieval Latin–Arabic glossary (Seybold, *Glossarium Latino–Arabicum*, eleventh century AD, where also *qaṣīda* is given as *armonia*). So the common bond between all three lyrics is the refrain of a popular *qaṣīda* lyric of the type quoted by al-Jāḥiẓ (cf. Beeston, 1980) and Ibn ʿAbd Rabbihi (cf. Farmer, 1942, *passim*), as being the staple of the singing girls: this refrain was taken up as a *kharja* in all three lyrics.

More usually, the *matlaʿ* of the model became a *kharja* in the imitation: Ibn al-ʿArabī (Stern, 1974, p. 189) imitated Ibn Quzmān's *zajal* in which the *matlaʿ* begins:

mallat wiṣālī *wal-l-malīh malūl*
wa-man yuwāfiq *maʿshūqan waṣūl*

Ibn al-ʿArabī's *muʿāraḍa* ends with these lines (though slightly modified, to make his point) as his *kharja*. Once more, however, the structure of the model has been modified in the imitation: an asymmetric *zajal* (in respect of the *simṭ*) and has necessarily been converted into a symmetrical *muwashshaḥ*. Here, the metre is decasyllabic with a half-way caesura. Let us assume that Ibn Quzmān's *zajal* had the primitive structure similar to that already adduced:

5	:	5
X	‖	*M*
X	‖	*M*
x	‖	*a*
x	‖	*a*
x	‖	*a*
x	‖	*m*

If this were the pattern of the *zajal* model, then Ibn al-ʿArabī's *muwashshaḥ* equivalent (with more complex rhymes and symmetrical *simṭ*) could have had this structure:

5 : 5	‖	5 : 5
X : *M*	‖	
X : *M*	‖	
	‖	*a* : *b*
	‖	*a* : *b*
	‖	*a* : *b*
x : *m*	‖	
x : *m*	‖	

Ibn Quzmān's *matlaʿ* = Ibn al-ʿArabī's *kharja*.

In another *zajal* (No. 108), Ibn Quzmān takes his own *matlaʿ* (*yā l-ashqar, yā ḥulay, yā sukkar*) and uses it as the *kharja* of *zajal* 107, introducing it once more with the words *fī ʿarūḍ*, which again must include "tune" as well as metre; but in this case there is a further complication: although the *simṭ* of *zajal* 107 (*fī ʿarūḍ* making up the first part of the *simṭ*) is the same length as the *simṭ* of *zajal* 108, and both would seem to belong to the "symmetrical" class of *zajal*, the *matlaʿ* is three syllables short in both cases.

We know from Ibn Sanāʾ al-Mulk that words and music of certain *muwashshaḥāt* did not apparently fit together quite as they should: he mentions (*Dār al-ṭirāz*, para 20) an example from Ibn Baqī where the *matlaʿ* has fewer syllables than it should have, and says that here the syllables *lā lā* should be vocalised. Maghribine *muwashshaḥāt* often include interpolations of *yā lā lā* or the like (reminiscent of the madrigalian *fa la la* of the English Renaissance: similar nonsense syllables are mentioned by al-Farābī [d. 350/961–2] in connection with singing exercises). This would solve the problem of the Quzmānian refrain: assuming that it commenced *yā lā lā* : *yā l-ashqar*, both *azjāl* would answer to this structure (*yā lā lā* being added to the beginning of *zajal* 107 in the same way):

6	:	6
X	‖	*M*
x	‖	*a*
x	‖	*a*
x	‖	*m*

Another *zajal* of Ibn Quzmān (No. 10) has the *matlaʿ*

dhāba naʿshaq-ki, lalayma
nujayma

The *simṭ* apparently corresponds with the first of these lines. According to rule, however, it should have corresponded with the end of the *matlaʿ*, which apparently lacks its first five syllables. These could have been farsed out by filler syllables, as before. The manner in which Ibn Quzmān's *zajal* might have been sung, using such syllables, is illustrated in Example 4, above, where it is matched with Alfonso's Cantiga 230 and a probable *gallego* precursor. Note there the remarkable correspondence between the proper names *Leonor* in the *gallego* cantiga of Roi Paes di Ribela and *Lālayma* in the Arabic: the temptation to see the former as the parent tune both for Alfonso's and Ibn Quzmān's lyrics is difficult to resist.

There are many lyrics which are *aqraʿ*, i.e. "bald", having no refrain. Here again, Maghribine performances (d'Erlanger, 1941) clearly suggest that the opening could be entirely vocalised to *yā lā lā* or something of the sort: so the recurrent refrain to a "bald" *muwashshaḥ* would have a meaningless text which was unwritten in the manuscripts, in common with the nonsense syllables discussed in the previous paragraphs in connection with the "balding" lyrics.

The *zajal* and *muwashshaḥ*, as has been seen, merge somewhat when one imitates the other. It seems likely that the *zajal*, based on a popular tune which formed the whole of its music, was the springboard for the development of the *muwashshaḥ*. The latter would take a popular refrain (sometimes in the Romance dialect) as its *kharja*, perhaps adding a fresh musical element for the often heterometric *aghṣān*. In turn, a *muwashshaḥ* might be imitated by a *zajal* of which the *kharja* would be the *matlaʿ* of the model, or simply the original refrain on which the *muwashshaḥ* had been based. The idea of the *kharja* being the starting point for the composition is well attested by Ibn Sanāʾ al-Mulk and is enshrined in the alternative word *markaz* (used by Ibn Quzmān) which is a musical term meaning "base".

From his eastern point of view, however, Ibn Sanāʾ al-Mulk failed to see the reason for using a popular *kharja*, for he complains that "some of the later poets are unable to compose a *kharja* and therefore employ a *kharja* of another poet"; but he does emphasise that it should avoid *iʿrāb* (i.e. the desinentials of classical grammar), and when composed in the Romance dialect he says it should be "garrulous, like naphtha and cinders, and in the manner of the Gipsies" (cf. Stern, 1974, p. 34). He mentions Ibn Quzmān's use of *laḥn*, and says that if this is used in the *kharja* it should be "hot and burning, close to the language of the common people and the phraseology of thieves" (*ibid.*, p. 33).

Ibn Quzmān mixes *laḥn* and Romance in some of his *azjāl*, but the linguistic mixture of the *kharajāt* ending several of the *muwashshaḥāṭ* is more intriguing. This may reflect the fact that the Muslims in Spain frequently took Christian wives: it is well known that the offspring of such a marriage would often be brought up in such a way as to perpetuate the sex-linked religious and linguistic differences; so it is easy to suppose that some of the *kharajāt* might originally have been fragments of Iberian song which the Christian *qayna* sang in her mother tongue at the end of the *muwashshaḥ*. The daughters of such a house would learn their mother tongue in a literal sense, in contrast to the "father tongue" of their Muslim brothers, and indeed the "nurse's tongue" of the Spanish nobility. This curious social and linguistic patchwork is quilted together wholly or partly in the Romance *kharajāt*. There are frequent allusions to *mamma* (see Excursus 2), the girl often asking her mother or confidante "What shall I do?" (*ke farey(o)*): this is a common device in the Galician *cantiga de amigo*. On the other hand, she addresses her lover as *habībī*, her lord as *meu sīdī*. It is also striking that the Romance *kharajāt* are mainly feminine, as opposed to those of the Arabic *kharajāt*, which tend toward the male point of view. A further point of interest is that whereas the Iberian Romance love lyric seems to emanate from a rural background, the milieu of the *zajal* and *muwashshaḥ* is urban (see Monroe and Swiatlo, 1977, pp. 161–3).

The *kharja* to a *muwashshaḥ* by Yusif ben Ṣaddiq (d. 530/1135) illustrates one level of this mixture:

Ke fare mamma?   Meu-l-habīb ?est ?ad yanā

("What shall I do, mamma? My darling ?is ?at the door": for the Hebrew characters see Stern, 1974, 144.)

A more obviously Arabic level is seen in the erotic *kharja* to an anonymous Arabic *muwashshaḥ*:

?Tan ?t'amaray illā kon ash-sharṭi
An tujammiʿ khalkhalī maʿ qurṭī

("I shall love you so much, but only if you'll have me with my anklets joining my earrings!" For the Arabic characters and discussion see Jones, 1988, pp. 85–8.)

The Romance phrase *tan t'amaray* seems to be confirmed by another *kharja* beginning with the same words (Stern, 1953, p. 18) though here the reading is *tmtr'y*, and *non* has been proposed for *tan* on the grounds that a negative is properly needed before *illā*. What is striking, however, is that very similar phraseology is found in two wholly Arabic *kharajāt* and the image is also found in an earlier poem by Abū Nuwās d. 195/810–1, whose place in the early history of the Hispano–Mauresque lyric is of particular importance (cf. Jones, 1988, and Excursus 1). This reinforces the conclusion that the *kharajāt* were based on popular refrains, Arabic, Romance and mixed, sometimes altered, perhaps sometimes deliberately made to sound "garrulous . . . in the manner of the Gipsies".

The earliest Romance rhyme schemes were remarkably primitive, as are those of the *qaṣīdāt*: it is in the *zajal* (which has been posited here as a coming together of these two elements) where the rhymes begin to be more elaborate, as reflected, perhaps, in some of the Cantigas. The *muwashshaḥ* (here assumed to be a later sophistication of the *zajal*) evolved still more complex rhyme schemes. The more basic elaborations are found in the Cantigas, and some rather more complex schemes can be seen in Catalan, Occitan and French lyrics. If a hypothetical line is to be traced, then Alfonso's encouragement of a variety of Romance traditions and his known borrowings from them might have been complemented by the transmission, in other directions, of tunes, with their concomitant rhyme schemes and musical structures from the Judaeo–Arabic side. After all, Don Todros Abulafia (d. *c.* 1310), a relative of the famous Hebrew *washshaḥ* of the same name, was an important member of Alfonso's court at Toledo, together with a host of Jewish and Arabic scholars.

At least four of the poet Todros Abulafia's Hebrew *muwashshaḥāt* have *kharajāt* borrowed from Ibn Quzmān's refrains (see Excursus 1) and another with a Romance *kharja* is addressed to "Rab [i.e. Don] Todros" himself (see Stern, 1974, p. 141). It is difficult to believe that at Toledo there was no interchange between Hispano–Mauresque forms and the Cantigas. And of course, the crossroads of the Aragonese kingdom, not to mention the *camino francés*, the pilgrim route to Santiago de Compostela, would have provided obvious paths for the eastward journey of elements of the *ghazal* to Aquitaine and elsewhere. Despite the deplorable relationships between the various religions and races, ranging from respectful tolerance to open loathing, there were ample opportunities for cultural exchange, even though this may not have been of an entirely straightforward nature.

Many years ago, H.A.R. Gibb pointed out that "Before any kind of transference is possible there must be a condition of receptivity on one or both sides — a willingness to take what the other has to give, an implied recognition of its superiority . . ." He commented that European receptivity to much of the possible literary influences "has been strictly limited both in time and scope" (*apud* Arnold and Guillaume, 1931, p. 181). Yet receptivity there was, for centuries after Alvarus of Córdoba, Peire Cardenal reflected that he wished that he could command the language of the Saracens while being faithful to Christianity, and have at once the law of Christ and the craft of the pagans:

dig vuelh aver de Sarrazi
e fe e lei de crestia
e sotileza de paia

(Riquer, III, 1493)

Yet despite this admiration, and although several Mauresque elements can be detected in the troubadour and trouvère traditions, the relationship between the cultures was as promiscuous as that imputed to some of the characters in the lyrics themselves: it was at the same time more indirect, and its by-blows were more miscegenated, than proponents of the "Arabic theory" might have hoped. This is illustrated by the position of the *muwashshaḥ*. It is curious that despite its enshrining the Romance *kharja*, it does not seem to have exerted any structural influence in turn: the characteristic three-part *ghuṣn* remained distinctly alien to the Romance lyric (and though this feature does appear in some *villancicos* of a later age, the "partial *simṭ*" which they display betrays the influence of the *zajal* rather than the *muwashshaḥ*).

It is extraordinarily difficult to sift the evidence relating to what was largely an unwritten substrate. It is tempting to take the easy way out and call for an unproven verdict for lack of evidence. This will be judged scholarly by some, but feeble by those who feel that the circumstantial evidence is often overwhelmingly suggestive.

I think that the limited evidence at our command (some of which is enlarged upon in Excursus 1, overleaf) can be taken to show that the interchange between the cultures was mostly at a level beneath the notice of literary sources: it was the vulgar *zajal*, successor to the "songs of the camel drivers" which provided the melting-pot, not the literate *muwashshaḥ*, despite its Romance *kharajāt* and the possible influence of its rhyme schemes. It was the popular "songs of the

Christians" which influenced, and were influenced by, the *zajal*, not the troubadour lyrics of Guillem IX of Aquitaine and his successors. The troubadours carefully avoided vulgar refrain songs, as manifest in the Catalan and Occitan *dançes*, so it is not surprising that troubadour lyrics fail to show any influence on refrain songs (but see Excursus 3). There is plenty of evidence that refrain songs and other lyrics existed in the Romance substrate, despite Dante's knowing nothing of Occitan lyric prior to Guillem: he, too, relied on literary rather than oral sources for his knowledge. For our part, we must be careful not to confuse the few bones of literary remains which we may unearth with the living flesh of the culture which, though itself perished, had an influence which is manifest in some of its descendants. Though they may have been objects of supposed contempt, the dubious songs of the boys, women and drunkards seem to have had more currency than the learned sages were (or perhaps are) prepared to admit.

Excursus 1

Alan Jones (1988) dismisses the musical dimension with the words "I remain totally unconvinced" (21, fn 23). This will not do: whatever the rights and wrongs of what I have said here and in Wulstan (1982), the interaction of music and prosody cannot simply be ignored, as has been seen. Some further examples regarding this interaction are appended.

Monroe and Swiatlo (1977) have collected the Arabic *kharajāt* found in Hebrew *muwashshaḥāt*. Several of these incontrovertibly show elision at vowel juncture, sometimes with a weak consonant (e.g. *ʿayin*, which was not properly pronounced in al-Andalus — see Monroe and Swiatlo, 150, fn 56) intervening. Their *kharja* 44 is a clear example, though some others admit of alternative explanations, e.g. resolution. The article seems now to require complete elision (synaloepha), elsewhere to have syllabic value, as in the extraordinary case of *kharja* 92 (Todros Abulafia). This requires a syllabic article in two internal instances where it might naturally be elided, but also in two places where *al-nābilī* occurs (in different senses) at line end, the article forming an enjambed rhyme in *-al* which cannot therefore have been agglutinated:

fa-n-nibāl
tarmuqu–nī
min laḥẓik al-
nābilī
wa-r-riḥāl
yafruqu-nī
min siḥrik al-
nābilī

(The arrows look at me from your noble gaze while camel-saddles are parting me from your bewitching charm.) (On the rhyme scheme, see below.)

It has already been observed that Todros uses refrains by Ibn Quzmān as his *kharajāt* in several instances. Merely to take one example, Monroe and Swiatlo, No. 41, the rhythms of Ibn Quzmān and of Todros are different, and different again from those of Ibn ʿEzra. Similarly, No. 51 (using a *kharja* also employed by Ibn Quzmān, but not noted by Monroe and Swiatlo) is not easy to reconcile rhythmically between all the instances of *muʿāraḍa.* These obviously reflect popular songs, and the waywardness of the metric of the *kharajāt* surely answers to that of the songs themselves, echoing several remarks on this matter by Ibn Sanāʾ al-Mulk. This must also apply to the Romance equivalents. Emendations in order to fit in with the strict quantities of what are often curiously untypical examples of *ʿarūḍ* are therefore doubly unwise, *pace* Jones (1988).

Similarly, the rhyme schemes of the main part of the *muwashshaḥ* are not necessarily a strict and infallible guide to those of the *kharja*, as Jones assumes. His *kharja* 1 has the parallel line ends *dolje* // *nokhte*, looking remarkably like Romance assonance. The rhymes of the *aṣmāt* correspond cleverly (in *-ji* and *-ti*), but do not rhyme between themselves. A more obvious instance of the problem of assonance to the Mauresque poet is seen in a Hebrew *muwashshaḥ* by Yusif al-Khaṭīb (fl. 422/1040, cf. Stern, 1979, p. 148):

Tan t'amarey tan t'amarey ḥabīb, tan t'amare
? ? ya dolen ta male

The poet, confronted with the assonance of the *kharja*, converted it into strict rhyme (in *-ri*) in the previous *asmāṭ*.

This loose rhyme or assonance is not only typical of the Romance or mixed *kharajāt.* An example may be seen in the previous quotation (p. 160) from Todros Abulafia (Monroe and Swiatlo, 92), where although the rhyme scheme of the *simṭ* is *abcd abcd* in respect of the *muwashshaḥ*, a concurrent assonance pattern of Romance type, *abab abab*, can also be seen. A similar rhyme scheme appears in a *kharja* which corresponds to the bilingual erotic example quoted earlier in the main body of the article. It occurs in the *Dār al-ṭirāz* of Ibn Sanā' al-Mulk, No. 14 (Anonymous); here the rhyme scheme is *aaaa bbbb*:

ḥabībī - ʿzam	*wa qum wa-hjam*
wa qabbil fam	*wa-jiʿ wa-nḍamm*
ilā ṣadrī	*wa-qum bikhalkhālī*
ilā aqrāṭī	*qadi-shtaghala zawjī*

("My darling, make up your mind. Hurry up and kiss my mouth, fondle my breast and raise my anklets to my earrings. My husband is busy." Cf. *Jaysh at-Tawshīḥ* No. 168, where the last part, beginning *wa-qum* . . ., is virtually identical.) It seems that these *kharajāt* reflect a popular song; as Jones points out (1988, 88 — and see below) Abū Nuwās quotes something similar at the end of one of his poems.

Monroe and Swiatlo mention several other *kharajāt* which seem to betray assonance, for example their No. 12 (Todros — *sākhis // yarāni*) and 34 (Ibn Ṣaddiq — *dalāli // ʿidhāri*). No. 86 (Todros) is also noteworthy, having *aabbbb* in respect of the *muwashshaḥ*, but *aabbcc* in respect of Romance. Even more remarkable, however, is the famous *kharja* used by al-Abyaḍ, followed by Yehuda Halevi (d. 1145), whose nearly chiastic rhyme is not noted by Monroe and Swiatlo (their No. 93):

bi-l-lāh rasūl
qul li-l-khalīl
kayfa s-sabīl
wayabīt ʿindī
khalfa l-ḥijāl
naʿtīh dalāl
ʿalā n-nikāl
wa-nazīd nahdī

(*aaab cccb* = *abbc dddc*: "By Allāh, messenger tell the lover what way to follow to spend the night with me under the covers I'll give him my locks by way of torment I'll add my breasts")

As already noted, Ibn Quzmān once uses the pattern *aabb* (*ccdd* etc.) in the *aghṣān* of *zajal* No. 4. This, to my knowledge, is unique. Even in the *maṭlaʿ* = *simṭ* sections, parallel rhyme of this kind is extremely rare in the *muwashshaḥāt* proper (see Stern, 1974, p. 24), despite the clear indications of it in *kharajāt*. The *rajaz* rhymes *aa bb cc* etc.: this could be the explanation for Ibn Quzmān's lone essay in this scheme, and might be the reason why it was eschewed in the more literate *muwashshaḥ*. Yet, the influence of Romance seems as likely a source. The connection between Ibn Quzmān and Todros, and between Todros (together with Ibn Ṣaddīq) and the court of Alfonso the Wise has already been stressed. (Incidentally, the exact kinship of the various members of the Abulafia family is far from clear: the *Jewish Encyclopaedia* gives little or no help in regard to the precise relationship of those bearing the name Todros.)

Although the notion of a pivotal position of the culture of Toledo is difficult to resist, and may explain the way zajalesque rhymes are to be found in the Cantigas, it does not directly explain the earlier interchanges: but it does provide a model whereby the conditions of receptivity, mentioned earlier, might well have prevailed at various stages in the history of the *zajal*, *muwashshaḥ* and Occidental lyric. An earlier style may be glimpsed in the zajalesque compositions (in Hebrew) by Ibn Tabbān (late eleventh century) and Ibn Gabirol (see Wulstan, 1982, p. 259) which predate Ibn Quzmān by a century or so. Earlier still, Abū Nuwās (see García Gómez, 1956 and Jones, 1988, p. 88) seems to employ devices which strongly resemble the elements found in *zajal* and *muwashshaḥ*. His use of quotation has already been noted: his employment of the *musammaṭ* style, in its fourfold variant (*murabbaʿ*) with *tasrīʿ* (opening rhyming couplet) is also important, for his scheme is:

zzzz aaaz bbbz

where the last *z* is often a quotation. This is very similar to the *zajal* scheme, where the opening is the refrain, and the subsequent *z* elements are the link rhymes. After the political upheavals and cultural uncertainties following the collapse of the Umayyads, and with with the arrival from Baghdad of the Persian tenor Ziryāb in Spain in AD 822 these innovations may have struck a chord, particularly since neither the Berbers nor the Mozarabs were particularly interested in Classical Arabic verse: the grafting of these elements on to the Romance *rondeau* form (incidentally, this was first posited by Monroe, 1974, pp. 30–1) would be a natural development: its popularity would give particular point to Alvarus' polemic of 854, mentioned earlier.

This, in turn, must have had at least some influence on Iberian lyric; but in particular, it inspired the more literary *muwashshaḥ*, with its characteristic *kharja*. The *nasīb* of the *qaṣīda* has already been noted as having an independent existence: moreover, it is specifically mentioned by Ibn Sanā᾽ al-Mulk in connection with the *muwashshaḥ*. It is not unlikely that these songs (rhyming *aaxa* = *mmnm*) were used as refrains in the earliest examples, before the idea of incorporating Romance and other popular refrains gained ground. It is suggestive that the development (which Ibn Bassām attributes to al-Ramādī [d. 403/1013]) of internal rhyme first occurred in the *matlaʿ=simṭ*. This would have been an almost inevitable consequence of using the popular refrains which have been discussed above. At the same time, this internal rhyme to the *simṭ* (*tadfīr*) is often fairly unadventurous, as has been seen: it was only when the internal rhyme was applied to the *aghsān* (this being called *taḍmīn*) that the inherent complexities of the *muwashshaḥ* were fully realised. At this point, perhaps, the debt to Romance poetry was repaid, via the troubadours, though the precise route whereby this development moved is as yet problematical.

To return to the question of rhythm. Ibn Sanā᾽ al-Mulk makes several references to music being the sole justification of the metric of some of the *muwashshaḥāt*. In paragraph 10 of the *Dār aṭ-ṭirāz*, he mentions an anomalous *muwashshaḥ* by ʿUbāda with an opening *qufl* (i.e. *matlaʿ*) of two elements, while the remaining *aqfāl* (i.e. *asmāṭ*) have three. This must be read in connection with paragraph 20, where he discusses *muwashshaḥāt* which cannot be reconciled with classical metric and paragraph 23, where he mentions the addition of nonsense syllables such as *lā lā* necessitated by the music. A particularly wide selection of such syllables may be seen in an extended setting of a panegyrical opening distich of a *qaṣīda* from the *Durrat al-tāj* ascribed to safī al-Dīn al-Ḥillī (see Wright, 1978, pp. 231–44: incidentally, the modified flat sign used there and in his other transcriptions — e.g. of the piece given as Example 1 here — is misleading, giving a microtonal look to the music. In fact, the notes in question are merely a pure major third above *C* or *F*). Vocalised syllables are characteristic of much Spanish song, and of course they give their name to the Galician *Alala* (though many kinds of Galician song make use of this device). It may be remarked that the refrain *leili, leilia doura* is similar to that which gives its name to the *layāli*, still sung in certain eastern *nawbāt* (*yā layli, yālayli ʿayni* — see the *New Grove* I, *s.v.* Arab Music, 524).

As Ibn Sanāʾ al-Mulk says (para. 20), the prosody (*ʿarūḍ*) often depends on the musical rhythm (*ḍarb* — he makes a pun between this meaning and that relating to the end of a metrical line, also playing on the signification of *ʿarūḍ* as the opening of such a line). Prosody, he says, depends less on "feet" than on the keys of the instruments, less on syllables than on their strings. He also mentions the "organ" (*al-urghān*) but it is not unlikely that this word is to be taken in the Greek sense of "instrument" (see López-Morillas, 1985).

This makes it plain that the "neglected and less frequently used metres" of Ibn Bassām, and those which "cannot be reconciled with classical prosody" according to Ibn Sanāʾ al-Mulk can only be justified in relation to music (al-Ḥillī says much the same concerning the *zajal* — cf. Hoernerbach, 1956, 10), which latter, as was seen in connection with Example 1, makes havoc of the longs and shorts of classical *ʿarūḍ*. In these circumstances also, a discussion of accent can have little proper significance if the notion of a musical "beat" is ignored: the beat may agree or conflict with the accent, and musical phenomena may indeed reconcile apparent accent clashes (see Excursus 2). It is thus wholly unrealistic to attempt to dismiss the musical dimension in connection with Hispano–Mauresque lyric.

Excursus 2

In connection with the curious way in which the children of a mixed household would often follow the religion of the parent of the same sex, it is interesting to note an example of the extremes to which this might be carried. Alvarus of Córdoba and others were part of an extremist movement which incited Mozarabs to insult the name of Muḥammad, a capital offence. Flora, the daughter of a well-placed Muslim, became part of this movement, and despite the fact that leniency was offered she persisted in flagrant conduct in order to gain what she regarded as martyrdom: she thus fulfilled her ambition, and was duly canonised (see Dozy, 1861, p. 317). Yet, when a daughter of such a household addresses her mother in a *kharja*, is the word *mama* Romance or Arabic? This point is discussed by Richard Hitchcock (1977): his thesis is that the question of accentuation is crucial. Once more, the musical side of the question is not without relevance. James Monroe has argued (Monroe and Swiatlo, 1977, p. 159) that the music of the *villancico* "Las mis penas" by Encina does not necessarily follow the verbal accents. The assumption that musical considerations may appear to conflict with the linguistic accent is true in general and up to a point. The specific example, however, is an interesting one in that the rhythm of Encina's music (which is mistranscribed in Anglés, 1947, p. 84) has a pattern of long and short notes which will bear almost any collocation of linguistic accents (in common with Alfonso's Cantiga 264 it is actually in quintuple rhythm, corresponding with *mukhammas* metre). Thus Monroe's assertion that the linguistic "Làs mis pènas" is contradicted by "Las mìs penàs" in the music is not entirely true: *both* patterns are satisfied by the music. This is a common phenomenon whereby the regular beat can operate in counterpoint to the "agogic" accent caused by a long note, and thus allow the music to reconcile apparent accentual conflicts. Thus, the question of accent and beat is far from straightforward; it is therefore unwise to read too much into the supposed prosodic accentuation of certain words; indeed, it is perfectly possible that the accentuation of *mama* was nicely equivocal in the original music.

Excursus 3

Few troubadour songs exhibit refrains. Those which do so are generally dance songs or lyrics apparently based on dance tunes. *Mei amic e mei fiel* (Paris Bibl. nat. fonds lat. 1139: both song and source have goliardic connexions, in my view) with its Latin counterpart *In hoc anni circulo* is one such: the subsemitonal cadence, arpeggio features and other traits rule out a chant origin; moreover, the length of the tune (each line has a final melisma which overruns the line end in the same way) seems to indicate that the metre of the model may have been enneasyllabic rather than heptasyllabic. This manuscript contains Aquitainian polyphony, many items of which seem to be based on secular *cantus firmi*, often evincing refrains. An interesting *cantio* therein is *Promet chorus hodie/ O contio* ending *Psallat cum tripudio*. The refrain and the reference to dancing give away its model. Spanke (1940) pointed to the many Latin songs and *conductus* of the period whose connexions with the lyrics of Guillem, Marcabru and other troubadours are very strong, though he assumed the vernacular had borrowed from the paraliturgical version rather than vice versa. That this is hardly the case is indicated by Guillem's *Companho farai un vers*, which is clearly based on *Promet chorus hodie*, or rather, upon a common model. The Latin *cantio* would hardly add a refrain and make a dance song out of a static lyric: on the contrary, by suppressing the refrain and altering the metrical and rhyme schemes, he refashioned a bucolic ditty into a high art lyric. The same process may be seen elsewhere in the early troubadour and trouvère repertory: it was not until later that the fashion for imitating the low songs brought them more obviously into the purview of the written sources.

Finally, I should like to apologise for the misleading error in Wulstan (1982) pp. 247–8 where I quoted the wrong song by Codax, which far from displaying the "Galician cadence" instanced here at Example 2, instead illustrates the flourish, possibly to be identified as being typically Arabic or Mozarabic, discussed in regard to Example 4 here. In the light of further refinement of my ideas, the rhythms in the transcriptions of the Codax and of Alfonso's Cantiga 250 given in Wulstan (1982) are subject to modification, but those of the other examples still stand.

Bibliographical references

Anglés, Higini. *La Música de las Cantigas de Santa María del Rey Alfonso el Sabio*, vol. II (*Transcripción*), Barcelona, 1942.

Anglés, Higini. *La Música en la Corte de los Reyes Católicos*, vol. II, Barcelona, 1947.
Anglés, Higini. *La Música de las Cantigas de Santa María del Rey Alfonso el Sabio*, vol. III (*Estudio Crítico*), Barcelona, 1958.
Arnold, Sir Thomas, and Guillaume, Alfred (eds.) *The Legacy of Islam*, Oxford, 1931.
Ballesteros y Baretta, Antonio. *Alfonso el Sabio*, Barcelona, 1963.
Beeston, A.F.L. (trans. and ed.) *The Epistle on Singing Girls by Jāḥiẓ*, Warminster, 1980.
Corriente, Federico, "The metres of the *muwaššah*, an Andalusian adaptation of *ʿarūḍ*, a bridging hypothesis", *Journal of Arabic Literature*, 13 (1982), pp. 123–32.
Dozy, Robert. *Histoire des musulmans d'Espagne jusqu'à la conquête de l'Andalousie par les almoravides (711–1110)*, vol. I, Leiden, 1861.
d'Erlanger, Rudolfe, Baron. *La Musique Arabe*, Tome III, Paris, 1938.
d'Erlanger, Rudolfe, Baron. *La Musique Arabe*, Tome VI, Paris, 1941.
Farmer, H.G. *Music: The Priceless Jewel* (Collection of Oriental Writers on Music, V), Glasgow, 1942.
Farmer, H.G. The Music of Islam. *New Oxford History of Music* (vol. I), London, 1957.
Ferreira, M.P. *O Som de Martin Codax*, Lisbon, 1986.
García Gómez, Emilio. Una extraordinaria página de Tifashī . . ., *Études d'orientalisme dediées à la mémoire de Lévi-Provençal* 2, Paris, 1952, pp. 517–23.
García Gómez, Emilio. Una pre-muwaššaḥa atribuída a Abū Nuwās, *Al-Andalus*, 21 (1956), pp. 406–14.
García Gómez, Emilio. *Todo Ben Quzmān*, 3 vols., Madrid, 1972.
Gennrich, Friedrich. *Rondeaux, Virelais und Balladen* (Gesellschaft für Romanische Literatur, Band 43), Dresden, 1921.
Hitchcock, Richard, "Sobre la ¿Mamá¿ en las jarchas", *Journal of Hispanic Philology*, 11 (1977), pp. 1–9.
Hoenerbach, W. (ed.). *Die vulgärarabische Poetik al-Kitāb al-ʿĀtil al-ḥalī al-Ḥillī wa l-murakhas al-ghali des Ṣafiyaddīn al-Ḥillī*, Wiesbaden, 1956.
Ibn Khaldūn. *The Muqaddimah*. Trans. Franz Rosenthal. 3 vols., New York, 1958.
Jones, Alan. *Romance* Kharjas *in Andalusian Arabic* Muwaššaḥ *Poetry*, Oxford, 1988.
López-Morillas, Consuelo. "Was the *muwaššaḥ* really accompanied by the organ?" *La Corónica*, 14 (1985), pp. 41–54.
Migne, J.P. *Patrologia Latina* (Patrologiae cursus completus, series Latina), *tomus 121*, 1882.
Monroe, James. *Hispano-Arabic Poetry*, Berkeley, 1974.
Monroe, James and Swiatlo, David. "Ninety-three Arabic Ḫarǧas in Hebrew Muwaššaḥs", *Journal of the American Oriental Society*, 97 (1977), p. 141.
Nykl, A.R. *Hispano-Arabic Poetry and its Relations with the Old Provençal Troubadours*, Baltimore, 1946.
Riquer, Martin de. *Los Trovadores: Historia, literaria y textes*, vol. III, Barcelona, 1975.
Robson, James and Farmer, H.G. *Ancient Arabian Musical Instruments* (Collection of Oriental writers on Music — IV), Glasgow, 1938.
Spanke, Hans. *Üntersuchungen über die Ursprünge des romanischen Minnesangs* (Zweiter Teil: Marcabrustudien — *Abhandl. der Ges. der Wiss. zu Göttingen, Phil. — Hist. Klasse*, Dritte Folge, Nr 24), 1940.
Stern, S.M. *Les Chansons Mozarabes*, Palermo, 1964, R, Oxford, 1953.
Stern, S.M. *Hispano-Arabic Strophic Poetry*, ed. L.P. Harvey, Oxford, 1974.
Wright, O. *The Modal System of Arab and Persian Music, A.D. 1250–1300*, Oxford, 1978.
Wright, Roger. *Late Latin and Early Romance in Spain and Carolingian France*, Liverpool, 1982.
Wulstan, David. "The *Muwaššaḥ* and *Zaǧal* Revisited", *Journal of the American Oriental Society*, 102 (1982), pp. 247–64.

Index

Index

Index

Index

Index

Index